Contemporary Issues in Luxury Brand Management

This book provides a comprehensive overview of the key themes surrounding luxury brand management and the core issues faced by luxury firms today. The luxury industry has undergone a series of dynamic changes in the past twenty years. Economic trends, digital transformation, and changing consumer habits are creating a new competitive landscape where traditional strategies will not necessarily provide continued growth and profitability.

Approaching luxury from a realistic brand management perspective, this book works step-by-step through a typical luxury course structure, covering sustainability, heritage, emerging brands, digital marketing and analytics, curation, intellectual property, and start-ups. Each chapter is illustrated by a relevant international case study and further examples, as well as reflective questions to help gain insight from contemporary practice.

With additional PowerPoint slides and a test bank of questions available online, this comprehensive textbook should be core reading for postgraduate students studying luxury brand management or luxury strategy.

Sylvie Studente is Assistant Professor at Regent's University London.

Eleonora Cattaneo is Professor of Marketing at César Ritz Colleges Switzerland.

T0399605

Mastering Luxury Management

The luxury sector is a rapidly evolving and competitive global industry, requiring premium brands to be dynamic and innovative in their business and management decisions to remain relevant. This series meets the need for thorough yet practical and accessible textbooks that address the complexity of the luxury industry and challenges facing its management.

Mastering Luxury Management is a valuable resource for Luxury Management courses, helping readers to acquire an in-depth understanding of contemporary theories and how they apply in practice, alongside recognising trends and developments that may shape the future marketplace. Individually, each text provides essential reading for a core topic. A range of consistent pedagogical features are used across the series, including international case studies that demonstrate practical applications in the luxury context.

Each text will be invaluable reading for advanced undergraduate and postgraduate students, in particular those studying for a Master's or MBA in Luxury Management or Luxury Brand Management, as they provide tools and strategies for a successful future career in luxury.

Strategic Luxury Management
Value Creation and Creativity for Competitive Advantage
David Millán Planelles

Contemporary Issues in Luxury Brand Management
Edited by Sylvie Studente and Eleonora Cattaneo

For more information about this series, please visit: www.routledge.com/ Mastering-Luxury-Management/book-series/LM

CONTEMPORARY ISSUES IN LUXURY BRAND MANAGEMENT

Edited by

Sylvie Studente and Eleonora Cattaneo

Routledge
Taylor & Francis Group

LONDON AND NEW YORK

First published 2023
by Routledge
4 Park Square, Milton Park, Abingdon, Oxon OX14 4RN

and by Routledge
605 Third Avenue, New York, NY 10158

Routledge is an imprint of the Taylor & Francis Group, an informa business

British Library Cataloguing-in-Publication Data
A catalogue record for this book is available from the British Library

Library of Congress Cataloging-in-Publication Data
Names: Studente, Sylvie, editor. | Cattaneo, Eleonora, editor.
Title: Contemporary issues in luxury brand management /
edited by Sylvie Studente and Eleonora Cattaneo.
Description: Abingdon, Oxon ; New York, NY : Routledge, 2023. |
Series: Mastering luxury management |
Includes bibliographical references and index.
Identifiers: LCCN 2022036826 | ISBN 9780367859282 (hardback) |
ISBN 9780367859305 (paperback) | ISBN 9781003015826 (ebook)
Subjects: LCSH: Luxury goods industry–Management. | Brand name products.
Classification: LCC HD9999.L852 C665 2023 | DDC 658.8–dc23/eng/20221125
LC record available at https://lccn.loc.gov/2022036826

ISBN: 978-0-367-85928-2 (hbk)
ISBN: 978-0-367-85930-5 (pbk)
ISBN: 978-1-003-01582-6 (ebk)

DOI: 10.4324/9781003015826

Typeset in Palatino
by Newgen Publishing UK

Access the Support Material: www.routledge.com/9780367859305

CONTENTS

ABOUT THE EDITORS

Sylvie Studente is Assistant Professor at Regent's University London. With over 20 years of research experience, she has led, and contributed to, a number of international research projects. Sylvie obtained her PhD in Human Computer Interaction in 2008 from the Knowledge Media Institute at The Open University, and has since completed a number of additional post-graduate studies in Education. Her BA and MSc are in the areas of Business and Computing. Her research interests span the areas of education, assessment, e-learning, and technology. Prior to her position at Regent's University, she taught at a number of other HE institutions, leading courses on interaction design, artificial intelligence, marketing, and project management. Sylvie also has industry experience in the fields of project management, artificial intelligence and interaction design in both business and education contexts. Alongside her duties at Regent's University London, Sylvie is the Chief External Examiner for Digital Business at the University of Westminster, and a doctoral supervisor for the University of Northampton. She is the course leader for the MSc in Digital Marketing and Analytics at Regent's University London, as well as a member of the Advisory Board for the Journal of Knowledge Management, Economics and Information Technology, and a member of the editorial board for the *Journal of Psychological Research.*

Eleonora Cattaneo is Professor of Marketing at César Ritz Colleges Switzerland. She obtained her PhD in Marketing from the University of Pavia in Italy, MBA from SDA Bocconi and BA from the University of Bristol. Her research focuses on rebranding, heritage branding and sustainable buying behaviour in the field of luxury. Her work has been published in Journal of Brand Management, Long Range Planning and Strategic Change among others. Prior to her position at Swiss Education Group, she was head of programme for the MA Luxury Brand Management at Regent's University and before that she was a faculty member at SDA Bocconi in Milan where she designed and led executive education and MBA programmes. Eleonora has extensive industry experience in the field of marketing as a consultant and senior advisor for global brands and leading luxury hospitality groups. She is a senior fellow of the Chartered Management Institute and a member of the Swiss Center for Luxury Research.

CONTRIBUTORS

Vincent F. Adegoke is Post Graduate Researcher in the School of Engineering at London South Bank University.

Nkechi Amobi Is a lecturer in law at Regent's University London, with professional experience in the fields of law and development. She obtained her PhD from the University of Leeds in Intellectual Property Law.

Eleonora Cattaneo is Professor of Marketing at César Ritz Colleges Switzerland. She obtained her PhD in Marketing from the University of Pavia in Italy. She has extensive industry experience in the field of marketing as a consultant and senior advisor for global brands, and leading luxury hospitality groups. She is a senior fellow of the Chartered Management Institute and a member of the Swiss Center for Luxury Research.

Bhavini Desai is Director of Content in Marketing & Brand at Regent's University London. She obtained her PhD form Brunel University in Information Systems Management. She has extensive experience and knowledge in marketing, management and data analytics.

Stephen Ellis is an academic based at University of Aberdeen. He obtained his PhD in the area of Organisational Development and an MBA from Henley Management College. His specialist areas are HR and Organisational performance.

Rebecca Fakoussa is Senior Lecturer in Business Entrepreneurship at Regent's University London. She obtained her PhD from Kingston University in the area of Family Business Start-ups

John Harrison is Senior Lecturer at Regent's University London. He teaches on and has developed a number of academic programmes across business strategy and marketing.

Steve Mancour is Managing Director of Social Media Sorcery, a firm which assists businesses with branding, marketing, analytics and PR. Steve has an extensive background in marketing an obtained his BA (Hons) in International Business.

Zubin Sethna is a Professor of Entrepreneurial Marketing and Consumer Behaviour at Regent's University London. a graduate of the University of Stirling (PhD). He currently leads as the Head of PG Programmes for MSc Marketing Psychology and MA Enterprise.

Thomas Smit is Group Chairman of Elegantes London Limited, a luxury perfumery.

Sylvie Studente is Assistant Professor at Regent's University London. She is also the course leader for the MSc Digital Marketing and Data Analytics Programme and Chief External Examiner for the University of Westminster in Digital Business. Her main area of expertise is UX Design, obtaining her PhD from the Knowledge Media Institute.

Patrice Seuwou is Senior Lecturer in Digital Business at the University of Northampton, where he is Programme Leader for the BSc (Hons) in Digital Business. He obtained his PhD from London South Bank University in the area of Computer Science and Informatics.

PREFACE

Sylvie Studente and Eleonora Cattaneo

The luxury industry has undergone a series of dynamic changes in the past 20 years. Economic trends, digital transformation, and changing consumer habits are creating a new competitive landscape in which traditional strategies will not necessarily provide continued growth and profitability. This book collects the research and practice output of academics and experts engaged in luxury brand management, focusing on the key issues that will shape the industry in the years to come. This book is specifically aimed at postgraduate students and higher education (HE) educators of luxury brand management programmes, as well as other brand management programmes. This book would also be of interest to marketing academics researching luxury brands and practitioners looking for case studies on how brands have managed specific issues such as sustainability and expansion into new markets. This book comprises nine chapters covering a range of themes within contemporary luxury brand management. Each chapter is supported with seminar discussion topics and study group exercises. The book is arranged into three key themes: People and History, Luxury Products, and Digital Business.

The first section of this book focuses on People and History. The first chapter in this section is titled 'Luxury throughout history' by Dr. Eleonora Cattaneo (César Ritz Colleges Switzerland). This chapter introduces the reader to a timeline of how luxury has been perceived throughout history to the present day, showing how it has changed from being the domain of a ruling class, to the current indulgence for any consumer with the disposable income to access it. The chapter asserts that 'history' is a key characteristic of luxury brands, enabling claims of authenticity as a component of heritage. The chapter raises the important question of 'What qualifies a brand as luxury?' and suggests that leveraging heritage holistically can create a powerful identity for luxury brands. This is followed by the chapter 'Luxury start-ups' by Prof. Zubin Sethna (Regent's University London) and Dr. Rebecca Fakoussa (University of Northampton). This chapter introduces the reader to the concept of 'Start-ups' and provides understandings on 'luxury'. The chapter invites the reader to investigate the structure of luxury start-ups using the 'when, where, what, and why' framework. In each case, theoretical constructs are provided, supported by case study applications. The final chapter in this section 'Contemporary people issues in luxury brand management' by Dr. Stephen Ellis (University of Aberdeen) and Thomas Smit (Elegantes London Limited) focusses upon the people aspects of creating, delivering, and managing a luxury brand proposition and experience. The chapter is structured into three sections: clarifying the concept of luxury in the marketplace, developing people in the luxury brand sector, and management development in the luxury brand sector. Each section of the chapter provides theoretical underpinnings which are illustrated through case studies and reflective questions

The second section of this book focuses upon luxury products. The first chapter in this section is titled 'Legal protection for luxury goods and the counterfeiting challenge' by Dr. Nkechi Amobi (Regent's University London). The chapter defines intellectual property rights (IPR) and explains how different types of IPR regulate how products can be used. Luxury goods industries rely on strong IPR frameworks for the protection of their products and services, affirm the originality and exclusivity of their products, and secure long-term investment in their innovations. The global luxury industry is unfortunately targeted by the counterfeit goods industry. Many counterfeit products infringe on the IPRs of luxury brand owners. The chapter examines the relevance of IPRs to luxury goods industries, by investigating how successful they are in securing monopoly or anti-copying rights for luxury goods. This is followed by the chapter 'The case for the wine experience' by John Harrison (Regent's University London) which provides history to the concept of 'luxury' wines. The chapter details fine wines as one of the top investments in the world, that can spread investment portfolios. In a portfolio of financial planning, wine is an alternative investment, which has an established track record for achieving solid income and has performed better than financial markets over the long term. Marketing of wine is also considered, and future concerns are outlined. The final chapter in this section 'Luxury and sustainability' by Dr. Eleonora Cattaneo (César Ritz Colleges Switzerland) highlights that, historically, the luxury industry was not focused on sustainability or corporate social responsibility. The chapter asserts that for luxury brands, the focus on quality over cost has typically been maintained along the entire value chain. The luxury industry's response to this was that the preservation of physical and biological resources had always been at the heart of all true luxury brands. Also, that due to limited production, strict control of demand and supply, limited use of machinery and preservation of craftsmanship, as well as the development of products expected to last a lifetime, unlike mass market brands, luxury brands supported rather than undermined sustainability. This chapter provides some valuable insights into how consumer preferences have been steadily moving towards a sustainable luxury industry.

The final section within this book, focusses upon Digital Business and incorporates three chapters. The first chapter in this section 'Social media marketing in luxury brand management' by Steve Mancour (Managing Director of Social Media Sorcery) provides an introduction to the use of social media marketing for luxury brands. The chapter introduces the reader to concepts such as advertising advantage, social proof, influencer, super fans, and other aspects pertinent to the effective and successful implementation of social media marketing for luxury brand management. The chapter also discusses challengers to luxury brand marketers. This is followed by the chapter 'Digital marketing and analytics for luxury brands' by Dr. Sylvie Studente and Dr. Bhavini Desai (Regent's University London). The chapter introduces the reader to the use of digital marketing within the luxury sector and the change in consumer behaviour resulting from digital consumption. The chapter provides examples of luxury brands who have shaped their marketing approaches to communicate with consumers via digital channels as part of their integrated marketing communications. The final chapter in this section 'The future of commerce with digital business' by Patrice Seuwou (University of Northampton), and Vincent Adegoke (London South Bank University) examines the implications for future business through the integration of innovative business models and digital strategies. Specifically, this chapter explores these issues by considering combinations of disruptive technologies utilised with digital marketing tools in providing competitive advantage.

ACKNOWLEDGEMENTS

We would like to thank all of those who have contributed to this collection of work:

Prof. Zubin Sethna, Regent's University London
Dr. Bhavini Desai, Regent's University London
John Harrison, Regent's University London
Dr. Nkechi Amobi, Regent's University London
Dr. Sylvie Studente, Regent's University London
Dr. Stephen Ellis, University of Aberdeen
Dr. Eleonora Cattaneo, César Ritz Colleges, Switzerland
Dr. Patrice Seuwou, The University of Northampton
Dr. Rebecca Fakoussa, The University of Northampton
Vincent Adegoke, London South Bank University
Steve Mancour, Managing Director of Social Media Sorcery
Thomas Smit, Group Chairman of Elegantes London Limited.
Amy Allan for assistance with proofreading.

People and History

CHAPTER 1

Luxury throughout history

Eleonora Cattaneo

1.1 INTRODUCTION

1.1.1 The concept of luxury

Throughout history, luxury has been associated with wealth, rarity, and aspiration (Brun & Castelli, 2013). In latin there are two similar words with overlapping meanings: *luxus*, meaning 'luxury' or 'excess', and *luxuria*, indicating 'rankness' or 'offensiveness' (Stegemann, 2006). These terms became *luxe* and *luxure* in French, with meanings that preserved the distinctions of the original Latin. The French word *luxe* developed the meanings commonly associated with luxury today: wealth and indulgence. The French phase *de luxe*, meaning 'luxurious', became the English word deluxe. Luxury does not have an equivalent expression in all languages; for example, the Japanese use *lugujuri* (phonetic adaption of lu-xu-ry) to refer to experiences in the stores of prestige brands (Kapferer, 2014). Scholars agree that a luxury brand must be able to meet six criteria (i.e., Kapferer, 1998; De Barnier et al., 2012):

- A hedonistic experience and products made to last.
- Offered at a price that far exceeds what their purely functional value would command.
- Bound to heritage, unique know-how and culture.
- Accessible only in very selective or exclusive distribution.
- Offered with personalised accompanying services.
- Representing status, making the owner or beneficiary feel special.

Others are less restrictive, proposing that a luxury product should meet three criteria: have a strong artistic element, be the result of craftsmanship, and have a global brand reputation (Chevalier & Mazzalovo, 2008). The consensus is that true luxury should have a rare and exclusive quality, characteristics that have remained unchanged through the ages. History and heritage are both associated with luxury (Beverland, 2004; Moore & Birtwistle, 2005; Christodoulides *et al.*, 2009), with several authors proposing that heritage and history are central to the success of luxury brands (Moore & Birtwistle, 2005;

DOI: 10.4324/9781003015826-2

Fionda and Moore, 2009; Hudson, 2011). This is supported by contemporary surveys of luxury consumers (Ipsos, 2014), which show that luxury brands are expected to have deep roots in history, as well as exceptional quality, know-how, and authenticity. Additionally, Cooper *et al.* (2015), indicate that there is an explicit connection between brand recovery and 'corporate heritage'. In cases of rebranding or relaunch the heritage factor is essential for success. History is therefore a key characteristic for a luxury brand, allowing it to claim authenticity and heritage. Some authors suggest that if a luxury brand does not have a history it has to invent one (Kapferer & Bastien, 2014). There are three types of history that a luxury brand can use to promote its history (Kapferer & Bastien, 2012):

- True history, authentic as long as it is capable of engendering a modern myth.
- A new, contemporary legend created to fit the brand narrative.
- Reappropriation of true historical elements in the service of a recent brand.

Being 'established' is not enough to qualify a brand as luxury, it simply makes it old. It is therefore important to signal additional qualities which can refer to people (the brand's founder for example), or unique craft skills (Kapferer & Bastien, 2014). The legacy of Chanel's founder Gabrielle 'Coco' Chanel is prominent in the contemporary brand's storytelling. There are Coco-named collections, quotes from her, and references to significant milestones in her career weaved into communications. 'Fashion is not something that exists in dresses only. Fashion is in the sky, in the street, fashion has to do with ideas, the way we live, what is happening' – Coco Chanel.

In 2019, Chanel's creative director Virginie Viard collaborated with film-maker Sofia Coppola for a catwalk show which recreated Coco Chanel's Paris apartment, 31 Rue Cambon. This is where the first Chanel shows were held almost a century ago featuring the mirrored staircase, where Coco would sit, unseen, to watch the models below. For the Haute Couture's Spring/Summer '20 season, Viard staged a runway recreating one of the key locations in Gabrielle Chanel's childhood: the cloister garden of the Abbey of Aubazine. The Italian designer, Elsa Schiapparelli, founded her brand in 1927 in Paris (Papalas, 2017). Her feminine and flirtatious styles were in contrast to Coco Chanel's minimalist designs, and she was known for her elaborate evening dresses. Her famous Lobster dress, a white organdy gown with a lobster printed on it, was the output of a collaboration with Salvador Dalì and caused quite a stir when it was worn by Wallis Simpson in 1937, shortly before her marriage to Edward VIII. Baxter-Wright (2012) stated: 'The juxtaposition of an innocent white floaty dress and a blood-red, supersized lobster placed strategically between the thighs, left little to the imagination'. Elsa Schiapparelli closed her couture house in 1954 and the brand lay dormant until 2006 when it was acquired by Tod's. Della Valle acquired the Schiaparelli brand and its archives in 2006. In 2012, the Schiapparelli Couture House reopened at the Hôtel de Fontpertuis, 21 Place Vendôme, Paris, where it had first started. The brand's identity today draws from Schiaparelli's irreverent spirit using elements of her early collections, and her presence is felt in much of the communication with a view 'to keep the codes alive but also drive the brand forward' (Roseberry, 2020).

1.2 A LUXURY TIMELINE

Some form of 'luxury' is believed to have existed since early mankind; in all societies, ownership of certain objects signalled status. Kapferer and Bastien (2009), use the example of Ancient Egypt which developed specific codes of luxury. The ruling classes, such as the pharaoh, the priests and their inner circle, expressed status through splendour in dress and exclusive products such as perfumes. In democratic Athens, attempts were made to control the indulgence of luxury with periodical clamp downs on excesses. Overall, the state preferred to tax the rich, promoting it as civic duty to 'serve the state as he (citizen) ought and as he best may, the rich man paying, the strong man fighting'.[1] The elite enjoyed lavish lifestyles: 'they have a life so full of delight as if they expect to die tomorrow, but their houses are so well built as if they believe they would live forever'.[2] Their contribution to the public purse earned them valuable social capital.

Luxury and Christianity were at odds throughout medieval Europe (Hunt & Murray, 1999). Since luxury was seen as an obstacle to eternal salvation, the clergy were swift to denounce ownership of jewellery, expensive fabrics and ostentatious swords. Monarchs enacted sumptuary laws to show their compliance, and in fourteenth-century England, under King Edward III, the colour and type of clothing, furs, fabrics, and trims allowed to persons of various ranks or incomes was strictly regulated. In France, Philip IV regulated the dress and the table expenditures of the social orders in his kingdom. The repression of luxury tastes was not specific to Europe; in feudal Japan, sumptuary laws were passed with a frequency and minuteness of scope that had no parallel in the history of the Western world (Shively, 1964).

Sumptuary laws were also a way for the aristocracy to restrain the extravagant consumption habits which the newly rich merchant class were acquiring a taste for (Freudenberger, 1963). If commoners were able to live more lavishly than the nobility, it could undermine the status of the ruling class, who had a social obligation to show inherited rank publicly through the display of expensive items (Muzzarelli, 2009). The Renaissance no longer considered the joys of life entirely sinful, although a way had not yet been found to separate spiritual and secular levels of enjoyment (Franchetti, 2013). As consumerism became an important social force in the course of the Renaissance, earlier efforts to ban certain goods according to social class became increasingly irrelevant. This was reflected in other cultures, with countries such as China, for example, progressively reducing restrictions after 1550. At the time of the European Industrial revolution, Chinese consumption of luxuries, such fine silk, tobacco and eating utensils, was on a par with the higher-income countries in Europe.

The origin of modern luxury can be traced back to the second half of the seventeenth century, in France. Louis XIV and his finance minister, Colbert, established the furniture, textile, clothing, and jewellery industries, forebearers of France's dominance in luxury today. Some early (1678), marketing tools can also be identified at this time in a court publication, *Le Mercure Galant*, which showed the latest 'must-have' fashions and hair styles. All luxury industries flourished in France under Louis XIV and furniture, fine art, dress, and jewellery set the benchmark for other European courts and rich elites (Vincent, 2005).

The economist, Thorstein Veblen, examined luxury consumption in his volume *The Theory of the Leisure Class* (1899). Veblen coined the term 'conspicuous consumption' to describe how people of the 'leisure' class bought goods whose primary function was to confer status. When it came to fashion, for example, an item of clothing sought to demonstrate both that it was expensive and that it would make physical labour impossible; a man's high hat or a woman's high heels signalled that the wearer, as a member of the elite, did not have to perform manual tasks. Veblen also considered activities such as learning dead languages, keeping pet dogs, or collecting furniture and art as 'conspicuous leisure'. These hobbies, and the accessories associated with them, demonstrated that a person had ample time to devote to frivolous pursuits. In the decades to come, luxury brands developed a similar culture of 'exclusion' which, to some extent, can still be observed today. Research on interactions in luxury stores show that respondents experience a feeling of being special – exclusive clients who are buying an exclusive product (Joy et al., 2014).

As in the past, luxury today is very much aligned to societal development. In the case of the twenty-first century, the desire for luxury has not abated, with the market for personal luxury forecast to progress at a CAGR of almost 3% in the period 2021–25, the slowdown of 2020 caused by the COVID-19 pandemic seeming a mere hiccup. However, demand has evolved from a simple craving to own a certain item, to a need to be engaged in an experience that creates an emotional connection, along with a request for brand sustainability and social responsibility. In more recent years, the borders of luxury have been redefined and it can no longer be considered the reserve of a minority elite. Luxury, in all its dimensions, is more accessible, with many brands making shows, product presentations, and launches available online. Entry-level items, the rise of rental and pre-owned items and now NFTs,[3] are making luxury accessible to a wider, and increasingly younger, audience. Brands have become conscious of the importance of finding the right balance between expanding to new and less affluent segments, while preserving the image of a luxury brand in the eyes of their core clientele.

1.3 LUXURY BRANDS TODAY AND HISTORICAL INSPIRATION

Luxury brands have always taken inspiration from history with a view to making 'a better future by developing elements from the past' (Karl Lagerfeld quoting Goethe). Styles, craftsmanship, and use of materials are periodically revived and incorporated into new designs. In the early twentieth century, Madeleine Vionnet, known as 'the architect of dressmakers', shaped her style aesthetic by combining elements of Greek sculpture and architecture, and turning to sculptures like the Winged Victory of Samothrace[4] for her creative collections. The square neckline associated with Anne Boleyn was revived in 2021, with Tudor-style square necks shown on the catwalks of Bottega Veneta among others, styled to complement ruffled sleeves and voluminous dresses. Traditional Swiss watchmakers still use equipment from the nineteenth century to perform age-old processes such as *guillochage*, a technique that produces precise decorative patterns. The watch dials of brands such as Patek Philippe, Audemars Piguet and Chopard are still entirely hand made using age-old methods. In 2018, Louis Vuitton launched a Riders of the Knights jewellery line, inspired by 'lands of legends and audacity'. It showcased 'the power of vision that drove several medieval heroines to transcend their status as women in order to forge their own destiny'. *La Royaume* necklace, the centrepiece of the collection, is shaped like a *gorget*, a chain mail throat-protector worn by knights in battle. As far as materials are concerned, Loro Piana supported the reintroduction of the vicuña[5] to Peru, reviving local ancestral practices to breed and shear sustainably. Today, Loro Piana is the world's number one processor of vicuña wool, the finest fibre that can be legally obtained from an adult animal, with an average diameter of just 12.5–13 microns.

1.4 BRAND HERITAGE

Heritage is more than a reference to the history of the company. It is a multifaceted construct which can help brands focus on different elements to engage customers. Urde et al. (2007) researched a number of heritage case studies and developed a model illustrating the characteristics which define a heritage brand (see Figure 1.1).

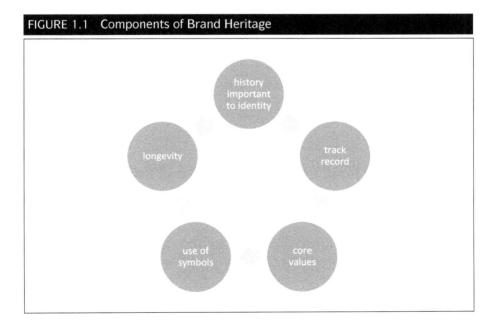

FIGURE 1.1 Components of Brand Heritage

They propose that brand heritage is 'a dimension of a brand's identity found in its track record, longevity, core values, use of symbols and particularly in an organisational belief that its history is important' (Urde et al., 2007). Many brands can claim a history, whereas a heritage can be translated into a corporate asset (Urde et al., 2007). Heritage is also an important value driver as it helps 'define these brands today and add value, especially when they are re-interpreted in a contemporary light'. A brand with a heritage creates and confirms expectations about future behaviour to stakeholder groups, and makes a promise that the brand will continue to deliver on these commitments (Aaker, 1996). Leveraging heritage can be a valuable differentiator for a brand; research has shown that brand heritage has significant effects on the perceived economic, functional, affective and social values of a brand (Wuestefeld et al., 2012). Heritage branding extends to store concepts which can be locations at the heart of a brand's identity and history. These heritage stores are a key component of the brand story. They are more than simply flagship stores (Dion & Arnould, 2011) or brand museums (Hollenbeck et al., 2008). They are an important signal of the brand's heritage.

Heritage branding extends to experiences, in which the service context is an integral part of the value proposition (Weidmann, et al., 2011). This includes the retail industry, especially brands with iconic flagship stores such as Harrods, and the hospitality sector with hotels, restaurants, and resorts. Harrods is described as 'an outstanding example of a department store, exemplifying the commercial confidence of the Edwardian era, and the successful adaptation of the department store to the British market'.[6]

For luxury heritage hotels, identity is inseparable from architecture. Therefore, preserving the condition of the building and other historical evidence, as well as managing the relationship with the surrounding environment, are key factors in maintaining the aura of the brand (Hudson, 2013). The Peninsula Hotel in Hong Kong opened in 1928 and although it has been refurbished to present-day standards, the old-world charm is expressed through spaces such as the lobby and Gaddi's restaurant which features grand chandeliers, brocade curtains, and white-gloved service. Heritage branding produces results in the service sector as well as products. Hudson (2015) found that 'qualitative evidence validates the notion that history [is] an important element of the consumer value proposition for the iconic hotel and contributed in a significant way to the ability to attain a price premium'.

1.5 THE IMPORTANCE OF HERITAGE FOR LUXURY BRANDS

Throughout history, the concepts of production and provenance have been important to luxury brand identity. Links to innovation and craftsmanship, in addition to handcrafted and traditional skills, emphasise the products' rare and unique values (McNeil & Riello, 2016). Provenance means a source of origin, claiming a historical footprint as evidence of authenticity (Collins & Weiss, 2015). The concept of authenticity is also related to heritage, and this has been shown to influence perceived value for the customer (Collins & Weiss, 2015). Luxury brands leverage production and provenance to create rich brand narratives, building personality and image (Collins & Weiss, 2015). The use of historical associations creates value for the customer and promotes authenticity, uniqueness, and reliability (Halwani, 2019).

The most successful luxury brands have managed to balance heritage with innovation, showing their younger consumers how, when, and where the products are made, through rich storytelling and showcasing crafts-manship. Louis Vuitton used this technique to develop 'Voyagez', an exhib-ition displaying iconic pieces that illustrated the history of the brand from 1854 to the present day. The exhibition, which toured a number of world capitals from Paris to Tokyo between 2017 and 2018, featured objects and documents from the Louis Vuitton heritage archives, as well as select articles on loan from the Palais Galliera and the Musée de la Mode de la Ville de Paris. In addition to bringing its past to life for a new generation, Louis Vuitton also adds modern applications to classic pieces such as the Louis Vuitton Echo, a smartphone-controlled luggage tracker. Gucci has taken its 'Artisan Corner' on tour, bringing the craftsmanship of the leather goods factory directly to its clientele in several Asian venues. The Artisan Corner displays a workstation with the tools used to craft leather, as well as background materials which illustrate the evolution of the products, from mood board to sketches. Gucci experts demonstrate the various stages of processing an item, from the selec-tion of the raw material to the final stages of workmanship. Heritage can also be leveraged by creating compelling stories to highlight brand milestones with engaging narrative, thus stimulating consumer conversations. Through these conversations, the relationship between the consumer and the brand, as well as among consumers themselves, can be strengthened (Escalas, 2004).

In 2016, Burberry produced a commemorative three-minute cinematic trailer-style film to mark the 160th anniversary of the brand. Historical events recreated in the film include Thomas Burberry's invention of the weather-proof fabric gabardine, designing military uniforms for World War I, and outfitting polar explorers and pilots. The CEO of the company stated: 'We wanted to tell the story of Thomas Burberry – pioneer, inventor, innovator, and the man behind the iconic trench coat – in our own words. We feel very proud to be sharing *The Tale of Thomas Burberry* – his spirit and his vision are still at the heart of everything we do at Burberry today'.[7] The trench coat stars consistently throughout the film, linking the origin of the brand to the present day, and the iconic plaid also makes several appearances. Although longevity is a key element of heritage and can play a crucial role in engaging consumers, a prestigious past is no longer a priority for the younger luxury consumer. A 2017 Deloitte global study of millennials found that 'quality and uniqueness' are the top factors attracting them to luxury products. Heritage storytelling may have to evolve in years to come to keep engaging with new consumers.

1.6 INSPIRED BY HERITAGE

Luxury brands that are able to claim a heritage generally leverage this exten-sively and consistently (Halwani, 2019). Recently launched luxury brands are recommended to invent a heritage (Kapferer & Bastien, 2014) to firmly anchor their image in history. This is not necessarily a choice that new brands have made in recent years. Daniel Del Core a former Gucci designer built his own brand launching his first collection in 2021 to enthusiastic reviews. Del Core was responsible for developing bespoke couture for Gucci's VIP clients and his own brand has a similarly exclusive target customer. When asked about his style and inspirations for the brand he responded, 'I don't do research in vintage stores';[8] the new brand's identity is explicitly contemporary.

Many recently launched luxury brands use cultural heritage to create their identity. This strategy has been implemented successfully when there is a lack of track record and heritage is 'borrowed' to fill the gap. The Shang Xia brand was established jointly by Chinese designer Jiang Qiong Er and the Hermès Group in 2009. The Chinese characters *Shang* and *Xia* mean 'as above, as below', and the intent is to represent the circulation between the two energies of Yin and Yang, past and future, tradition and innovation, craftsmanship and contemporary design, in 'a symmetrical, balanced beauty between seemingly diametric poles'.[9] The brand offers furniture, homeware, apparel, leather goods, jewellery, accessories, and tea sets which 'bridge the gap between the tangible and the intangible, tradition and present… with a distinctive combination of contemporary design and exquisite hand craftsmanship'.[10] The brand's Da Tian Di collection is inspired by traditional Ming-style furniture. However, the usual rounded outer lines have been developed into a more complex square outline with rounded interior lines. Traditional techniques are used to infuse zitan wood (prized Chinese imperial wood) with a velvet-like texture and each piece from the collection requires about six months' work. The Bridge tea pot collection uses a new weaving technique for a white porcelain tea set based on the traditional bamboo porcelain technique which seamlessly melds one material into the other.

1.7 CHAPTER SUMMARY

In this chapter, a timeline was introduced of how luxury has been perceived throughout history to the present day, showing how it has changed from being the domain of a ruling class, to the current indulgence for any consumer with the disposable income to access it. Claiming a history is important for luxury brands today as it validates qualities such as authenticity, craftsmanship, and personalisation. Consumers consider these essential in a product or service that is expected to be rare and exclusive. History, as an important element of the concept of heritage, has also been discussed. Leveraging heritage holistically can create a powerful identity for a luxury brand.

CASE STUDY 1 Van Cleef & Arpels

The ownership of jewellery and rare gemstones as status symbols can be traced back to the Roman era (McNeil & Riello, 2016). Women would wear gold necklaces or rings imported from Spain, Egypt, Britannia, and Dalmatia, enriched with pearls or gemstones from the Middle

East or India (McNeil & Riello, 2016). Gemstones, gold, and silver continue to signify material achievement but are also used to communicate deeper meanings through items such as engagement and wedding rings (McNeil & Riello, 2016).

The jewellery worn in medieval Europe reflected an intensely hierarchical and status-conscious society. Royalty and nobility wore gold, silver, and precious gems. Lower ranks of society wore base metals, such as copper or pewter. Colour (provided by precious gems and enamel) and perceived protective power were highly valued. Until the late fourteenth century, gems were usually polished rather than cut, and size and colour determined their value. Enamels – ground glasses fired at high temperature onto a metal surface – allowed goldsmiths to colour their designs on jewellery. They used a range of techniques to create effects that are still widely used today. Furthermore, there is a profound theme of the appeal of the exotic in relation to luxury items in history. Oriental luxuries, such as precious stones and pearls, became items of prestige due to their rarity (McNeil & Riello, 2016). The Orient was depicted in history as an exotic land filled with riches, an example being the 'peacock throne' owned by the Mughal Emperor Shah Jahan (McNeil & Riello, 2016).

Luxury jewellery brand, Van Cleef & Arpels, is known for crafting pieces that incorporate extremely rare gemstones. In 1960, the brand purchased a 300-year-old rare pink diamond from India called the 'Princie', that was eventually sold at auction for $39m in 2013 (Doulton, 2015). Craftsmanship is at the core of the brand, with techniques such as the patented *Mystery Set* used to mount precious stones (rubies, sapphires, emeralds, and diamonds), with no prong or other metal component visible. The technique is so complex, that it can require up to eight hours of work to achieve the perfect cut and can only be performed by a select number of master jewellers. The brand has also successfully been producing fine watches since 1910, incorporating gemstones into the designs to create delicate pieces that draw inspiration from historical designs.

The brand claims to be faithful to the values of creation, transmission, and expertise, exemplified through their 'Spirit of Creation' philosophy, which guarantees understated elegance, grace, refinement, asymmetrical design, and innovation through its product designs (www.vancleefarpels.com). Longevity tends to reflect multiple elements of heritage (Urde, et al., 2007). Van Cleef & Arpels has maintained a continuous link to its early years. The headquarters are still located at 22 Place Vendome in Paris, where Alfred Van Cleef, son of a diamond broker and cutter, opened a small boutique in 1906 with his brothers-in-law Charles, Julien, and later, Louis Arpels. Today, the brand has a Heritage collection offering vintage Van Cleef & Arpels pieces to clients in a themed 1906 heritage room. 'The heritage room tells the history of the brand to clients via pieces from our collection where clients can see the craftsmanship, the tools and the moulding' (www.vancleefarpels.com).

History is an important component of the heritage brand identity, influencing current and future operations (Urde et al., 2007). Van Cleef & Arpels' contemporary Navette Mystery Collection draws inspiration from flora and fauna, a favourite theme for the brand. In the 1930s, the brand developed a series of brooches featuring butterflies, flowers, and birds. The new collection uses a 3D effect evocative of the plumage of a bird or the petals of a flower, adapting a technique for emeralds and diamonds to produce designs such as the *Pomme de pin*, a rare piece depicting a delicate cluster of pinecones. The brand's High Jewellery collection is a direct link to history and heritage, targeting ultra-high net worth customers with bespoke pieces and themed collections. The Snowflake High Jewellery collection is inspired by flakes of snow, an inspiration for Van Cleef & Arpels since the 1940s, and features round diamonds combined to form winter motifs.

The continuity of core values helps companies to incorporate heritage as part of their corporate strategy, depicted as a promise used in communication, that forms part of their identity and heritage (Urde, Greyser & Balmer, 2007). Van Cleef & Arpels has maintained the original values of expertise, creation, and transmission to express a 'poetic view of life'. Brand extensions are chosen carefully to ensure consistency and maintain the exclusive and rare image of the brand. In 2008, Van Cleef & Arpels collaborated with Inter Parfums in the fragrance market, developing a perfume to closely align with the high-end jewellery offer (WWD, 2008). The scent was named *Féerie* (fairytale), and the fragrance used notes of mandarin from Southern Italy, iris from Florence, jasmine from Egypt, vetiver from Haiti and rose from Bulgaria (WWD, 2008). This linked the composition to the brand's constant quest to find rare gemstones all over the world. The bottle design depicting a fairy was inspired by the brand's jewellery and used to portray a story of magic and fantasy (WWD, 2008), in line with the core values of the brand.

CASE STUDY 2 Boutique hotels

Eight of Singapore's boutique hotels are found in the officially designated Historic District of Chinatown. The area has its origins in a town plan initiated by Stamford Raffles, who claimed Singapore for the British East India Company in 1819. Chinatown's character is defined by shophouses, a traditional form of architecture with the ground floor devoted to commerce and the upper storeys to private residences. Shophouse styles combine different elements of Chinese, Malay, Indonesian, and European influences. In 1986, after decades of demolitions and replacement by modern buildings, the Singapore Urban Redevelopment Authority (URA), developed a Conservation Master Plan, which included the preservation of substantial portions of the Chinatown landscape. The luxury Duxton Reserve hotel unites a row of heritage shophouses, restored to contemporary luxury standards, with major references to Chinatown's history expressed as 'echoes of 19th century elegance reimagined in the historic heart of Singapore'.[11]

The lobby includes large theatrical golden fans and strong hues of black, gold and yellow, layered with Oriental screens and calligraphy wallpaper. The Duxton Duplex Suite features an original spiral staircase and the Pearl Suites showcase dressers inlaid with mother-of-pearl. The design elements reference the importance of history to the brand's identity and the service component, while in line with modern requirements, also offers a traditional tea ceremony.

Seminar exercises

Discussion topics:

1. Discuss how attitudes to luxury have evolved over time. What has changed?
2. How can a brand incorporate heritage elements and still remain relevant for younger consumers? Thinking of your own relationship with luxury brands, to what extent is heritage a factor in motivating you to engage?
3. Brands use a variety of different cues to signal their relationship with an original, iconic founder. Is this an effective way of communicating heritage? Are there any risks associated with this strategy?

Group exercises:

1. A luxury product should have a strong artistic element, be the result of craftsmanship, and have a global brand reputation (Chevalier and Mazzalovo, 2008). Using two examples of luxury brands, discuss which in your opinion meet all three criteria.
2. Many brands can claim a history, whereas a heritage can be translated into a corporate asset (Urde et al., 2007). Discuss this statement using two examples, one of a brand that is not able to leverage heritage as a corporate asset and one that is.

Notes

1 J. H. Vince, *Demosthenes, English translation* (Cambridge, MA, Harvard University Press; London, William Heinemann Ltd.), 1930.
2 Diogenes Laertius, *Lives and Opinions of Eminent Philosophers*.
3 NFTs are intangible digital items. With NFTs, a physical item can be 'tokenised' to create a digital certificate of ownership that can be bought and sold. As with cryptocurrency, a record of ownership is stored on a shared ledger known as the blockchain.
4 The Winged Victory of Samothrace is a marble Hellenistic sculpture

of Nike (the Greek goddess of victory), created in about the second century BC. Since 1884, it is displayed at the Louvre and is one of the most celebrated sculptures in the world.

5 The vicuña is a wild South American camelid which lives in the high alpine areas of the Andes. Vicuñas produce small amounts of extremely fine wool, which is very expensive as the animal can only be shorn once every three years.

6 www.rbkc.gov.uk/

7 Christopher Bailey interviewed in Vogue UK, 1 November 2016.

8 Vogue, 25 February 2021.

9 www.shang-xia.com/EN/brand.html

10 www.shang-xia.com/EN/brand.html

11 https://duxtonreserve.com/

References

Aaker, D. (1996). *Building Strong Brands*. FreePress, New York.

Baxter-Wright, E. (2012). *The Little Book of Schiaparelli*. Carlton Books, Glasgow.

Beverland, M. (2004). 'Uncovering "theories-in-use": Building luxury wine brands'. *European Journal of Marketing*, 38(3/4), 446–466.

Brun, A. and Castelli, C. (2013). 'The nature of luxury: a consumer perspective'. *International Journal of Retail and Distribution Management*, 41(11/12), 823–847.

Chevalier, M., and Mazzalovo, G. (2008). *Luxury Brand Management: A World of Privilege*. John Wiley & Sons.

Christodoulides, G. et al. (2009). 'Measuring perceived brand luxury: An evaluation of the BLI scale'. *Journal of Brand Management*, 16(5), 395–405.

Collins, M. and Weiss, M. (2015). 'The role of provenance in luxury textile brands'. *International Journal of Retail & Distribution Management*, 43(10/11), 1030–1050.

Cooper, H., Miller, D., & Merrilees, B. (2015). 'Restoring luxury corporate heritage brands: From crisis to ascendency'. *Journal of Brand Management*, 22(5), 448–466.050.

De Barnier, V., Falcy, S., & Valette-Florence, P. (2012). 'Do consumers perceive three levels of luxury? A comparison of accessible, intermediate and inaccessible luxury brands'. *Journal of Brand Management*, 19(7), 623–636.

Dion, D., Arnould, E.J. (2011) 'Retail luxury strategy: assembling charisma through art and magic'. *Journal of Retailing*, 87(4), 502–520.

Doulton, M. (2015). Diamond sales: Records broken as frenzy for rare rocks takes hold, Financial Times. www.ft.com/content/4b46768c-a532-11e2-8777-00144feabdc0

Escalas, J. (2004). 'Narrative processing: building consumer connections to brands', *Journal of Consumer Psychology*, 14, 168–180.

Franchetti, C. (2013). 'A reconsideration of werner sombart's "Luxury and Capitalism"'. *International Review of Social Sciences and Humanities*, 5(2), 135–137.

Freudenberger, H. (1963). 'Fashion, sumptuary laws, and business. *Business History Review*'. 37(1–2), 37–48.

Fionda, A. & Moore, C. (2009). 'The anatomy of the luxury fashion brand', *Journal of Brand Management*, 16(5), 347–363.

Halwani, L. (2019). 'Making Sense of heritage luxury brands: consumer perceptions across different age groups'. *Qualitative Market Research: An International Journal*, 22(3), 301–324.

Hollenbeck, C.R., Peters, C., and Zinkhan, G.M. (2008). 'Retail spectacles and brand meaning: insights from a brand museum case study', *Journal of Retailing*. 84(3): 334–353.

Hudson, B. (2011). 'Brand Heritage and the renaissance of Cunard', *European*

Journal of Marketing, 45, 9/10. 1538–1556.

Hudson, B. (2013). 'Brand Heritage and Heritage Tourism'. *Boston Hospitality Review*, 1(3), 12–16.

Hudson, B. (2015). 'The pricing effects of heritage at an iconic hotel'. *Boston Hospitality Review (online)*.

Hunt, E. and Murray, J. (1999). *A History of Business in Medieval Europe. 1200–1550*. Cambridge University Press, Cambridge.

IPSOS (2014). *World Luxury Tracking Survey: Mature and Emerging Countries*, Paris.

Joy, A., Jianfeng Wang, J., Sing Chan, T., Sherry Jr., J.F., and Cui, G. (2014). 'M(Art)worlds: Consumer Perceptions of How Luxury Brand Stores Become Art Institutions'. *Journal of Retailing*, 90(3), 347–64.

Kapferer, J. N. (1998). 'Why are we seduced by luxury brands?' *Journal of Brand Management*, 6(1), 44–49.

Kapferer, J. N. (2012). 'Abundant rarity: The key to luxury growth', *Business Horizons*, 55(5), 453–462.

Kapferer, J. N. (2014). 'The future of luxury: Challenges and opportunities'. *Journal of Brand Management*, 21(9), 716–726.

Kapferer, J. N. and Bastien, V. (2009). 'The specificity of luxury management: turning marketing upside down'. *Journal of Brand Management*, 16(5), 311–322.

Kapferer, J. N., and Bastien, V. (2012). *The Luxury Strategy: Break the Rules of Marketing to Build Luxury Brands*. London: Kogan Page Publishers.

McNeil, P. and Riello, G. (2016). *Luxury: A Rich History*. Oxford: Oxford University Press.

Moore, C. and Birtwistle, G. (2005). 'The nature of parenting advantage in luxury fashion retailing – the case of Gucci group NV'. *International Journal of Retail & Distribution Management*, 33(4), 256–270.

Muzzarelli, M. (2009). 'Reconciling the privilege of a few with the common good: sumptuary laws in medieval and early modern Europe'. *Journal of Medieval and Early Modern Studies*, 39(3), 597–617.

Papalas, M. (2017). 'Fashion in interwar France: the urban vision of Elsa Schiapelli'. *French Cultural Studies*, Doi: https://doi.org/10.1177/0957155817693512.

Roseberry, D. (2020). Interview with the artistic director of Schiapparelli, 20 February 2020, *Financial Times*.

Shively, D. (1964). 'Sumptuary regulation and status in early Tokugawa Japan'. *Harvard Journal of Asiatic Studies*, 25(1964–1965), 123–164.

Stegemann, N. (2006). 'Unique brand extension challenges for luxury brands', *Journal of Business & Economics Research* 4(10): 57–68.

Urde, M., Greyser, S. A., Balmer, J. M. T. (2007). 'Corporate brands with a heritage', *Journal of Brand Management* 15(1): 4–19.

Veblen, T. (1899). *The theory of the leisure class*. New York, NY: Macmillan.

Vincent, M. (2005). 'Le Mercure Galant: Présentation de la première revue eminine d'information et de culture, 1672–1710'. (Sources classiques, 57). Paris, Champion, 2005.

Weidmann, K., Hennigs, N., Schmidt, S. & Wuestefeld, T. (2011). 'The importance of brand heritage as a key performance driver in marketing management'. *Journal of Brand Management*, 19, 182–194.

Wuestefeld, T. et al. (2012). 'The impact of brand heritage on customer perceived value'. *International Journal of Marketing*, Special Issue February 2012, 51–61.

Weil, J. (2008). Van Cleef & Arpels evokes Luxe (Online). Available from: https://wwd.com/feature/van-cleef-arpels-evokes-luxe-1706143-1629904/

CHAPTER 2

Luxury start-ups

Zubin Sethna and Rebecca Fakoussa

2.1 INTRODUCTION

Looking back in history, we know that both Socrates and Plato had noted that it was inevitable that luxury would become a defining element of civilised society. According to Professor Howard Stevenson of Harvard Business School, entrepreneurship is defined as 'a process by which individuals – either on their own or inside organisations – pursue opportunities without regard to the resources they currently control' (Stevenson, Roberts, and Grousbeck, 1989). This may seem somewhat philosophical until you start to de-construct the words. This definition is all about the entrepreneurial actor focusing on grabbing an opportunity whilst a perceived 'short window' presents itself, but under an umbrella of resource constraints.

2.2 START-UPS

A 'start-up' is a term which became quite popular in the 1990s during the dot-com boom era. This is where an entrepreneur will seek, develop, and validate a scalable economic model, and has sole control of the capital, whether that be financial, social, or human. Many entrepreneurs will, of course, keep much of the capital being spent to a bare minimum (bootstrapping), until the enterprise becomes self-sustaining from generating their own cash flow. With luxury start-ups, many entrepreneurs need to find and activate more resources than they control personally in order to satisfy the demands that their target audience requires. This creates another issue; the combination of a lack of access to required resources (the three types of capital we talked about earlier), combined with the pursuance of a novel opportunity, is inevitably going to lead to a risk of sorts! The entrepreneur needs to assess this risk and find potential solutions depending on which perspective the risk comes from – demand, finance, technology, or execution. The literature on entrepreneurship has grown tremendously over the past 30 years and the

DOI: 10.4324/9781003015826-3

'enterprise narrative' is predominantly built around two differing views: the narrow view and the broad view.

According to early commentators such as Amin et al. (2002), Dees et al. (2001) and Dart (2004), there is a strong relationship between entrepreneurship and economics, and thus, exploring and later exploiting market creation opportunities, can be 'satisfying demand in new and not so new markets' (Bjerke and Hultman, 2013). This is commonly referred to as the 'narrow view of entrepreneurship' and sometimes referred to as 'the American view'. The 'broad view' of entrepreneurship denotes that 'it' belongs not just to an economic domain but to the 'whole' of society, and therefore the term is applied when creating anything new. This is equally supported by a plethora of commentators, notably Bjerke (2007), and Steyaert and Hjorth (2003), and is sometimes known as 'the Scandinavian view' (Bill et al., 2010). However, the literature on 'luxury' has struggled to find a consensus for the definition of the luxury concept (Wirtz et al., 2020), and according to Ko et al. (2019) there is generally no accepted definition. The word 'luxury' has often been defined very simply as: 'a state of great comfort or elegance, especially when involving great expense'. Interestingly, as per Ko et al. (2019), the 'narrow set of dimensions' include 'high product quality, high price, exclusivity, and positive customer emotions'. One could argue then that the 'broad set of dimensions' could include social hierarchy, hereditary luxury, and guardianship/stewardship inheritance. So, in bringing these two definitions together, you find that that 'luxury start-up' is the epitome of elegance, the very core of comfort, and a picture of perfection! Luxury start-ups cherish the idea of their customers, or should we say clients, ensuring that there is living perfection in their lives. The global luxury goods industry, which includes cars, jets, drinks, fashion, cosmetics, fragrances, jewelry, and handbags, has increased in value for many years, estimated at $281 billion in 2021 (Statista, 2021a). Entrepreneurs strive to develop products which become sought after status symbols which they hope that clients will acquire and use often. In providing examples of what it means to enjoy a luxury experience, we have recent start-ups such as Brimoncourt Champagne, the Tesla Model S Plaid, and Starr Luxury Jets, all making a significant impact in the luxury start-up space. This rise in demand can be clearly seen in emerging markets, with D'Arpizio and Levato (2017) reporting that the global luxury market grew to almost 1.5 trillion USD in 2017. However, during 2020 and the global pandemic, the global personal luxury goods market has contracted between 20–35% (Bain, 2020).

2.3 WHAT IS 'LUXURY'?

What exactly do you envisage when thinking about the word 'luxury'? At this point, it is worth noting the existing models of 'levels of luxury' (usually visualised with a pyramid), of which one of the most renowned is Kapferer (2012) as well as Rambourg's (2020) model which both suggest that the luxury space can be viewed from a multi-layered perspective. Kapferer's (2012) narrower categories include: unique luxury, luxury, premiere, and standard.

Rambourg's (2020) model takes a slightly broader perspective with his categories which include: bespoke, ultra-high end, super premium, premium core, accessible core, affordable luxury, and everyday luxury. People are at the centre of luxury concepts regardless of whether we are talking about tangible products or intangible services. Luxury service attributes can be easily defined. A comprehensive definition says, 'economic activities performed by one party for another through access to labour, skills, expertise, goods, facilities, networks, and systems; they are time-based, and no transfer of ownership takes place in service transactions' (Wirtz and Lovelock, 2016, p. 21).

The key question here, is what do these terms really mean to customers of luxury products/services and how do they define luxury? It all, of course, starts with the entrepreneur! What is their prior experience and expertise? Without wishing to re-invent the wheel, we suggest that a good way of making some sense of these levels is by their application to real-world entrepreneurs which is what we will do throughout this chapter.

The differentiation could appear to be linked to the different elements of Maslow's hierarchy of needs. The historical understanding can potentially be construed as the top of the pyramid (self-actualisation) being the conduit into the luxury space. However, given recent works by Rambourg (2020), it seems that a shift has occurred from self-actualisation to belonging. This means that entrepreneurs serving every level of any such pyramid need to be fully cognisant of the potential for targeting consumers in a more inclusive way; a way in which the entrepreneur includes everybody who wants to 'belong', not necessarily only those who have the immediate financial means. All of this of course means that you (the entrepreneur) need to consider who your consumers and customers are (Sethna and Blythe, 2019). The answer to this question is simple; all those people with status who want to enjoy your brand, and those also aspiring to be part of your brand.

Entrepreneurs wanting to start-up in the luxury space therefore need to be aware of several concepts:

- **Trust and Relationships.** 'Luxury' is very much dependent on the individual's perspective of what luxury is. While established brands build on their heritage and might target certain related niche areas, they are able to do so based on the already established trust and longevity of the relationship, sometimes built over generations. Luxury start-ups need to position themselves carefully and consider where and how they want to position themselves within the minds of the luxury consumer.
- **Type of luxury and the positioning of enterprise**. There is a vast continuum of consumers and their related behaviours, which goes to make up what could be loosely known as luxury. Furthermore, there is a shift away from the historical/traditional notion of luxury as indulged by the ultra-high-net-worth individuals, to consumers who simply want to belong and are willing to pay for this – even if it means that indulgence is beyond their financial means.
- **Location and technology**. Luxury start-ups may find themselves being heavily dependent upon using both location and technology, to support them to identify and service a niche market.

2.4 THE 'WHEN, WHERE, WHAT AND WHY' OF LUXURY START-UPS

To further investigate the structure, makeup and nature of the 'luxury start-up', we need to examine the different elements of which a start-up comprises. Broadly speaking, the key questions for consideration include:

1. When? – getting the timing right
2. Where? – channel/route to market
3. What? – industries/offerings and discovery
4. Why? – benefits (narrow and broad) and overall purpose

By starting to answer these questions, you will develop an overview of the different elements that are needed at the start of your entrepreneurial journey and which you as an entrepreneur will have to contend with, all the while considering that this is *your* luxury enterprise. Each of the following sections is divided into two parts: theory and practice. This will allow you to understand the theoretical concepts first, followed by the practical applications and their implications for a range of luxury enterprises ranging from tech to transport and wood to waste. Compared to a historical notion of luxury brands, luxury start-ups lack something major – heritage – which some would say is a key element of luxury. We have tried to steer clear from the 'classic' luxury sectors of fashion, hotels, foods, or private planes/yachts (which are often steeped in heritage), and instead have brought you a selection of inspirational enterprises from across the primary, secondary, and tertiary sectors. These examples cover a variety of online to offline businesses – all heterogeneity of luxury start-ups – and this will help you to develop and contextualise your understanding of firms within the luxury market.

Using each of the sections (when, where, what, and why), please find below Table 2.1 to give you an overview of the different case companies that you can find throughout this chapter.

TABLE 2.1 Cases for each of the sections	
Section	**Case company**
Section on *When*	www.brikk.com/ Business: gold and diamond encrusted technology Country: USA
Section on *Where*	https://starrluxurycars.com Business: luxury car hire specialist Country: UK
Section on *What*	https://xibitxr.com/ Business: augmented reality furniture Country: Germany
Section on *Why*	www.sea2see.org/ Business: sustainable glasses Country: Switzerland

2.4.1 'When?' Getting the timing right

Business history has shown us time and time again, that organisations use luxury goods and services to differentiate themselves from the crowd, and in turn provide stability and often significant long-term profits. On the flipside, luxury purchases remain highly appealing to many, if not afford-able by all. Originating from the mass consumption of traditional luxury products, through the social and technological production period, entering a period of high-growth amongst the new urban classes in Europe (Broit, 2011), Rambourg (2020) noted that the utility of luxury consumption ranges from fitting into society to feeling happy and empowered and complete. Back in the 1960s to 1980s, many of the players in the 'luxury' market were 'them-selves small and medium-sized enterprises, owned and managed by families and organised like crafts, without the financial and marketing resources to meet the demand' (Donze and Fujioka, 2015). It is important for start-ups to regard the 'super-premium' luxury market as a different entity to the usual luxury market. There are many different factors to consider when it comes to the super-premium luxury market. For one, the fluctuations tend to be larger in this market, which makes it vital to secure the correct timing of the entry point.

Over the past 80 years of post-industrial revolution, we have witnessed the launch of numerous products and services, and where the primary agent for failure has been a misjudgment as far as 'timing' is concerned. Luxury products and brands are not immune to failure and need to continu-ously remind themselves of the process of building on past failures when braving new encounters. The effects of failure are multiple and there are many arguments both for and against, pros and cons (Neck and Corbett, 2018). Undergoing the process of failure certainly intensifies our cognitive processes which include thinking, knowing, remembering, judging, and problem-solving. These are higher-level functions of the brain and encom-pass language, imagination, perception, and planning.

Starting a new venture can be frightening and/or daunting. When do you know it is the right time? Taking that leap of faith can be difficult espe-cially knowing that the whole industry has been slowly changing to include vertical integration. It might be an organic and slow start, as you turn a hobby into a part-time and then full-time business, or you might invest heavily in resources and go 'all in'. Either way, at some point you just have to start and then keep going. Remember that you may also need to identify any particular or emergent business and/or consumer trends.

Case study for When – BRIKK

BRIKK, USA – gold and diamond encrusted technology (www.brikk.com/)

Founded in 2009, by Cyrus Blacksmith in Los Angeles, USA, BRIKK designs and manufactures couture products and accessories for tech-nology and lifestyle industries (Crunchbase, 2020). BRIKK appeared in the popular press in 2015, where the $349 Apple Watch was billed for purchase for $75,000 as it was a 24-carat gold and diamond-encrusted version. More than just a brand, BRIKK exists to ensure sophistication in every aspect of life. BRIKK brings the opulence (www.brikk.com). According to their website: 'More than a single gold-plated iPhone, solid titanium wheels, or a diamond encrusted watch, BRIKK is an all-encompassing lifestyle designed to flaunt a gilded life' (BRIKK, 2021). It can be considered a technology luxury design firm as it encrusts by artisan hand and constructs luxury items from companies such as Apple, Nikon, and Sony technologies with different carat metals such as gold or titanium as well as diamonds. BRIKK has stockists around the world in Los Angeles (USA), Hong Kong, Paris (France) and Shenzhen (China) as well as its own concierge service. Their website states: 'BRIKK only uses the finest of materials. From near imperial jade to purple diamonds, BRIKK customises its products to match the taste and personal fashion of all their clients. Everything is handcrafted by gifted artisans, resulting in the perfect extravagance every time. Special products will often be run in sets of 77 to further underscore their uniqueness and make them eternally extraordinary. Always in vogue, BRIKK is the definition of splendid rarity' (BRIKK, 2021).

BRIKK designs luxury versions of all items, where personalisation is possible and customisation is encouraged. Items range from Lux AirPods to Apple Watch and iPhone docks as well as items from other brands including Nikon and Sony. BRIKK created a premium version of Sony's DualShock 4 Controller for the PlayStation 4 (Classic and Deluxe versions), using conflict free diamonds, 24 and 18 carat gold, as well as the option of full customisation with a variety of bespoke options like platinum plating, titanium buttons, ruby embellishment and gaming-focused upgrades. Prices were at 8,495 and 13,995 USD (Li, 2018).

In addition to delivering high quality items globally, BRIKK also offers a one-year BRIKK global warranty and has multiple service centres for cleaning and repair, as its focus is on opulence and limited artisan luxury. 'All of BRIKK's products are designed to be nothing less than fabulous, with the sole purpose of making their devices the envy of the masses. The stunning elegance of BRIKK's heptagon-based logo makes each and every product immediately recognisable, demanding respect. Available only to the select few, BRIKK is luxury on display' (BRIKK, 2021).

Getting their timing right has been crucial for BRIKK. They chose their 'when' based around new products in order to deliver their personalised approach. Their expansion examines different tech products and follows the demands of their customers, providing artisan solutions of opulent elegance for emerging gadgets, mobiles, and toys. BRIKK has created a super-premium luxury brand.

Whilst timing is important, remember that it is merely a function of finding the right balance between supply and demand and the route to market, which we cover in the next section.

Questions to ask yourself:

- Have you done enough research to know if there is a market for your product/service?
- Are you aware of the emergent trends where you'll need to give credence to timing?
- Did you know that you can start and then adapt along the way?
- If not now, then when?

2.4.2 'Where?' Getting the right channel/route to market

'Bricks versus clicks' (physical versus online presence and the vertical integration that many firms have engaged in) is a common phrase. However, where are you planning on being, and where will you actually be? Any (bed)room, garage, village, town, city, or capital can be the best place to start, but making that decision depends on a multitude of factors and can potentially be quite hard. Remember that this is about the where – your route to market. You might be located online, or perhaps you feel you're a 'born global'. In case you're unfamiliar with the term 'born global', the London Business School defines it as 'business organisations that, from inception, seek to derive significant competitive advantage from the use of resources and the sale of outputs in multiple countries' (www.london.edu, 2008). Of course, availability and/or lack of financing may be a contributor to the decision (Warhuus, Frid, and Gartner, 2021). Alternatively, you might need a physical location where you would consider the likely footfall (Khare, Awasthi, and Shukla, 2019) and also the representative surrounding buildings. You might be a digital entrepreneur and have remote workers yourself (Aroles, Granter, and Vaujany, 2020), and a team based around the world in different time zones, or you might think that face-to-face in the same office is key. Choosing the 'where' – your effective route-to-market strategy – can be crucial to initial success (Gabrielsson, Kirpalani, and Luostarinen, 2002; Goyal, 2018). It will not only enable the company to develop operational plans for a strong customer focus but also to align its strategic goals and value offerings. In management speak, this is about balancing customer needs with revenue growth and profitability (Hawkins and Hoon, 2020), something which every entrepreneur must be cognisant of.

In terms of developing a strong customer focus, designing a 'buyer persona' (Lehnert, Goupil, and Brand, 2021), might really help you understand where to pitch your idea and where best to start up. Alternatively, if you are reliant on certain natural resources (Lazarus et al., 2015) or artisan crafts, you may or may not be location bound (Lechuga-Cardozo et al., 2019). In amongst those considerations, you will find out where your customers are and whether you need to be there with them too. This is especially applicable for a transient target market of high-net-worth individuals (HNWI) and/or ultra-high-net-worth individuals (UHNWI).

The total number of HNWIs continues to grow at a significant rate of around 7% per year, surpassing the 20 million bar of HNWIs around the world (based on Capgemini's definition of an HNWI as an individual with 1 million USD in wealth to invest). By contrast, the definition of an ultra-HNWI is a HNWI with investable assets of 30 million USD or more.

These buyer personas may help an organisation to further craft its offering. Statista (2020) shows the distribution of ultra-high-net-worth individuals in selected countries in 2019, with a total 80,508 individuals with net assets of at least 50 million USD who are residing in the United States, the highest number of any country. Entrepreneurs may find the dominance of men in ultra-high-net-worth populations – a global trend – somewhat useful. In contrast, the female share of ultra-high net worth in the United States in 2014 stood at 13%, comparable to 14% of the United Kingdom and 12% of Germany seen in Europe. Entrepreneurs could use the Wealth Report available at www.visualcapitalist.com (Neufeld, 2020), which shows the countries with the highest number of UHNWIs, to help craft their offering to a target population. Interestingly, this also gives an indication of how the number of UHNWIs is projected to change in years to come.

Case Study for Where – STARR

STARR Luxury Cars, UK (www.starrluxurycars.com)

Starr Luxury cars was founded by Ikenna Ordor, who positioned his business in London, UK. He targets the luxury travel market, and his website claims they have the 'largest luxury car fleet'. Ikenna, who grew up in Nigeria until the age of 14, is the youngest of seven children. However, having started to study in the UK, he initially launched an entertainment company in the north of England (Olalekan, 2019). His business idea evolved and changed due to his clients demands. They asked for transportation, and Ikenna was happy to oblige. He specialised in travel, starting with luxury transportation in the capital of the UK. He now has a fleet of 'over 80 cars available and offers a nationwide delivery' (StarrLuxuryCars, 2021a). Their cars include luxury marques such as Aston Martin, Bentley, Bugatti, Ferrari, and Lamborghini. Starr Luxury offers these cars as self-drive hires or chauffeur-driven experiences. In addition, they can be used for events, including music videos, TV and filming, weddings, promotions, and special occasions. Ikenna realised that clients wanted experiences which money couldn't as yet buy, and which could be location independent. However, his clients were initially location sensitive and lived mainly in London. Ikenna sensibly decided to build his business around his customer base. Whilst the company is located in Mayfair, central London, the business provides a seamless experience for its many international clients and operates nationally and internationally.

While their locations are important, their own location choice does not influence their customer experience. They will provide the experience a customer wants, from anywhere, using technology of course. Starr Luxury Cars has been designed to be semi-automated and accessible any time of day from anywhere. Clients can access the website and pay for a vehicle without having to speak to anyone, 24/7, 365 days a year, and customers can have cars delivered to their area or address of choice. Importantly, as a lesson for entrepreneurs, Ikenna describes his business as an 'asset light' experience. He notes that his service means customers do not have to concern themselves with car repairs or maintenance, meaning that customers can arrive at any location and immediately enjoy the experience.

Starr Luxury Cars offers clients other enhanced services too, including chauffeur-driven Lamborghinis, helicopter rides over London, and meet and greets with a Formula 1 racer (StarrLuxuryCars, 2021b). As a part of his 'buyer persona' build, he considered that HNWIs and Ultra-HNWIs wanted to celebrate their money with classic James Bond-esque cars, helicopters and boats, but with the modern ease and immediacy of booking through peer-to-peer platforms, like for instance Airbnb. Ikenna's business is now looking at further locations and has its sights set on expansion. Based on Ikenna's target market, other locations around the world where people seek fun and luxury lifestyles will continue to be targeted, showing how important location is. Who was it who once famously said, 'it's all about location, location, location!'? While Starr Luxury Cars sets its sights on the next target locations, including Monaco, Geneva, Paris, Dubai, renowned for both their tourist market and the local market, you might want to consider location, its importance to your business, and more importantly, to your customer.

Starr Luxury cars has created a premium core luxury brand.

Questions to ask yourself:

- Where do you see yourself in five years?
- Where are your customers?
- Where are your suppliers/customers/clients/workforce?

2.4.3 What? The right product/service offering

Start-ups can of course be across any industry sector – from banking to fashion, technology to travel, and everything in-between! The global luxury goods industry includes cars, jets, drinks, fashion, cosmetics, fragrances, jewellery, and handbags. The key to remember is that ultimately the shareholders are the consumers. In the current climate in 2022, with many firms battling with what a post-COVID post-normal world will look like, it seems that both sustainability and a move towards more responsible consumption are equally important. The actions taken by an entrepreneur will of course then have implications for the product/service portfolio, and ultimately the performance of the firm (Sproul, Cox, and Ross, 2019). Another way of looking at performance is profitability (Tenucci and Supino, 2020), which would suffer if the 'offering' is out of kilter with market needs/demands, especially when sustainability is so important in our fast-developing circular economies (Matschewsky, 2019).

Some larger brands at times diversify their portfolio by using mergers and acquisitions of more niche luxury brands. For example, this is largely how LVMH has amassed its fortunes – note that as of writing in 2022, Bernard Arnault became the world's richest man with a fortune of $186.3 billion. In going through this process, many companies adopt lessons-learned practices by developing product-service systems (PSS), to further transform gained experiences into useful knowledge (Chirumalla, 2016). Interestingly, it seems that age, and potentially hormones, are likely to have an impact when it comes to acquisitions. Young male CEOs appear to be combative: they are 4% more likely to be acquisitive and, having initiated an acquisition, they are over 20% more likely to withdraw an offer (Levi, Li, and Zhang, 2010). Even with a recent flurry of various mergers and acquisitions, including Etsy's acquisition of Depop for 1.6 billion USD, which would ordinarily suggest that there are some very rich rewards to be had, there are still some firms who are unwilling to sell, due to their values-based operation or indeed their heritage. In amongst this, is a thriving resale market for luxury items. Whilst Kering earlier in 2021, backed a new 178 million Euro financing round for luxury resale platform Vestiaire Collective, rival LVMH Moët Hennessy Louis Vuitton, the world's largest luxury group with brands like Louis Vuitton, Dior, and Fendi, said it does not plan to get involved at present.

According to Statista (2021b), the US, Germany, and the UK, revealed that 'fashion and accessories' is the most popular category when it comes to gifting or buying in all three countries while France leads in the number of leading luxury products companies globally.

Case Study for What – Xibit

Xibit Augmented Reality, Germany (https://xibitxr.com/)

Abdeljalil Karam and Zakaria Jaiathe co-founded Xibit in 2019 in Berlin, Germany. Xibit, considers itself the market leader in mixed-reality brand experiences, specialising in visualising furniture in a space pre-purchase. One of the elements that makes this start-up so exciting is the 'what'. Jaiathe worked for SAP as a software engineer for about six years, growing his skills from a full-stack developer to a virtual reality (VR)/augmented reality (AR) specialist. While he had a great career and comfortable life, he wanted more. So, he quit his role and used his skills to co-start Xibit.

Xibit set out to reinvent how people design, consider and acquire their interior environment. Using cutting-edge technology, Xibit is a mixed reality platform. You can stand in your room, office, or space, and can add chosen products virtually into the room before you choose to buy. This means you can really 'see' what a table, chair, light, or other item would look like virtually within your given area. Augmented reality technology allows you to visualise furniture products before you purchase them. Gone are the days of measuring your space (sometimes incorrectly), checking the aesthetic design and comparing prices or brands. 'Xibit is the first cross-brand furniture marketplace natively designed with augmented reality for the convenience of customers. Deciding which furniture to purchase is overwhelming. We work on removing the effort to measure, find the right product, and check if it fits in a matter of minutes' (Xibit, 2021).

Xibit styles itself as a sustainable marketplace. It aims to reduce the logistics and shipping of unnecessary products as well as minimise dissatisfied customers consuming products they do not like by using augmented reality. Further, they sign-post to the added-value they bring to their customers: 'As a customer you can find all furniture in one space, making furniture buying easier but also to see immediately how different items interact with each other in your chosen space. Once you have this visualization you can also share a video of your designs with your chosen Network. Thereby collecting opinions and influencing your purchasing decision' (Xibit, 2021).

Xibit has built trust with world-class companies such as McKinsey, SAP, and Techstars (Alldus, 2020), and has been so successful that it has won a string of awards including Global Luxury Innovation Award™ 2020, and the Beautiful Software Award 2019 shows that Xibit has identified the 'what'. Their industry experience and support of the customers' choices demonstrates a deep understanding of the industry and its customers' requirements. Xibit have created an accessible core luxury brand.

Questions to ask yourself:

- What industries do you care about? What interests you?
- How much do you know about your own product/service offering?
- Do you have a hobby that you could turn into a business?
- What is a problem or issue that you, or others, face that you can offer a solution to?

2.4.4 Why? The value created and captured

Opportunity recognition is the cornerstone of many entrepreneurial start-ups. It can be conceived as 'an activity that can occur both prior to firm founding and after firm founding throughout the life of the firm' (Hills and Singh, 2004). This includes 'seeking, recognizing, fostering, expanding and creating opportunity, together with the activities involved in value creation and capture when exploiting opportunity' (Morris et al., 2013). It is a concept that the entrepreneur believes will create more value than currently exists in the market, but it has to be genuine.

There are different ways that entrepreneurs might approach thinking about, and realising their own start-up, the value they create, and the benefits that it provides to their customers. Their start-up exists because an opportunity exists, and one which they can exploit. They could identify a gap in the market and try to close it to ultimately profit from a customer need. On occasion, and especially after disasters (for instance the Covid pandemic), there are opportunities which present themselves (Gur et al., 2020). Alternatively, using a variety of techniques, they might create an opportunity from scratch by having a business idea, or using a breakthrough technology. Many start-ups consider the notion of price sensitivity, whereas luxury start-ups might choose to focus on economics, quality, and purpose. You are creating a brand/product/service that is more luxurious than others, but the function (unless you are in the tech or musical sector) is arguably the same. Luxury travel, soap or sunglasses are still functional but use higher grade materials or have artisan craftsman. And now, more than ever, luxury is also concerning itself with purpose and sustainability.

So, ultimately, it's all about the value that's created and/or captured. Let's dip into value creation first. A luxury start-up strives to provide benefit through the product, packaging design, and the features which differentiate its brand. With this brand building comes a notion of security and longevity. The more that clients/customers engage, the more the brand develops its customer knowledge and this cycle repeats through promotion. This newfound confidence enables the firm to provide utility functions through its distribution channels, both offline and online, and often with shorter order cycles with logistics. The exclusivity for many luxury start-ups with their intricate and often highly tailored and individualised client/customer service programmes enables an enhanced buyer experience.

From a value capture perspective, there are several strategies that a luxury start-up could utilise. In order to differentiate themselves, many luxury businesses have started implementing a unique business model. For instance, take Cartier as the first luxury watch brand to advertise on WeChat via an influencer campaign in 2016. Attaining patents, licenses, and permits is fine but there has always been some tension around the somewhat contradictory concepts of license and luxury. Ask yourselves whether it is wise for a start-up to make such a strategic decision to license – which involves fundamental choices about the configuration of its value-chain, which can undoubtedly involve short-term profitability and possibly scale as well, but all as a result of partially surrendering operational control. Other value-capture perspectives include attracting clients away from your competition by creating customer switching costs, establishing exclusive relationships with suppliers/distributors, building on a 'resource-based theory' by acquiring resources or assets that cannot be easily replicated, developing proprietary knowledge, achieving sustainable differentiation, and taking a stance which has ethical luxury written all over it. In this regard, start-up luxury can learn a lot from established players.

Since the beginning of 2020, the Valentino Fashion Group, and the Armani Group, have set a target of zero discharges of harmful waste by seeking to eliminate all hazardous chemicals from the production processes. By using a chemical test management system adopted in all of Armani's factories, they can use a group-wide test request form to enable real-time tracking of such materials. A company known as 'Evolved by Nature' (EbN), attracted investment from Chanel. EbN creates high-performing textiles from liquid-silk, providing a natural alternative to toxic chemicals that are often used in manufacturing processes and thus promoting green technology. Aims and objectives are important and are being set by many players, for example Ralph Lauren has promised to use 100% sustainability-sourced key materials and to increase the proportion of female employees by 25% by 2025 (Ralph Lauren, 2020). Moncler has set various standards through a mandatory Supplier Code of Conduct which requires full transparency for material sourcing, factories, and manufacturing processes. The code also very clearly states that suppliers must not employ anyone under the age of 15 or below the legal age for employment in the country concerned, whichever is higher (Moncler Supplier Code of Conduct, 2016). Similarly, the Kering Group (owners of Gucci, Balenciaga, Saint Laurent, and Bottega Veneta), have clearly stated that they will only hire models who are at least 18 years old, and furthermore Gucci have signed the United Nations Standards of Conduct for Business to tackle discrimination against LGBT+ people (United Nations, 2017). Similarly, the LVMH Group (which includes Fendi, Givenchy, Louis Vuitton, and Christian Dior), has been taking part in a French Task Force initiative to set out a three-year plan that incorporates defined gender equality targets. It has not escaped the attention of the luxury sector that the physical and mental health of fashion models should be an area which they invest in, and Kering and LVMH have created a joint website providing key advice (Fashion Network, 2018).

As you can see, answering the 'why' question is not easy. It's not an orderly process. An entrepreneur's best chance of success is to be well-versed in the method, so that no matter what the situation, they always know exactly what to reach for, from deep within their toolkit.

Case Study for Why – Sea2See

Sea2See, Switzerland (www.sea2see.org/)

Sea2see was launched in 2016 in Switzerland, by François van den Abeele, a father and entrepreneur with a deep passion for oceans and nature. Made entirely with recycled marine plastic waste collected in collaboration with fishermen from West Africa, Spain, and France, Sea2See produces optical frames and sunglasses starting at €99 and watches from €149 (Sea2see, 2021a). Sea2See combines ecological luxury with design and production of optical frames and sunglasses in Italy and their watches in Switzerland. François' motivation, investigations, and investment in R&D have helped him to succeed in manufacturing premium eyewear made entirely with abandoned fishnets and ropes, collected by fishing communities, thereby reducing ghost-fishing and ocean contamination (Regent's University London, 2020). Sea2See has proved that it is perfectly possible to mix luxury with 'profit, people, and planet'!

Sea2see (2021b), describes in detail the process of how they use UPSEA™ PLAST to produce 100% of their eyewear and watches – upcycling waste to create new products which have been Gold-certified from Cradle to Cradle™. This certification adds to Sea2See's customer experience, as it is the world's most advanced, science-based standard regarding designing and making products for the Circular Economy. Currently, their website boasts that over 425 tons of plastic have been collected and a variety of niche collaborations have been instigated. The company uses approximately 1 kg of marine plastic waste, which once collected and recycled, makes one pair of eyeglasses. However, the value creation does not stop there. The packaging and logistics are both also environmentally friendly, and shipping is managed in a thoughtful way for their fashion and eco-conscious customers (Sea2see, 2021c). At the heart of the business, their vision statement speaks volumes about their work: *Envision the change you want to SEA … and wear it!*

François has big plans for Sea2see and sees them at the forefront of leading a change in sustainable luxury products. As a result, there is hope that consumers will start understanding that waste can be transformed into luxury and premium products.

Realising that there is more than just profits and consumption can help start-ups identify their 'why'. More and more companies globally are trying to be conscientious about the different forms of waste including plastic and textiles. With sustainability at the heart of what they want to do, this leads to eco-disruption of traditional industry sectors, while embracing the luxury sentiment. Sea2see is an affordable luxury brand founded on planet, profits, and people. (The 3 Ps are referred to as the triple bottom line).

Questions to ask yourself:

- Why do you want to start a business or a new venture?
- What is the purpose for you, as an entrepreneur, and for your customers?
- Can you use your idea to be profitable, good for the planet and for people?

2.5 Summary

This chapter on luxury start-ups initially looked at what luxury 'is' and has subsequently taken you through the different types of luxury you might find within the luxury sector, before examining the different aspects of start-ups in the luxury space. Using the *when, where, what, why* approach, the chapter examined the different aspects of building a luxury start-up. Throughout the chapter you were able to identify the different constituent parts of a start-up and link them to a variety of international start-ups within different areas of luxury.

The chapter presents the diversity and complexity of founding and running a start-up, particularly in the luxury sector which is steeped in heritage and tradition. Creating a long-lasting luxury brand can be difficult. The data around start-ups suggests that most businesses fail within the first three years, and many more businesses fail within the first five years of being created. To be more precise, data in the USA suggest around 6.5 million businesses launch every year, but start-up failure rates continue to hover around 90%. In the US, just over 21% fail in their first year, 30% in the second, and 50% by the fifth year (Bureau of labor, 2019). However, other countries also demonstrate the challenges of having a start-up. Failure rates are echoed around the world, suggests Startup Genome, who are a world-leading research and policy advisory organisation, working across six continents in over 40 countries. Their 2019 report claims that 11 out of 12 start-ups fail (Startup Genome, 2021).

Indeed, even whilst we were writing this chapter, some of the original case studies had to be changed because of the companies going bust. This highlights not only the value of understanding your 'basics' (when, where, what, and why), but understanding the potentially changing demands of your target market and customers, as well as developing expertise in your chosen niche. Whether you grow your business from passion or an identified gap, your ability to survive as a business, and ultimately boom, is key.

Looking forward, or forecasting as the start-up would say, the global luxury goods market is expected to increase from 309.6 billion USD in 2021, to 382.6 billion USD in 2025 (Statista, 2021b). In addition, Statista (2021b), reports: 'Even though online sales of luxury goods are expected to cannibalize the brick-and-mortar share over the next few years, the importance of the physical store continues to increase …' Interestingly, digital-born luxury companies are now opening physical stores to increase traffic to their eCommerce stores, enhance brand legitimacy, provide the touch-and-feel lacking in an online store, and improve local community engagement. An overall Luxury 4.0 model is emerging, which is characterised not only by the growth of the online sales channel but also by the digitalisation of a consumer's entire luxury shopping journey.

Historically, many start-ups in the luxury sector have laid their focus on artisan, creativity, uniqueness, or exclusivity. However, start-ups now need to incorporate sustainability as well as consider targeting the most valuable commodity of all – time. Time is an important luxury, and no standard monetary value can be placed on it. In order to further guide you through the different levels of luxury illustrated at the beginning of the chapter, we created a summary of different levels of luxury based on Rambourg's (2020) model. We hope that using the 'when, where, what, why' approach will support you in understanding key elements of start-up, and the different international luxury case studies support the underlying ideas.

CASE STUDY 1 Private & Regent, a private education company

Private & Regent is a luxury education provider based in Mayfair, London, offering bespoke education for children of all ages. They offer a unique style of teaching that helps change the life of your child through creative and imaginative means. Born in the foothills of the Himalayas on a family farm and raised in Yorkshire, Sara Jerusalem Khan established Private & Regent in 2019, as a distinctive learning approach which is playful yet rigorous and enhances a child's potential to progress. has managed to incorporate key moments of her life and identity into every aspect of the company to harness individualism and quality. Her specific method is a celebration of old and new, and at the heart of Private and Regent's philosophy lies the focus of not only increasing knowledge but working on confidence and emotional empowerment.

Luxury at Private & Regent means offering a complete individualised package of educational services ranging from exam preparation, pre-prep to GCSEs and advice tailored to both the parent and their child's needs. Targeting families who value education and success, inclusive to all ages, Private & Regent offer bespoke services, including tutoring, The Confidence Booster Programme, homework support, exam preparation and techniques. The range of their bespoke services are developing as the demand from the market grows. They are also able to offer other extra-curricular activities such as classes in poetry, horse riding, and yoga, as well as bespoke childcare and baby-sitting services, The Governess package and nanny services. Each service is hand-picked for the child and their needs. Private & Regent further sets itself apart by positioning their customers as *members*. Khan believes that you are a member of the organisation, not just a client. This highlights a very clear entrepreneurial mindset and a special approach taken towards their customers.

While the headquarters are based in London, members could be based anywhere geographically. Private & Regent exclusively only uses strategy of word-of-mouth to identify and attract new members and based on their success to-date, they are evidently very good at it! Typically, this can range from targeting the 'HENRY' (high earners, not rich yet) segment, to those who have extensive family wealth and are very accustomed to bespoke educational services. In addition, the Private and Regent tutors can act as 'flying faculty' and thus, upon request, are also available to travel internationally to visit members and their children. This type of extraordinarily bespoke service for their members and their children is rarely seen in ordinary private tutoring services. Finally, Khan is a dedicated proponent of integrating social values into her business by making sure that she is uses philanthropic means as a way to demonstrate these organisational principles. Private & Regent donates 2.5% of all profits to a charity of her members' choice.

CASE STUDY 2 DeepTech start-up using translucent wood technology

Woodoo are motivated by their passion to pursue both a societal and environmental agenda, as well as their desire to help innovate the wood industry. Woodoo, a DeepTech technology start-up, bridges synthetic biology and organic chemistry and was born following five years of intensive research in cellulosic nano-technology. Using low-grade woods, they create innovative smart surfaces by blending nature and technology to design patented groundbreaking new materials. Woodoo developed a patented process to turn low-grade woods into hard and translucent surfaces and materials. This luxury, ultra-high-tech invention renews what digitisation and emotions mean in cars, private jets, and yachts. Woodoo's pioneering materials can now be found in tables on-board a Dassault private jet and in high-end Mercedes car dashboards, totally tactile, and digital (Girod, 2020).

Timothée Boitouzet, the French co-founder of the start-up Woodoo, states on his website: 'We are inventors of biomaterials'. In an interview he provides a narrative for the motivation behind starting Woodoo, 'the materials that we build with today, were invented thousands of years ago but are utterly unable to cope with the environmental and demographic challenges of the 21st century'. Further, he notes that in order to accommodate the rising urban population, something had to change – thus Woodoo was born. So, what does their patented method actually involve? They have developed a technical process to remove the weak lignin parts of a wood board's structure, replacing it with a custom polymer. Using a thin strip of wood less than a millimeter thick, you will be able to observe a slight transparency. Their ingredients are mainly bio-based polymers which, once injected into the wood, allow it to pass 10 to 20% of the light and make it more resistant (Anon, 2016). The result is a sustainable, waterproof material with the strength profile of metal and the cost profile of low-grade wood. This can be used in a multitude of ways to add technology and sustainability, and to demonstrate luxury as well as durability.

Woodoo add value to the automotive and retail industries and retail who are constantly looking for new materials to optimise the experience of their users, while reducing weight and emissions. Woodoo's innovative smart surfaces are perfectly suited to these uses. This success has been recognised! Woodoo is one of the most awarded tech start-ups in Europe, with over 30 accolades since 2016. The future for Woodoo looks interesting, as the highly versatile product can be sold into different b2b sectors to add value to their products. There are many directions that Woodoo could take. Their website suggests that they might find ways to replace other less or non-sustainable materials using their technology, such as plastic, glass, and metals. So, whilst luxury is now just one sector interested in their products, they may next target the construction industry. Globally, new environment standards are being imposed to reduce the use of increasingly scarce wood species. This is where Woodoo can support the industry, offering luxury and design as an alternative to premium wood, without harming the planet.

Seminar exercises

Discussion topics:

1. WHEN	Starting up might seem daunting. Take a 'thought-shower' and collectively with your group write down all the items you might put in place prior to deciding to start a business. What would you need to consider before you start? What are your key assets? What do you think are your biggest fears and barriers? Identify the similarities and differences and consider at least two ways of overcoming each issue. Use this to consider, individually, when is the time right for you?
2. WHERE	Think about different channels and locations. Should you be based online or offline? For physical locations, consider the advantages and disadvantages of regions (Europe, Americas, Asia etc.), countries (UK, USA, Nigeria, Egypt, India, China, etc.), and different areas within a country (capital city, large or small towns, village/rural etc.). Construct a table with your ideas on advantages, disadvantages, and notes on each area. Use this to discuss in a larger group what you think are the biggest challenges when considering your route-to-market. What do you need to consider and look for?
3. WHAT	Reflect on your own consumption of luxury services, goods and items, and how you perceive luxury start-ups. Write down at least five luxury products (and their associated brands) that you consume. What do you value and look for in these brands? What is important about them to you? Exchange the ideas you have about those brands with others in your groups and compare and contrast your answers.
4. WHY	Consider the different ways entrepreneurs might approach a start-up: maybe a gap in the market, a cause that they care about, or having a business idea from scratch or using a breakthrough technology. Identify one approach and choose three potential start-up ideas in your group. Make sure you consider different ways of coming up with the ideas and approaching this task. Extra: Identify and write down any social, legal, economic, political, technological, and/or environmental causes that are important to you. Consider how you can link these to your entrepreneurial ideas. Maybe you can link it to the core values of the business (i.e., Sea2See) or support causes through philanthropic initiatives or donations (i.e., Private & Regent).

Group exercises:

1. Select a luxury start-up of your choice (any sector, country, or type of luxury) and create a presentation to address the following:
   - Describe – Overview of start-up
     - (What is the company? Who founded it? Where? Are they offline or online? What do they do/sell/make? What type of luxury? Size and scope of business etc.)
   - Evaluate – when did they start up – explain the context that you consider relevant to the business idea.
   - Evaluate – where did they chose to start up – add details and considerations to the context.
   - Evaluate – what industry are they operating in? Who are they competing against?
   - Evaluate – why did they start up? What is their purpose?
   - Analyse – do you think they could have been more successful if they had started at a different time and/or in a different location? Explain your rationale.
   - Analyse – look at their current industry, then moving forward, what are the trends and factors they need to be aware of?
2. Research – carry out research into different luxury start-up contexts around the world. Consider up to date sources and the changes over time, if needed. Use the points below to create visualisations (either an infographic or referenced slide/ mind map) detailing the following:
   - Which countries have the most luxury start-ups? (Consider the different definitions of luxury.)
   - Which areas or regions provide the most support or capital (financial, human, social, or physical) for a luxury start-up? Explain your rationale and back up your ideas.
   - Create a list of at least six luxury start-up competitions or awards internationally.
3. Having seen how others do it, it is now your turn to plan your start-up. In groups, plan how you will create your own luxury start-up. Discuss how you will come up with the idea (identifying a plan or idea from scratch) and what each team member would bring to the table. Are any skills missing?

Create a pitch deck covering the following:

- What is the idea (product/service) and who are you targeting?
- When would you launch it? When would be the 'best' time to launch it and what does the competition look like?
- Where would you launch it and why? (Consider a vision and a mission statement.)
- What gap in the market are you filling? What industry are you in?
- Why does this business exist? Are you 'giving back' or 'doing good'? Do you want to add other aspects, such as people or planet, or are you just focused on profit?
- Consider how you would get funding for your idea.

References

Alldus (2020). Accessed at https://alldus.com/blog/podcasts/aiinaction-zakaria-jaiathe-xibitxr/

Amin, A., Cameron, A. and Hudson, R. (2002). *Placing the Social Economy*. Routledge, London.

Anon (2016). Transparent wood for the house of the future? Accessed at: www.techniques-ingenieur.fr/actualite/articles/du-bois-transparent-pour-la-maison-du-futur-32984/ Last accessed: 27.07.2021

Aroles, J., Granter, E. and Vaujany, F-X. (2020). Becoming mainstream: the professionalisation and corporatisation of digital nomadism, *New Technology, Work and Employment*, v35 n1, pp. 114–129.

Bain & Co report (2020). *The Future of Luxury: Bouncing Back from Covid-19*.

Bill, F., Jansson, A., & Olaison, L. (2010). The spectacle of entrepreneurship: a duality of flamboyance and activity. In F. Bill, A. Jansson and L. Olaison (Eds) *(De)Mobilising the Entrepreneurship Discourse:Exploring Entrepreneurial Thinking and Action*, Published by Elgar publishing, London, pp. 158–175.

Bjerke, B. (2007). *Understanding Entrepreneurship*. Edward Elgar Publishing, London.

Bjerke, B. and Hultman, C. (2013). The role of marketing rational and natural business startups. in Zubin Sethna, Rosalind Jones, and Paul Harrigan (Eds) Entrepreneurial Marketing: Global Perspectives, Emerald Publishing – Bingley, pp. 63.

BRIKK (2021). Homepage. Accessed at: www.brikk.com/ Last accessed: 27.08.2021

Briot, E. (2011). From industry to luxury: French perfume in the nineteenth century. *Business History Review*, v85 n2, pp. 273–294.

Bureau of labor (2019). Data set accessed at: www.bls.gov/bdm/us_age_naics_00_table7.txt

Chirumalla, K. (2016). Organizing lessons learned practice for product-service innovation. *Journal of Business Research*, v69 n11, pp. 4986–4991.

Crunchbase (2020). Brikk Designs And Manufactures Couture Products And Accessories For The Technology And Lifestyle Industries. Accessed at: www.crunchbase.com/organization/brikk Last accessed: 17.07.2021

D'Arpizio, C. and Levato, F. (2017). *Luxury Goods Worldwide Market Study*, Fall–Winter 2017, Bain&Co report.

Dart, R. (2004). The legitimacy of social enterprise. in S. Zubin, R. Jones and P. Harrigan (Eds) *Entrepreneurial Marketing: Global Perspectives*, v14 n4, pp. 411–424.

Dees, J.G., Emerson, J. and Economy, P. (2001). *Enterprising Nonprofits: A Toolkit for Social Entrepreneurs*. John Wiley & Sons Inc, New York, NY.

Donze, P-Y. and Fujioka, R. (2015). European luxury big business and emerging Asian markets, 1960–2010, *Business History*, v57 n6, pp. 822–840.

Fashion Network (2018). LVMH shines the spotlight on gender equality by joining new task force. (Accessed on 10 August 2020) https://uk.fashionnetwork.com/news/lvmh-shines-the-spotlight-on-gender-equality-by-joining-new-task-force,956446.html

Gabrielsson, M., Kirpalani, M. V. H. and Luostarinen, R. (2002). Multiple channel strategies in the European personal computer industry, *Journal of International Marketing*, v10 n3, pp. 73–95.

Girod, S.J.G. (2020). Discover What Inspires Today's Luxury Entrepreneurs Accessed at www.forbes.com/sites/stephanegirod/2020/09/25/discover-what-inspires-todays-luxury-entrepreneurs/?sh=5a1ca3b24ac8 Last accessed: 27.07.2021

Goyal, V. (2018). Sweets of Olive (SOO): Tasting Success through sales and distribution management, *South Asian Journal of Management*, v25 n1, pp. 150–174

Gur, F.A., Bendickson, J.S., Madden, L. and McDowell, W.C. (2020). Entrepreneurial opportunity recognition in the face of disasters, *International Journal of Entrepreneurial Behavior & Research*, v26 n4, pp. 671–693.

Hawkins, L., and Hoon, S. (2020). The impact of customer retention strategies and the survival of small service-based businesses, *IUP Journal of Marketing Management*, v19 n1, pp. 7–34.

Hills, G.E. and Singh, R.P. (2004). Opportunity recognition. *Handbook of Entrepreneurial Dynamics: The Process of Business Creation*, v259, p.272.

Kapferer, J. N. and Bastien, V. (2012). *The Luxury Strategy: Break the Rules of Marketing to Build Luxury Brands*. Kogan page publishers.

Khare, A., Awasthi, G. and Shukla, R.P. (2019). Do mall events affect mall traffic and image? A qualitative study of Indian mall retailers, *Asia Pacific Journal of Marketing and Logistics*, v32 n2, pp. 343–365

Ko, E., Costello, J.P. and Taylor, C.R. (2019). What is a luxury brand? A new definition and review of the literature, *Journal of Business Research*, v99, June, pp. 405–413.

Lazarus, E., Lin, D., Martindill, J., Hardiman, J., Pitney, L., and Galli, A. (2015). Biodiversity loss and the ecological footprint of trade, *Diversity*, v7 n2, pp. 170–191.

Lechuga-Cardozo, J. I., Leyva-Cordero, O., and Nunez-Garcia, A. (2019). Internationalisation strategy in the handicraft industry: the Galapa-Columbia case, *RAN*, v5 n2, pp. 99–106.

Lehnert, K., Goupil, S., and Brand, P. (2021). Content and the Consumer: inbound ad strategies gain traction, *Journal of Business Strategy*, v42 n1, pp. 3–12.

Levi, M., Li, K., and Zhang, F. (2010). Deal or no deal: Hormones and the mergers and acquisitions game. *Management Science*, v56 n9, pp. 1462–1483.

Li, N (2018). Gaming opulenceThis Gold-Plated, Diamond-Encrusted PS4 Controller Costs 14,000 USD. Accessed at https://hypebeast.com/2018/10/brikk-sony-playstation-4-lux-dualshock-4-controller

Matschewsky, J. (2019). Unintended circularity? Assessing a product-service system for its potential contribution to a circular economy, *Sustainability*, v11 n10, pp. 2725.

Moncler Supplier Code of Conduct (2016). Accessed on 10 July 2020 at www.monclergroup.com/wp-content/uploads/2016/07/SupplierCodeofConductENGdefinitive-1.pdf

Morris, M. H., Webb, J. W., Fu, J. and Singhal, S. (2013). A competency-based perspective on entrepreneurship education: Conceptual and empirical insights, *Journal of small business management*, v51 n3, pp. 352–369.

Neck, H. M. and Corbett, A. C. (2018). The scholarship of teaching and learning entrepreneurship, *Entrepreneurship Education and Pedagogy*, v1 n1, pp. 8–41.

Neufeld, D (2020). Mapped: The World's Ultra-Rich, by Country Accessed at: www.visualcapitalist.com/map-worlds-ultra-rich-by-country/ Last accessed: 08.09.2021

Olalekan, F. (2019). Meet the successful Nigerian entrepreneur who owns the Airbnb of luxury cars in UK Accessed at: https://nairametrics.com/2019/08/21/meet-the-successful-nigerian-who-owns-the-airbnb-of-luxury-cars-in-uk/ Last accessed: 17.07.2021

Ralph Lauren (2020). *Global Citizenship & Sustainability Report*. (Accessed on 10 Aug 2020 – https://corporate.ralphlauren.com/on/demandware.static/-/Sites-RalphLauren_Corporate-Library/default/dwd8688705/documents/2020_Global_Citizenship_Sustainability_Report.pdf)

Rambourg, E (2020). Future Luxe: What's Ahead for the Business of Luxury. Canada, Vancouver: Publishers group West.

Regent's University London (2020). In conversation with Francois van den Abeele, CEO & Founder of Sea2See Accessed at: www.regents.ac.uk/events/in-conversation-with-francois-van-den-abeele-ceo-founder-of-sea2see Last accessed: 27.07.2021

Sea2see (2021a). Homepage. Accessed at: www.sea2see.org/ Last accessed: 27.07.2021

Sea2see (2021b). Accessed at: www.sea2see.org/pages/process Last accessed: 27.07.2021

Sea2see (2021c). Accessed at: www.sea2see.org/pages/packaging Last accessed: 27.07.2021

Sethna, Z., and Blythe, J. (2019). *Consumer Behaviour 4th Edition*, SAGE Publications, London, UK.

Sproul, C., Cox, K., and Ross, A. (2019). Entrepreneurial Actions: implications for firm performance, *Journal of Small Business and Enterprise Development*, v26 n5, pp. 706–725.

Steyaert, C. and Hjorth, D. (Eds.). (2003). *New Movements in Entrepreneurship*. Edward Elgar Publishing.

Statista (2020). Number of ultra high net worth individuals in selected countries in 2020 Accessed at: www.statista.com/statistics/204095/distribution-of-ultra-high-net-worth-individuals-for-selected-countries/ Last accessed: 08.09.2021

Statista (2021a). Global Personal Luxury Goods Industry – Statistics & Facts Accessed at: www.statista.com/topics/1110/global-luxury-goods-industry/ Last accessed: 08.09.2021

Statista (2021b). In-depth: Luxury Goods 2021. Statista Consumer Market Outlook Accessed at: www.statista.com/study/61582/in-depth-luxury/ Last accessed: 08.09.2021

StarrLuxuryCars (2021a). Homepage. Accessed at: https://starrluxurycars.com/ Last accessed: 27.07.2021

StarrLuxuryCars (2021b). Website – Shop. Accessed at: https://starrluxurycars.com/shop/ Last accessed: 27.07.2021

Startup Genome (2021). Homepage about us. Accessed at: https://startupgenome.com/about-us Last accessed: 27.07.2021

Stevenson, H.H., Roberts, M.J., Grousbeck, H.I. (1989). *Business ventures and the entrepreneur*. Richard D Irwin Publishing, Homewood, IL.

Tenucci, A. and Supino, E. (2020). Exploring the relationship between product-service system and profitability, *Journal of Management and Governance*, v24 n3 pp. 563–585.

United Nations (2017). Tackling discrimination against Lesbian, Gay, Bi, Trans and intersex People – Standards of Conduct for business. (Accessed online on 12 August 2020) www.unfe.org/wp-content/uploads/2017/09/UN-Standards-of-Conduct.pdf

Warhuus, J.P., Frid, C.J., and Gartner, W.B. (2021). Ready or not? Nascent entrepreneurs' actions and the acquisition of external financing, *International Journal of Entrepreneurial Behaviour and Research*, v27 n6, pp. 1605–1628.

Wirtz, J., Holmqvist, J. and Fritze, M.P. (2020). Luxury services, Journal of Service Management, v31 n4, pp. 665–691.

Wirtz, J. and Lovelock, C. (2016). *Services Marketing: People, Technology, Strategy*. Singapore: World Scientific Publishing Company.

Xibit (2021). Website about. Accessed at https://xibitxr.com/about/ Last accessed: 27 July 2021.

CHAPTER 3

Contemporary people issues in luxury brand management

Stephen Ellis and Thomas Smit

3.1 INTRODUCTION

3.1.1 Clarifying the concept of luxury in the marketplace

It is important to understand what luxury presents in the marketplace and how this needs to be communicated to its global audience. According to a survey by American Express and The Harrison Group, reported in Luxury Daily (2019), luxury is defined by three elements:

1. The luxury experience – elegant stores and flawless delivery.
2. Close relationships with the sales associates – built up over lengthy relationship management.
3. Exclusivity – this experience is not available to all and definitely not mass market.

For the consumer, the brand is the luxury experience. According to this survey, luxury customers prefer stores that are elegant and tend to value close relationships with select sales associates. They want an experience of purchasing that is as pleasant as owning a luxury item. They believe it is worth paying more for items of the very best quality, and they value exclusivity. To reinforce this understanding of a luxury experience, Kapferer and Bastien (2009) argue that to be a true luxury brand, the product or service must be able to meet six simple criteria.

1. A hedonistic experience and products made to last.
2. Offered at a price that far exceeds what their purely functional value would command.
3. Bound to heritage, unique know-how and culture.
4. Accessible only in very selective or exclusive distribution.
5. Offered with personalised accompanying services.
6. Representing status, making the owner or beneficiary feel special.

DOI: 10.4324/9781003015826-4

What this vision of luxury implies for those who work or seek to work in the area, will be addressed later in this chapter in terms of the knowledge, attitude and skills required for success. Whilst luxury brands tend to have a higher price point and added overall value (AOV) by definition, many luxury brands can, and do, still lose a large proportion of their customers in any given year. Those same brands also struggle to retain the top 50% of their customers, so there is a real opportunity for improvement through the effective management of the people involved in delivery. Hence the ultimate proposition for a luxury offer has to be personal with high touch, delivered through highly developed people and systems. A brand that is infused with a heritage usually stands for authenticity, credibility, and trust, which can provide strong leverage for that brand, especially in global markets (Aaker, 1996). The emotional connection can be strengthened with the target market by re-establishing this favourable connection to the past.

There is also a widely shared concern among industry insiders that luxury has lost its meaning, with too many companies peddling so-called 'luxury' goods that would not meet the criteria contained in Figure 3.1. With the meaning of luxury not well understood by many consumers, or even some luxury companies, there is an opportunity now to return to what we believe to be the key pillars of luxury:

- Quality
- Craftsmanship
- Design
- Unstinting attention to detail
- Uniqueness
- Authenticity
- Correlation of price and value

We will return to these key pillars in more detail later, but the only way to achieve this, we would argue, is through significantly ramping up the development of the people involved in luxury-brand delivery. A major challenge for luxury brands is how to communicate their true luxury values through their people. However, this is also a fantastic opportunity for brands that lean into the future. Girón (2017), points out that in the luxury universe, the constant challenge is to transform creativity into profitability – creativity is the hallmark of all great luxury brands which comes from the people behind the brand. 'It is always people who make a brand' (Kapferer and Bastien, 2012).

3.1.2 The impact of people factors in the luxury brand arena

As luxury companies struggle with often conflicting demands of the virtual and experiential physical luxury worlds, the entire organisation needs to be dedicated to the brands' true luxury values. On the people side, above all, luxury companies need to hire right, train right, and create the ongoing and sustainable culture of excellence that is needed to build and maintain a luxury brand. The way that people are recruited, supported and developed will in the end lead to varying degrees of success or failure for all business organisations. This is especially true for the luxury brand arena where outcomes are particularly susceptible to damage from poor people management. The sales process in this sector is often driven through long-term relationships and relies heavily on the discretional effort of the people behind the brand. Overlooking how they are managed and developed is tantamount to business suicide.

To better understand the environment in which leaders need to lead, is to better understand luxury. Employees in all sectors, whether selling off-the-shelf items or bespoke luxury items, should understand the difference between needs and wants. Horst Schulze who is known in the hospitality industry as the father of Ritz-Carlton states: 'When I recruit general managers for my hotels, and they have passed all the tests and interviews I have the final say. I simply ask one last question: do you want to be the general manager, or do you need to be the general manager?' The correct answer is 'need'. Many people would *like to* have a fabulous lifestyle but not everyone *needs* it. It should be a hunger to achieve or to own, otherwise the want becomes an illusion.

Having left Dusseldorf at the age of 13, on a boat destined for New York City, Schulze's first job was at the Waldorf in New York where he worked as a bellhop. Her Majesty Queen Elizabeth II made her first visit as monarch to New York after her coronation. Schulze clearly had the need to achieve in life, for at the banquet hosted by President Dwight D. Eisenhauer, Schulze, wearing coat tails and white gloves, was head waiter serving Her Majesty by the time he was 23 years old, and, in 1985, he co-founded the Ritz-Carlton Hotel Company. Schulze introduced the first academy of its kind in the hotel industry, the Ritz-Carlton Academy. Training was ongoing and the hunger for more information and more knowledge made the Ritz-Carlton one of the world's most luxurious hotels worldwide.

3.2 DEVELOPING PEOPLE IN THE LUXURY BRAND SECTOR

3.2.1 The key challenges

The luxury brand sector is developing at pace. As a consequence, those who choose to work in the luxury world are required to be on what might seem like a continuous conveyor belt of improvement (Ellis, 2006). Standing still in this industry is effectively going backwards as the competitive pressures to be innovative, creative, and constantly refreshing the offer, drives success. Avoiding staleness is also a key challenge in an industry which often values heritage and tradition alongside constant innovation. Even if the established products or services have a relatively long lead with established client groups, they must be constantly refreshed and updated to ensure that technology, fashion, legislation, or any other external factors, do not leave them outdated. Product knowledge for employees must therefore be comprehensive. Clients are often highly knowledgeable and will look to their provider for the confidence that this product or service is right for them both now and in the future. Employees need to be knowledgeable about their own product line and its constituency, but also about those of competitors, real and potential. What is increasingly important is the likely direction of future trends, as clients in this sector will not be pleased to be sold a product that is quickly outdated or subsumed by revisions.

Alongside this, employees delivering luxury service propositions must be able to demonstrate the ability and desire to meet a supremely high level of client expectations. Purchase decisions in the luxury market are often highly discretionary, and as such, the quality of the service offered and client relationship management become crucial. Indeed, it is often the personal relationships that define the luxury offer, leading to a strong background of goodwill to fall back on temporarily, should a problem occur in the supply chain. There are many examples of world-famous companies with significant international brand exposure, failing, in some cases very badly. We believe there is often a common thread that these companies' leadership have been guilty of, that caused significant shareholder value depreciation, depleted staff morale and loss of customers/clients.

3.2.2 Some illustrative case examples

How do you rebrand your high-end fashion label after it becomes associated with hooliganism? Or resurrect your beer when it acquires the nickname 'wife beater'? As many businesses know, reputations take time to build but can be shattered in seconds. However, there have been some remarkable turnarounds by well-known companies, which have rescued their languishing brands. From Lego to Stella Artois, we can take a look at what went wrong and how these companies changed their fortunes for the better.

It's been a bit of a rollercoaster ride for the pilsner beer, brewed in Belgian since 1926. Back in the 1990s, Stella's sponsorship of Channel 4 broadcasts and outdoor cinema events, combined with the clever tagline 'reassuringly expensive', positioned it as an upmarket beer brand. Come the mid-noughties, however, and it was more closely associated with lager louts than beer connoisseurs. Part of the problem was supermarkets' practice of selling discounted crates during the summer and key sporting events. Despite it not being any stronger than many of its rivals, the moniker 'wife-beater' has been hard to shake. Sales inevitably slumped as a result. Stella's answer to the problem has been to create a range of beers under the softer umbrella 'Artois' brand. In addition to Stella, it started producing Peeterman, a wheat beer of 4% strength, and Bock, a 6% lager. It followed these by launching its own brand of cider, marketed as Stella Artois Cidre.

Just over 10 years ago, Burberry's famous check design was actually banned in pubs and clubs for its association with hooliganism. Today, the company boasts brand ambassadors including Emma Watson and Cara Delevingne. What has been behind the transformation? Angela Ahrendts, former chief executive of the fashion label, is credited with steering Burberry from baseball caps to high fashion. After she took over in 2006, she handed creative control to Christopher Bailey, and bought back 23 licences Burberry had sold to allow other businesses to use its check on anything and everything. During her time at Burberry, the company value rose from £2 billion to more than £7 billion.

Claire Ritchie, director of International Fashion Studies at the London College of Contemporary Arts, highlighted two strategies that have worked particularly well for Burberry's renaissance – the use of technology and personalisation. Burberry is a brand that comes up time and time again when promoting good practice. They have been very clever in terms of how they have integrated technology into their brand. The art of the trench campaign is a good example of clever use of social media. Luxury brands are predominantly about heritage, tradition, and craftsmanship, so it's about how you balance that with technology. In terms of personalisation of the product itself, you can order straight from the catwalk and have your initials or name etched into the garment's labels.

Finally, as a similar case to consider, it is often quoted that the luxury brand Harley-Davidson relies more on the loyalty of its client base than the reliability of its product (Light, 2020). However, they made a series of errors in the last ten years by introducing smaller and cheaper bikes, in an attempt to shift their core market to younger, less wealthy clients. One can see the logic in wanting to move away from a client group that is literally dying out, but in doing so, it has also sacrificed the long built-up loyalty of these older clients. Many of these had enough knowledge to be able to correct any minor delivery faults on their new bikes and enjoyed doing so.

In all three of the case examples above, we think there is a common thread. That thread is poor leadership or management; taking their eye away from the original intentions, values and 'spirit' of the brand, and making poor marketing decisions as a result. These cases show the dangers of making such moves, but also show that they can be recovered if the leadership of the organisation is strong enough, and sufficiently connected to its true values and attributes, to restore the brand to prominence.

3.2.3 Building or rebuilding a luxury brand through your people

As shown in the cases above, it is possible to build, or rebuild, a luxury brand if the performance has declined. Any brand can be damaged beyond repair in a very short period of time if the staff are not able to live up to the promise and standards expected. Staff therefore must absorb, and contribute to, the values and attributes of the brand, through early and ongoing training. There are increasingly effective ways of developing employees for the luxury brand arena. Obvious avenues are traditional training programmes, offsites, awaydays, client visits, and supplier visits. Less traditional developments such as online skill and knowledge building, secondments, job-sharing, special development projects, coaching, and mentoring, are increasingly coming to the forefront. These changes are often down to the speed of business development in the sector where product life cycles are shortening and market sectors are becoming more defined and ever more niche.

Cheales (1994) details the inevitable long-term costs of poor management, training, and communication skills. He argues that companies spend tens of millions of pounds trying to get new customers yet are unable to maintain and retain their customer base. The reasons, he argues, are many; however, the number one reason for losing a customer is customer service. This does not only happen at the time of purchase; it is also of great importance how a dissatisfied customer is dealt with. As a motivational speaker, Cheales, who has travelled the world delivering his classic and casual on-stage performances, argues that it ultimately came down to communication. His motto is, 'one unhappy customer equals 1000 never customers'. Conversely, one happy customer will spread the word and generate new customers, future loyalty, and money in the bank. Cheales concludes that in today's world of mobile phones and smart technology, it is a puzzle why some chief executives share their mobile telephone numbers and others not. It suggests that those who do not are less connected and less willing to step in to solve any issue their clients might have.

The same principle applies to employees. Warren Buffet is famous for visiting the shop floors of his investments and insists that 'service with a smile' is profitable for the company and profitable for the employee. Employers spend so much time and money to recruit those that they believe will be successful, propel the company forward, drive profits, and achieve increase share prices in multiple hundred percentages. We believe that in most cases, this is fundamentally wrong; the simple question that executives should ask themselves is, what do we have to do to develop and retain our existing talent? The answer is not simple, but we should learn from those who have achieved the impossible in the recent past. Harold Geneen is such a leader, a world-renowned business manager in his day who turned a faltering ITT into a giant conglomerate, dealing with everything from 'Wonder Bread' to Avis cars, while sales skyrocketed from $766 million to $22 billion. His management techniques were so successful that ITT was dubbed the 'Geneen University'. One of his managerial principles with regards to the employment and hiring process, was to hire the best and pay the most. If the remuneration was extremely generous, it would be difficult for competitors to hire them from the various businesses that Geneen managed. Conversely, the employee would find it challenging to leave and give up a lucrative career with terrific benefits. Put simply, employ the best, train and retain them. Obviously, in return for the above market compensation he would demand above market performance.

Cross-training is an essential part of developing the employee, to increase their understanding of the various parts of the business and to broaden their experience. Developing your people is only part of the solution though; how they are treated day to day and getting the whole organisational culture correct, is also crucial. The case examples at the end of the chapter on the Augustine Hotel, and Grays of Westminster, will give you a chance to investigate and comment on this aspect in more detail. The need to rebuild business after the pandemic shock, allied to the vast increase in e-learning opportunities, is in many ways a match made in heaven for luxury brand employers seeking to significantly improve their training performance.

Statista (2019) reported that the average spend on training per employee in the USA was around $1400 per year in 2019 and the amount of working time taken was around 35 hours. That's not a sustainable picture given the pace of change we are witnessing – one week of training to support 52 weeks of delivery is not a sum that we think makes any sense. A more sensible figure might be at least 10% of employee time spent updating or training. That would require development time of around five weeks per year, which is way beyond the current norm but a goal we should aim for.

Apart from the fact that current investment in training is simply way too low, in the new e-learning world we can expect that the costs and working time of workplace learning give exciting opportunities to get more out of the investment – but only if the training programme is well conceived and appropriate. Many retailers are facing new challenges with lockdown restrictions being lifted in most countries, and as one analyses the value proposition that luxury offers, we see a new emphasis on 'conversational retail'. Engaging with, and educating the customer, are two separate functions. We would argue that the younger generations communicate more via social media, and little or no time is allocated for training individuals on how to engage face-to-face with a prospective customer. They are often generally more able to send text messages, and less able to develop a meaningful business relationship through appropriate eye contact, a firm handshake, and a genuine, welcoming smile.

We should not underestimate the significance of product knowledge, but the social skills of developing commercial relationships and networks are also crucial in the luxury arena. Dagmar Smit, co-founder of Elegantes London, one of the world's most prestigious luxury perfume houses has this to say: 'Elegantes is not for everyone and not everyone is for Elegantes'. She is emphasising that her employees need to have skills and attitudes that may not necessarily be required in non-luxury businesses, in order to fully exploit the aspects of conversational retail and to understand the features of the product being sold, the benefits and the story behind its creation. This comes long before there is any discussion about price, or indeed a purchase decision being made. A direct comparison in the United Kingdom between Harrods and Harvey Nichols indicated that more emphasis was placed on conversational retail by Harrods. Astonishing as this may be, Harrods spent only 3% of working hours in face-to-face training, compared to Harvey Nichols at 2%. This indicates to us that there is a massive gap to be bridged.

There is a clear need for a framework of development for the luxury sector to use as a guide as to what type of development to invest in. Without a clear framework, how do we know that the time and cost of any development is appropriate? We can rely on gut feel but that is not always wise. The ASK (Attitude, Skill, Knowledge) model (Nagendra et al., 2013), outlines a simple framework that can be adapted to meet our needs.

The simple 'ASK' model can be used for designing a way to develop people. I have used it previously in designing Master's-level programmes for health service professionals. It works well to help the commissioning client identify precisely what areas of development need to be prioritised. The model can have a more sophisticated application by confirming what the requirements are at the basic, intermediate, and advanced level, in each section of the business. Further work can lead to a distinction between new starters, experienced employees, and those who can coach others. The model

FIGURE 3.1   The 'ASK' model – applied to luxury brands

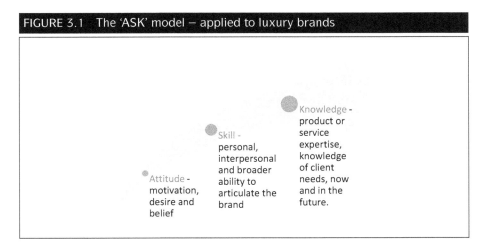

Knowledge - product or service expertise, knowledge of client needs, now and in the future.

Skill - personal, interpersonal and broader ability to articulate the brand

Attitude - motivation, desire and belief

fits with almost any context but would need to be adjusted carefully by managers for the luxury brand arena.

In terms of 'Attitude', those working in the field of luxury need to be aware of the priorities and imperatives around luxury products and services, such as the desire for 'special' treatment. The heritage aspects might also require more than would be expected in the non-luxury area. The 'Skills' required in luxury brands centre heavily around client care and relationship management. Communication and, importantly, listening to client need and desire is vital. Those who are highly skilled in influencing will also be at an advantage, for the client will often look to the luxury brand provider to advise and consult. The 'Knowledge' requirements in luxury brand are many and varied, but clear understanding of the product/service, and its attributes and philosophy, are basic requirements. High level knowledge of what might be called the 'constituency' of the luxury product or service would also be expected. This would entail, for example, knowledge of the heritage or provenance aspect, and crucially, how the offer fits into the target client lifestyle or cycle of key events.

3.2.4 The qualities needed of a luxury brand employee

Below, we will make some suggestions in each of the categories and describe some brief case examples, to delineate how those working in the luxury brand business must strive to make themselves distinct from other sectors. Frei and Morris (2020) point the direction that many leaders are becoming aware of in terms of improving their employee's performance, suggesting the need to 'unleash', rather than control, their behaviours.

3.2.4.1 ATTITUDES REQUIRED OF EMPLOYEES IN THE LUXURY BRAND BUSINESS SECTOR

- Client-first service approach.
- Willingness to avoid 'staleness' or complacency.

- Confidence from an awareness of the luxury marketplace requirements.
- Understanding and ability to describe clearly the competitive advantage of competitive brands by describing the difference and value proposition.
- First-hand experience of the luxury brand, i.e. when selling a luxury garment, the employee should be wearing such a garment.

3.2.4.2 SKILLS REQUIRED FOR THE LUXURY BRAND EMPLOYEE

- Ability to work in a team and to support others.
- Listening and acting on instructions from managers or client judgement to 'do the right thing'.
- Relationship management to create new pipeline relationships and build on existing ones.
- Research skills to predict future trends and spot opportunities.
- Sales skills, particularly upselling, on selling, and referral.
- Ability to work in a luxury culture and understand the environment of luxury.
- Ability to coach and mentor others.
- When working for a group-based company (e.g. LVMH), broad enough experience to recommend other brands from the stable; for example, when buying a suit, can the salesperson recommend a briefcase or shoes from another company within the same group?

3.2.4.3 KNOWLEDGE REQUIREMENTS FOR THE LUXURY BRAND EMPLOYEE

- Full understanding of the product or service, and those of other parts of the group.
- Knowledge of the marketplace and competitor information.
- Awareness of future trends and opportunities.
- Technological understanding of the area.
- Knowledge of their own professional specialism, e.g. finance, HR, marketing, legal, etc.
- Knowledge of the key influencers of the niche market that the business operates within.

In each of these areas and more, the individual business needs to work out a matrix to define and set their own clear requirements, reflecting the stage of the business and the individual employee. Managing the employees progress through the development becomes a significant part of the job of their manager.

3.2.5 Self-reflection questions

Considering the ASK model, picture the needs of three people in a typical luxury brand business. For example, this could be a clothing retailer. Ask yourself what would be a good 12-month development plan for each of the following?

1. A new entrant graduate with limited understanding of the business or products.

2. An experienced supervisor moving to a new department within the same business.
3. A store manager looking to improve sales and revenue for the business.

For each one of the above, what would be your top three priorities for their development? What learning model or vehicle would be the most appropriate in each case? If you are not sure of the best type of training or learning to employ, the next section gives you some ideas to consider.

3.2.6 Typical methods of staff development

Developing staff in-house offers the advantage of adding to the culture and team spirit. Many more innovative ways of sustaining and developing high performance are outlined by Daisley (2019). He suggests, among other ideas, walking meetings to avoid people turning off and to keep energised, 'Monk Mode' mornings (a distraction free problem-solving time) and 'pre-mortems' to iron out any barriers or potential hold-ups before starting a new project. These are just a few of the ways in which development can become part of normal activity and not seen as something extra to be done. Other training and development methods widely used include:

- In-house development programmes to build the culture and approach of the brand.
- External professional development, e.g. accounting or technological.
- General development programmes, such as MBA or leadership courses.
- Mentoring and coaching.
- Refresher training.
- Awaydays/offsite workshops/teambuilding.
- Online learning (self-managed or led by internal/external staff).
- Pre-model launch development; for example, whenever Bentley launch a new model, frontline sales teams are given the opportunity to experience the car at Millbrook (UK), on tracks designed to demonstrate new features.

Each of the above has its advantages and disadvantages and is more or less appropriate for the specific learning need. However, the experience of the last two years has led many people to adjust to, and value, the possibilities of online development, which has the flexibility to be built around the employees' other commitments. Remember, earlier we were suggesting that five weeks of development per year would be a good target. Coaching and mentoring has seen a recent rise, as employers seek to maximise the benefit of experienced staff sharing their approaches. Some new perspectives on this phenomenon are provided by O'Farrell (2021). Her belief is that only through effective coaching can managers free up their teams to become more independent and be able to problem solve well. However, we should not assume that all experienced staff have the ability or desire to become effective coaches. It is a separate skillset which may need to be invested in before coaching can become effective and productive. There are a number of organisations and coaching associations – for example, The Chartered

Institute of Personnel Development (CIPD), and many universities are available to help with scoping the coaching needs of any luxury business. External courses in coaching have great benefit by giving employees confidence through certification and practice, before they start to become coaches in the business.

3.2.7 Evaluating the development spend

Whatever the business budgets for its development needs, spending on training and development can always be increased, as employees' appetite for improvement needs to be strong. Where employees do not wish to improve or be developed, that can be a significant issue for the sustainability of the business. However, if the costs are going to be significant, there needs to be clarity on what benefits are being secured so we can be certain that we are getting the biggest 'bang for our buck'. Evaluation of people-development work is always something of an estimate as it relies so much on the context and application of the development in the place where it counts – the business. Simple attempts at evaluation could look like:

- Training days per year (we have already seen that at an average of five it is far too low).
- Percentage of staff being developed at any one time – if this is significantly below 100%, we would have an issue, as this implies that some people are already perfect!

Such evidence is a start, but not necessarily meaningful or helpful. For example, what if we doubled the number of training days but they were not focussed on the real priorities? This would hardly be an improvement, but this kind of measure might falsely suggest that it was. The CIPD confirm our view that any evaluation of learning and development has to be tied to the objectives of the business and what the intervention is trying to achieve. My experience as a management development specialist for many years is not generally that positive in this area, as many organisations are not clear about how their learning and development spend directly impacts their priorities, and this is a poor start. CIPD research alone shows that around 25% of organisations have no real draw through from their learning and development function and business objectives, while the same number don't even try to evaluate it (CIPD, 2021).

More sophisticated ways of evaluating training are required and are becoming increasingly available. The more advanced 'learning organisations' are already active in this area, but the CIPD suggest that as a minimum, the following three aspects of evaluation should be prominent:

Impact – where learning and development (L&D) can work with the organisation to show how the learning interventions have impacted performance – these can include links to key performance indicators (financial and operational).

Transfer – where L&D can work with the organisation to show how any learning undertaken on L&D events has been transferred back into the employee's role and work area – these can include performance goals and how new skills and knowledge have been used.

Engagement – where L&D can demonstrate how stakeholders are engaged with learning. This can be at an organisational level where a positive learning environment is the goal, at team levels, or at an individual level (the 'happy sheet' is an individual reaction to an individual event).

We would add: the ability to gain feedback from clients and the training professionals involved, the employees' ability to absorb and apply to learning leading to an increased ability to adapt and change quickly. These are true and valid indicators of the value of the training intervention; however, the culture surrounding the training also has to be taken into account here. If training is seen as a punishment or a requirement because something is wrong, then employees may rightly be defensive and not in the right mental place to benefit. Training should not be seen in this way, but as part of an ongoing journey to improvement. To go back to basics on the value of learning and development in organisations, especially in the luxury market, we should consider the views of Tom Peters (1990), one of the leading management gurus of the 1990–2000s. In his view, the fact that we have to ask about the value of any training spend means that we don't really understand the question. He would argue that all training is good, job related or not, as it keeps the employees mind engaged, which is a key consideration in a service environment.

3.2.8 Further self-reflection questions for this section

Consider the following requests for development that have come in from your department heads. How would you respond to each one if you were the company learning and development manager?

1. My department has had a quick turnover of staff for a variety of reasons, and I need to get my new guys up to speed. What can I do to improve the situation?
2. One of our established sales team wishes to be supported for an MBA programme. This will be quite expensive and needs her to be freed up one day per week during term time. I can't really cover her time off, but the budget is healthy, what options can I give her?
3. I want to take the department away for a team-building event. They have had a good year of sales, but I want to set them some really challenging targets for Q4 and I think this will really help me to gain buy in.

3.2.9 Seminar/group activity for this section

In small groups, brainstorm your responses to the following questions:

1. What qualities do you feel are essential for an employee looking to work in the luxury brand industry?
2. How can these qualities be developed and maintained?

3.3 MANAGEMENT DEVELOPMENT IN THE LUXURY BRAND SECTOR

3.3.1 Opportunities for effective management

As we have already argued, companies need to hire right, train right, and create a culture of excellence to build and maintain a luxury brand. This is where the development of managers must be designed effectively to fire up the brand. The managers of any luxury brand business need to be constantly updating their competence, alongside the added responsibility of supporting their staff to deliver. Some areas will be more important for this group, such the ability to understand and plan financial aspects of the business, develop succession plans or recognise product life cycles. Strategic decision making is also a key requirement for luxury brand manager. Handy (2016) speaks with authority of the need to be able to see quickly the impending future demise of a product or service, and be ready with the replacement, revision or extension that the market is looking for, even before it knows it. Opportunism is then translated into business benefit, but it relies on management knowledge and sound market intelligence. Therefore, the ability to see into the future with a degree of certainty is a clear requirement of effective management in the luxury sector.

3.3.2 Family ownership of the luxury brand

Some luxury brands may be able to count on client loyalty and its heritage to a degree, however, this does not mean that products can be preserved in aspic forever. In the sector it is not uncommon for a business to be connected closely, or remotely, to a family or set of families, who are often the originators or long-term backers of the business. This can distort the way that the business operates, as the family influence might be significant in terms of acceptable development directions.

Take one case with which we are familiar – Charles Smith Bootmakers. In 1892, Charles Smith started his workshop in Northampton, the heartland of British leather goods manufacturing. His son took over the thriving business, at which point some of their clients, who were members of royal families in England and Europe for almost 50 years, became a household name in the polo and horse-riding fraternity. The focus was specifically on riding, hunting, and polo boots. Each pair of boots were luxury and, of course, bespoke. In 1984, Charles Smith the second passed away and the business was taken over by his only child, June Tilley, who had no experience of the industry and unfortunately no real business acumen. By 1986, Charles Smith Boot Makers Limited was insolvent. The need for succession planning cannot be more emphasised in family businesses, and emotions, no matter how strong, should not play a part in the decision-making process.

Another example is Sheridan & Co, a design agency established in 1983, in Leicestershire, by Michael and Julien Sheridan. The Company was primarily led by Julian on the creative side and Michael dealing with overall management and finances. Today, Sheridan & Co have their Head office in

Leicestershire and offices in London, Shanghai, and New York. Since 1983, Sheridan & Co has become one of the world's leading retail design agencies. Their clients include LVMH, Calvin Klein, Dolce & Gabbana, Dior, Gucci, Bucherer, and many other prestigious luxury brands. The founding couple have two children, Freddie and Julien. Freddie joined the business as creative director. In early 2019, Julien stepped down as managing director being replaced by Sophie Pinder, a graduate from Trent University in Nottingham. This was a tough decision but the family, having worked together for so many years, were open, practical, and not emotional about the appointment of Sophie.

It is clear from this example that by careful coaching, teaching, and training, the time had come for Julien to step down and for Sophie to take the reins. If the decision was made purely on emotional grounds, and Freddie appointed as CEO, that would have been a very bad decision for the business, employees, and clients. This was a win-win situation as Freddie could continue as creative director, applying his creative genius, with Sophie managing the business as she had learnt, to accomplish success. The importance of 'The Peter Principle' in the workplace and in particularly, family and businesses cannot be over emphasised. According to the Peter Principle, it is stated that people generally get promoted to their level of incompetence, i.e. they prove themselves at one level but then cannot step up well to the next.

There may also be issues around succession planning where family owners and members are concerned. Family members will have the advantage of greater access to the owners but will carry the added burden of maintaining family tradition and expectations. Often it is sensible for key family members who are intended to lead the business in the future, to be sent to other business environments or development programmes before they arrive at their planned destination. It is often wise to learn from mistakes made elsewhere, and the spotlight will be sharply on any family member coming into a management position.

Having worked with a number of family-owned businesses both inside and outside of the luxury brand envelope, we can reflect on the special challenge faced by a family member coming into a parent's business. The parent often expects more than they would from other managers and people often find it hard to live up to these expectations. Added to this there may be issues of trust or favouritism between family members and non-family to consider. Managers, whether from within the family ownership or not, will also need the skills and mindset to challenge poor performance and develop a high-performance culture to support the brand. In-house training will be an invaluable tool to create and reinforce the desired luxury brand culture, whilst external training interventions will bring with them fresh ideas and challenges. Building high performance is often about being clear on standards and expectations and taking action where outputs fall short of these clear ambitions. The impact of important, personal, family relationships on this process must be understood and mitigated. Family ownership will impact on succession planning but should not be detrimental to allowing those who inherit to play to their strengths and not be forced into positions of power beyond their capabilities or desire simply due to family loyalty.

3.3.3 Widening the 'Jaws' in luxury brand – a key management task in the luxury business

There is a widely known business concept known as the Jaws Ratio, which describes the relationship between costs and revenues in the business over time. In the high-end, high mark-up luxury business, it is important to remember that revenue is not everything and the costs of doing high-end business can easily get out of control. This is where the Jaws concept comes in. In Figure 3.2 you can see this demonstrated. The chart follows four years of a business and starts as in many cases with negative Jaws, i.e. expenses are above the revenue line. You can see that as the business develops over time, the situation improves, and positive Jaws are achieved by reducing expenses and growing the revenue line. The gap between the two lines are the 'Jaws', and the manager's job is generally to make them as wide as possible, as that will generate the surpluses required for further investment, rewarding the shareholders or employees. Operating with negative Jaws, no matter what the reason, can only be a temporary situation as the business will eventually run out of cashflow.

In the luxury brand sector, the expenses of set up and ongoing business are likely, by the nature of the business, to be higher than for non-luxury. In addition, the sales volumes may not be as high in terms of units, as the offer is unlikely to be 'mass market'. Indeed, the very essence of many luxury brands relies to a degree on exclusivity and rarity. In this situation, the positive Jaws gap must be sufficient to generate the required returns and managers need to have a twin focus at all times on the cost and revenue sides.

3.3.4 Opportunities for management development in the luxury sector

Before we consider how managers in luxury sector should be developed, we should step back and ask what are they going to be judged on? Of course, bottom line results (widening 'Jaws'), are usually the final arbiter; however, these are really the outcomes or scorecard of good practice and may be influenced by a range of factors way outside the managers control or influence, as we have seen recently. Most businesses, luxury or otherwise, will

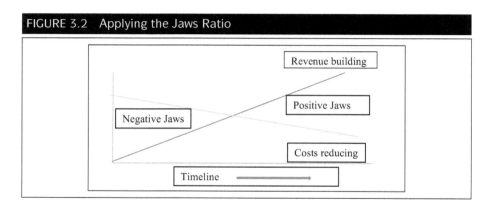

FIGURE 3.2   Applying the Jaws Ratio

have had a pretty awful year in 2020–21, and bottom-line results would have been below expectations, but this was clearly not down to poor management alone. There are a number of indicators of good and bad management, and these are what we should be focused on. Managers will in the end be judged by their impact on the business, but how is this achieved?

3.3.5 Judging management performance in the luxury sector

Performance of the sector managers is tied to that of their organisation, so the following list of key performance indicators are ones that we think need to be considered:

- **Organisational reputation** – in luxury brand this is vital. What does the brand stand for? What are the values, and are they being exhibited every day?
- **Organisational performance** – what do we use to measure this? Commercial, social or other factors? (Hint – what are the objectives? Are they all about finance or are other things equally significant, such as market dominance, diversification, etc.?)
- **Organisational culture** – what is it like to work there? How does the management drive and improve the culture, make it client centric and sustainable?
- **What happens when a leader leaves?** – What is their legacy? If managers leave a poor situation behind, in the relatively close world of luxury brand, it will not be unnoticed.

You should easily see the crucial role played in all of the above factors, by the people that managers are responsible for. Above all, getting the culture right is a significant challenge to managers in all sectors but especially in the luxury brand world, where strong and effective relationships between clients and staff are vital.

3.3.6 The culture iceberg in luxury brand businesses

Organisational culture is defined in many ways but for most people it comes down to what it is like to deal with the organisation. Most managers have the task of managing culture and it is not an easy ask. They actually set the culture every day when they interact with staff or clients. How they communicate, how they look and what they do under stress, all give signals to others about what the culture of the organisation is going to be. I always advise people thinking about joining any organisation to go along and sit in the canteen or reception area for an hour or so. You will see from the way people behave, dress, and talk to each other, what the culture of the company is like and whether you will be able to fit in or change it! However, remember that culture in any organisation is often referred to as an 'iceberg'. That is because you can only see the 10% or so of visible, or surface, culture indicators. This will include the brand, all the marketing collateral, the way people look and behave in front of clients, but the real culture is often deep below the waterline, generally dangerous and unseen (see Figure 3.3).

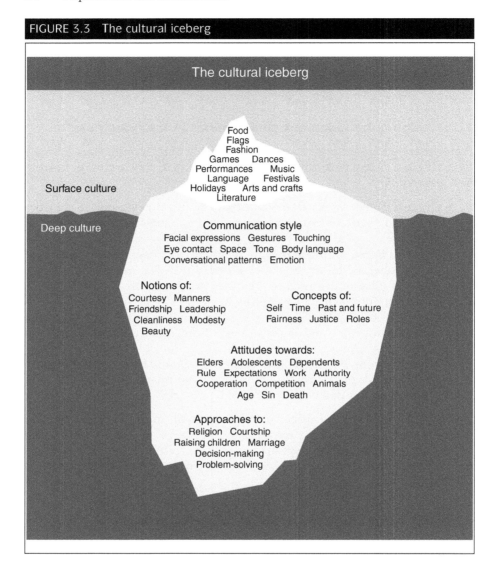

FIGURE 3.3   The cultural iceberg

The application of this concept to the luxury brand sector is very instructive. Where relationship management is a key factor in the business, and those relationships extend over many years, there is no way that a fake culture and lack of authenticity can be hidden. The luxury business relies so heavily on reputation that this becomes a much more significant factor than in other business sectors where other factors such as price, speed, or technology might be far more to the fore.

3.3.7 Management development tools and techniques

Just as in the section on people development, there are many ways that managers can be supported to improve their skills. Lewis and Malmgren (2019) outline much of the new territory for effective leaders of the future. Many areas that have not been so well explored are where leaders and managers can have a real impact such as:

- Defining the new leadership mandate – what are we expecting from our managers that we did not expect before?
- Working around information overload to stop it crushing creativity.
- The impact of fear on risk taking.
- Long- versus short-term consequences – managing for today but looking out for the future.
- Customer impatience and desire for immediacy amidst uncertainty.
- Mindfulness and anger issues.

Some of the methods are quite traditional but the use of e-learning also opens the door to less obvious improvement programmes. The list below suggests some of the less obvious options available to luxury brand businesses:

- **Scenario planning** – often done as a management team to 'dry run' different strategies or challenges.
- **Crisis management sessions** – an extreme version of scenario planning, but useful to consider what happens, or what approach to take, in response to such things as technology failure, hostile takeovers, or new competition, for example.
- **Action learning** – in teams on specific projects – this is a more long-term and action-focused intervention that more mature organisations tend to like. It allows managers to work together and reflect on their learning as the project develops and usually requires an external facilitator.
- **Job sharing or job shadowing** – this allows new perspectives to be gained, prepares managers for their next role, and builds in some resilience in case managers move on.
- **Secondments** – local or international, internal or external. Great for confidence building and knowledge sharing. Allows managers to see the different approaches used by different areas of the business.
- **Team building activities** – becoming less common due to the expense, but vital in developing the culture and shared values around the organisation.
- **Off-site workshops** – focus on key business challenges or new ventures. This is a great way to pre-empt problems, and ensure buy in, where the envisaged change might be controversial.
- **Visits to suppliers or vendors** – essential for managers to see the end-to-end process of the product or service they are delivering. Speaking to those at various stages of the supply chain will provide dividends when the manager briefs their staff or speaks with clients about product specifications.
- **Mystery shopper activities** – testing the customer experience. The ultimate test of how managers are coping. Managers would be expected to assess, and act on, the feedback from the mystery shopper.
- **Problem solving through others** – this is a key skill for all managers in the sector. They must be able to empower their teams with confidence

to deal with day-to-day issues and challenges. Without mastering this skill, all problems will land with the manager, and they will eventually be snowed under.

Any, or all, of these interventions will be applicable at different stages of the manager's development, and dependant on the specific needs of the business. As we saw before, the evaluation of investment in such activity is not always clear but having a strong process for supporting the managers of the business, in our minds, will never be the wrong thing to do.

3.3.8 Utilising empowerment in a luxury brand business

Great managers move their organisations forward by 'empowering' their people to act. What does this mean?

- Allowing employees to make mistakes and learn from them.
- Requiring employees to think things through and 'solutionise'.
- Motivating/challenging people to achieve more.
- Increasing the skills of the workforce through development.

Where client service and high expectations are key drivers, the need to empower your staff to act on your behalf to achieve positive outcomes, is a no brainer. Gates (2019) detailed how the empowerment of women, in particular, can provide a significant uplift to business. There are, of course, downsides to the use of empowerment as shown below but it is a clear advantage to the luxury brand business manager to have staff who can act on their own initiative and 'solutionise' (see Figure 3.4).

Empowerment holds many opportunities, as outlined above, and a few real dangers. It is up to the manager of the luxury business to ensure that they mitigate these dangers as far as possible, because acting without an empowered workforce will make it virtually impossible to achieve the level of client engagement that a luxury business requires. Empowerment of employees in

FIGURE 3.4 The pros and cons of using empowerment in a luxury brand setting

The positive side of empowerment for luxury brand businesses:
- More engaged employees
- Better ideas
- Improved organisational performance
- More attractive culture and place to work
- Greater and better teamworking
- More competitive

The possible downsides:
- Disruption as new ideas compete
- Less consistency
- Managers authority declines
- Employees might not be as capable as you think
- Needs more support, time and development
- More room for error

the luxury setting must include interdepartmental brainstorming workshops in order to understand any negative issues that need to be addressed and turned into success. In the hospitality sector, for example, the sales team are tasked with the responsibility of increasing occupancy. The positive side of this might be increased revenue but could also be poorer service if it is not handled well. Increasing revenue through greater occupancy, without increasing the number of departmental staff and other resources, such as the in-room dining, bar and restaurant services, spas, gyms, and housekeeping, would create future problems. Empowering staff to talk through these situations, and set out the requirements, would be of great benefit.

In one particular case that we know of, the sales team had to take turns working in housekeeping, including sanitising toilet facilities, washing up in the pantry, working in the kitchen preparation room and learning how to iron tablecloths. It soon became evident that the negative impacts of increased occupancy had to be reversed. The upside experience resulted in the sales teams (banqueting, private dining, events planning, and general reservations) experiencing first-hand the different components in a luxury hotel. The benefits were quickly noticed when they experienced the quality of the food, the fine linens, artwork on the walls and the enjoyment of Italian and Turkish marble. The entire sales team collectively increased their efforts to increase room rate revenue, rather than just occupancy rates, and room discounts were abolished.

The use of empowerment to allow staff to work out problems themselves, and suggest constructive solutions, is often overlooked as a free and often vital resource. Many organisations use staff suggestion schemes to encourage this; however, we experienced an unexpected negative consequence in one organisation where employees were given monthly awards for the best idea implemented. In this company, which was a motor vehicle manufacturer, one employee had a seemingly unlimited supply of bright ideas (many of which were excellent) but only submitted one per month, as that was all the scheme allowed him to do! He won the prize most months but would not agree to join the management team and continued to 'ration' his great ideas for many years.

3.3.9 Self-reflection questions

1. Knowing what you do about the luxury brand sector, what is different about their need to develop their managers compared to non-luxury sectors?
2. Where the brand is closely connected to a family, or set of families, how does this impact on the development of the brand's managers?
3. What can managers do to manage culture when it is a very independent phenomenon?

3.3.10 Seminar activities

1. Think of a time when you have not received good service from a retail environment. Whether it was a luxury brand or not, what seemed to be

the cause of this poor level of service? Was it down to the staff member – were they lacking in attitude, skill, or knowledge? Compare your example with the group and see if you can come to a proposed solution.

2. If you were employed as a mystery shopper for a luxury brand business, what would you do? What would you look for as indicators of the 'right' culture amongst employees?

3.4 MANAGING PEOPLE FOR COMPETITIVE ADVANTAGE IN LUXURY BRANDS

3.4.1 Resurrecting the value of luxury brand through people

We have already mentioned that there is a widely shared concern among many luxury insiders, that luxury has begun to lose its meaning, with too many companies peddling so-called 'luxury' goods that would not pass the criteria we detailed earlier in this chapter. The leading hotels of the world group (LHW), for example, was founded in 1928 with 11 luxury European hotels. In 1960, they had 60 members, and today have 375, so the element of exclusivity has inevitably diminished. Pierre Cardin, initially an icon of Haute Couture from the 1950s, can also be accused of watering down the cache and impact of its luxury brand, through licencing the logo throughout the 1980s to a range of products, including BIC pens. The market has arguably been watered down by greater wealth and accessibility, and with the meaning of luxury not well understood by many consumers, the opportunity is available now to return to the key pillars of luxury brand, by a much more sophisticated and targeted development of those involved in all aspects of the luxury business.

3.4.2 The employee value proposition (EVP) for a luxury brand business

Recovering from the past two years of very painful business conditions will require all employees to refocus on their employee value proposition (EVP). Attracting and retaining talent will be a challenge for all, but in the highly demanding arena of luxury services, this will be especially tough. Naresh (2022) comments that employees, and potential employees, now have more refined requirements as to where they want to work compared to before the pandemic. Attracting and retaining talent will be the key HR battle ground for recovery. To attract and retain in the new world of employment requires:

- More holistic experiences based around a range of incentives that don't start and end with the financial.
- Recognition of the individualistic aspects of employment, i.e. don't treat the employee as a number, but see what they need to be fully engaged, both now and in the future, and tailor the package accordingly. Allowing them to pick and choose from a cafeteria style benefits package would be a good start, but the choices have to be meaningful and valid for each employee, which is often not the case.

- Flexibility in workplace and time is now the new normal, so employees will expect to be able to choose, at least to a degree, some aspects of their employment relationship. The 9am to 5 or 6pm, five days per week, is not going to work for many. This requires new levels of trust on both sides of the relationship. Luxury service delivery will need to recognise the importance of flexibility more than ever.
- Inclusivity of employees by strengthening the bond between the employee and the organisation. Involving family members, open days and supporting community-based events are good ways to start here.
- Potential employees may well ask questions about what they will be doing, where and when, how they will be supported, etc., and the luxury business cannot rely on their brand being enough to draw the talent in.
- The talent pool may need to be widened to include non-traditional hiring regimes, flexible and fixed-term contracts, and luxury employers will need to look at new hiring practices.
- Above all, the renewed emphasis on 'purpose' is becoming more prevalent. The best placed employees want to know that they will be working towards a laudable goal and set of outcomes, that are way beyond mere 'shareholder value'.

Developing a luxury brand version of an attractive EVP is therefore a crucial requirement of managers in the industry, where business outcomes are so dependent upon relationships and the willingness of staff to go the extra mile.

This is an area where it would be very easy to sit back and lose out by relying on the draw of a heritage brand to attract employees as it previously did. This might initially be a helpful position but not sustainable, if other, less established brands are in front with a much better developed EVP.

3.4.3 The key pillars of luxury brand – a people perspective

Although it is impossible to list all of the current and future types of luxury brand business, it is possible to narrow down most of their features, to distinguish them from the non-luxury market. By considering these, we can then play back the requirements of the people who run and maintain the business.

- **Unsurpassed Quality** – clients in the luxury sector are discerning. Any lack of quality, real or perceived, will not be tolerated and managers will be expected to intervene sharply if this is experienced, to protect the brand's standing.
- **Craftsmanship** – highly skilled and time-consuming processes will often be utilised by the luxury business, and investment in developing and maintaining these skills has already been highlighted as a key feature of the sector. There could be geographical locations associated with the skillset and the business manager will need to be aware of this. Craftsmanship is often decentralised from large cities and centralised in communities and villages. Many examples exist, such as Northampton for leather goods, Stoke on Trent for ceramics, and Waterford in Ireland

for crystal. The tradition of craftsmanship begins with apprenticeships. For example, handblown crystal is a skill, a talent, and an indication of desire from the individual, as it takes an investment of between six to eight years to become a Master Glassblower.

- **Design** – often referred to as 'form over function'. Luxury versions of products or services are designed to be more than is required, and to be enjoyed for the design aspects as much as for the performance of the product. Volvo motor cars factory in Gothenburg, Sweden, has a poster with the words, 'it cannot be beautiful if it does not function well'. Assar Gabrielsson was the engineer and Gustav Larson the designer. It is rumoured that in early 1926, the two men had a huge argument because the design was beautiful, but there were issues about the door opening.
- **Unerring attention to detail** – this means the elimination of defects, predicting the problems and eradicating them. Clients expect high levels of service but even higher levels of service recovery when things do happen to go wrong.
- **Uniqueness for the right reasons** – luxury brands exploit their uniqueness and that is what justifies the premium price tag. Clients looking for the best price are not really the luxury brand's target market. Value is important and a degree of exclusivity will justify the price differential. Managers need to be aware that sometimes 'less is more'.
- **Authenticity** – particularly for the 'heritage' brands, the purchaser is buying into a lifestyle or choice, where the tradition and background is as important as the consumption now. Indeed, a product such as fine wine or specialist timepieces, might be seen as an investment for the future. This cannot be risked by removing degrees of authenticity to reduce costs or substituting technology without due care. For example, if the client is expecting, and paying for, something 'hand built', even though it could be made more easily by automation, this must not happen. This is particularly difficult if production is outsourced to other organisations. Managers must be wary of diluting the brand for convenience.
- **Rarity or exclusivity** – particularly using the media and PR, the 'presence' of the product or service must be closely managed. The luxury brand is not seeking mass market appeal but needs to be visible in the right way and at the right time. Sponsorship of events needs to be considered carefully to meet the ongoing brand traditions and not be driven just by 'clicks'.
- **Correlation between price and value** – luxury markets and clients are not looking for the cheapest options but there will be an expectation of value. If I am paying 'above market', I can expect above market levels of quality and service. So, employees and managers must also be of higher standards.

We need to reinterpret luxury from simply labels and conspicuous consumption to a quest for goods and services that are personal, authentic and unique. From the key features identified above, we can see that the people who wish to work in the sector have to be in tune with a range of factors that would not be present or required in the non-luxury market. As a result, they need to be managed and developed with these aims and features in mind. It could be argued that the demands on those working in the sector outweigh those from other areas, which is something that needs to be declared openly at the entry stage. All of the features outlined above rely heavily on the people aspects of the business. As we have mentioned previously, the relationship between the business and the client group are key. Relationships are always about people and how businesses are able to make connections, support clients when times are tough, and see opportunities to exploit when the time is right.

3.4.4 Managing luxury brands strategically

Managing the luxury brand business with strategic intent is a crucial requirement for sustainability, which also relates to the people aspects that we have already discussed. There are many broad aspects of business development that could be featured here, but we have chosen to focus on just four that we think are likely to be the most influential to underpinning success, and to reemphasising the importance of the people aspects in each case. However great or sophisticated a business strategy may be, the people involved are the ones who make it happen. There is a well-known quote attributed to the professional boxer now long retired, but who was once the world heavyweight champion, Mike Tyson. When he was being challenged by Evander Holyfield, who was of course after his crown, he was asked how he would cope with a person using a different strategy, devised to defeat him. His response was simple: 'Everyone has a great strategy until they get a punch in the mouth'. What he meant was that a strategy is only ever as good as the ability to achieve its implementation. Effective strategic implementation requires your people to be on board, and fully engaged, so in relation to strategic priority areas, we wanted to highlight the people aspects that a manager needs to consider:

- People issues in financial management
- People issues in strategic planning
- People issues in product life cycle management
- Environment, sustainability, and governance (ESG)

3.4.5 People issues in the financial management of a luxury brand

Financial management rightly features in most general management development programmes, such as typical MBAs and professional accreditation. However, separating financial aspects from people aspects often leads to the wrong type of thinking and poor decisions. As an example, I was once working for a huge financial services organisation with a global presence and the ability to outsource any administrative or data processing tasks to any of their numerous locations. It made absolute financial sense to do this, so managers in the UK and elsewhere were asked to identify the processes to be offshored and costs subsequently squeezed out. Unfortunately, the basis of the decision was purely financial and not in any way dependent on people issues. Managers therefore targeted the processes with the highest headcount to offshore, as that would give the biggest cost savings. The consequence of this was that processes that were very technical and not easily transferable due to the high level of tacit knowledge required, were sent offshore; the tacit knowledge was lost and the subsequent performance in these areas suffered. The lesson from this is that people issues, such as who will be impacted and how we can cope without them or their knowledge, must form part of the decision-making process, not just the bottom-line financial impact which will be short-term in any case, as the processes that were erroneously transferred inevitably seek to come back.

3.4.6 People issues in strategic planning

In our view, the demise of much of strategic planning is accelerating as it fundamentally requires very accurate forecasts of future business environments and opportunities. The level of accuracy for three to five-year plans is now decreasing to the extent that they are very low utility. Nonetheless, there must still be a compelling vision for the business that can be communicated well, then adjusted and implemented by skilled managers. The only way that businesses can really plan for the future is to have a set of options, or a wider boundary of action that they can work towards, giving direction, but also freedom to veer off if the market requires this.

Figure 3.5 demonstrates that rather than a fixed five-year plan, a more realistic strategy is about setting the right boundaries for the direction of the business. As the timeframe increases, the boundaries have to expand as we cannot predict the future with much accuracy. At times, the direction of the business might come close to these boundaries and the senior management then have a clear decision to take. Do we allow the direction to cross the boundaries and therefore take us in a different (possibly superior) strategic direction, or do we take steps to bring the business back to our original

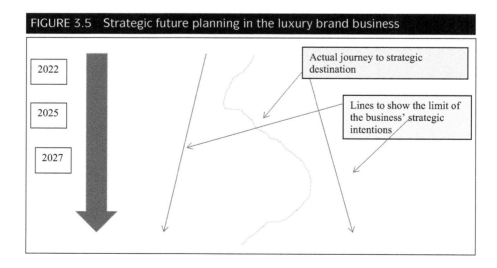

FIGURE 3.5   Strategic future planning in the luxury brand business

strategic intent? What are the consequences of this approach for the people within the business?

- Employees need to be absolutely clear about the business' top line vision and boundaries, as these will have implications for their behaviour.
- People in the business will need to be flexible enough to work towards the vision and strategic direction in terms of their skillset and abilities.
- Managers must be capable of leading between the boundaries that they have clearly defined.

3.4.7 People issues in product life cycle management

People who use the product or service are often the best placed to provide input for future design and functions, connections to other brands and concepts, and areas where the quality or application are not optimal. However, where do they communicate this vital information? If the employees have strong relationships, they can be an effective pipeline of product development information. Staff will need to be kept fully abreast of new developments through a comprehensive training process and updating when required. The combination of research and development, and new product ideas, must be kept in line with any legacy products where older versions may need to be reverse engineered to provide new solutions for clients.

Behind every luxury brand is a story which translates into the final delivery of a product or service. Employees need to be fully aware of the story and their part in it. The personalities, or people, behind the product story adds greatly to the kudos or value proposition and must never be underplayed. Training will once again be the key that unlocks the employees' ability to tell and utilise the story, perhaps of legendary inventors, pioneers or risk takers whom the client wishes to emulate. The story must have passion and serve to build the desire to be part of the ongoing narrative.

3.4.8 Environment, sustainability, and governance (ESG) in the luxury marketplace

The corporate world has moved on from producing statements around corporate and social responsibility (CSR) and had to embrace more impactful ESG policies. The aim is to work towards protecting environmental priorities in the course of their business operations. They will consider ways in which they can improve sustainability in resources used, and how they themselves are governed, to ensure that risks are minimised and that the appropriate checks are employed to balance competing interests.

The luxury world has a deeper responsibility here, by the nature of the industry. Producing luxury items or providing high-end services, cannot be done at the expense of environmental or ethical considerations. More importantly, the industry needs to be seen to be contributing its fair share to any business reforms that hold the sustainability of the planet to the fore. Consumer groups are increasingly active and luxury goods might well be a target group if they are considered extravagant, exclusive, and detrimental to the common good. There are protests aimed at a range of business areas and they often quickly become a cause celebre which can have lasting negative aspects for the brand concerned. People are obviously at the heart of any ESG policy, declaration, or standards. If the luxury business creates a comprehensive ESG policy, it is only of value if employees are required and enabled to act accordingly. Attention must also be paid to suppliers' practices, as the business needs to be confident that all the ESG positives are present throughout the supply chain – ignorance will not be a strong defence if this is found not to be the case. It is incumbent upon top and senior management to engage fully with all employees and companies in the supply chain, to fully understand the importance of having policies in place to prevent further erosion of the environment. One such example can be found at Denby Potteries in Derbyshire. The water used in the production of their ceramics is filtered multiple times post-production, and when pumped back into the network, is cleaner than originally used.

When dealing with corporate social responsibility, and focusing purely on the social aspect, it is important for top management to recognise their duty, responsibility, and accountability towards society as a whole. Microsocieties are found on the shop floors, in offices, fields, and factories. The workplace has to allow for this microsociety to flourish, to be a place of comfort and enjoyment. This goes far beyond white sound, air-conditioned offices, and a nice staff canteen. It is important to breed a culture in the workplace where employees of all levels feel appreciated and can share the joys and sorrows in equal measure. Having an open-door policy cannot be more emphasised as staff members need to feel comfortable to speak out when necessary. Corporate governance has improved significantly during the last 30 years, particularly since the publication of the Cadbury Report published in 1992. Although essentially dealing with financial management and in particular risk management, the report also addresses governance at the highest level. The mood had swung from responsibility to accountability and was the first attempt to create awareness of the importance of governance and its impact on the environment and society. In this report, significant reference was made to the oil industry in Nigeria, and how the absence of corporate governance led to significant corruption, cheap labour, and a deleterious effect on the environment and the society.

3.4.9 Reflective questions for this section

1. Review the key pillars of a luxury product or service. How does your preferred luxury business stand up to these?
2. How can strategic planning be worthwhile with the level of changes experienced in all sectors of the market?

3.4.10 Seminar work for this section

As a small group, discuss how luxury brand businesses can attract and retain their employees. Where should they be looking for new recruits and for their managers?

3.5 Chapter summary

In this chapter we have attempted to highlight the crucial role that the employees have in today's luxury brand business arena. Employees carry the brand with them at all times, and managers have a role in reinforcing the brand so that it maintains its presence and never goes stale. Senior managers in the luxury world have the added responsibility of strategically reviewing the business on a regular basis and ensuring that existing goals are still relevant and desirable. Sometimes heritage businesses are understandably very reluctant to let old propositions go. In many luxury businesses there will be an identifiable, established, and solid DNA built into the business model that transcends the people that work in these businesses. It should therefore be very difficult to fail even generationally, however, sometimes the need to progress and develop new avenues is just as important as hanging on to old values that the market no longer supports.

Ethicality, or more broadly ESG, is also a crucial area in the luxury brand marketplace. Consumers are constantly on the look-out for products where the sourcing is thought to be unethical or employees are potentially being exploited. Where such evidence occurs, it is often a battle to remove any stigma left behind to damage the brand, and managerial ignorance, however true, is generally not a good excuse.

In the case studies we have introduced, we hope that you will be able to see how to apply some of the ideas and concepts that have been outlined here.

One important aspect that we wished to leave you thinking about, is that managing and working in the luxury brand business arena should not be seen as daunting or drudgery. It is a real privilege for most people to be in an industry that can deliver such outstanding experiences and real pleasure to its client base. Yes, it can and will be challenging to live up to the highest expectations, but it should also be fun. Employees and managers need to wake up each day wanting to be their best, and provide the service levels that they can, when they are fully supported and well developed. That is the only sustainable way to drive the future of the luxury brand business, whatever the sector. As we have seen the EVP for a luxury business needs to be defined and refined as the business progresses. The future of luxury business might also benefit from the allure and reputation of a strong brand presence in the face of growing uncertainty in many areas, and mistrust of service providers who are new to market. A well-established brand can be a reassuring and comforting home for clients seeking greater feelings of security.

CASE STUDY 1 The Augustine Hotel, Prague

The Augustine Hotel in Prague is a multi-award winning, ultraluxurious hotel, that consists of seven historical buildings, three of which were deemed to be demolished and the remaining four protected by UNESCO as buildings of significant historical importance. However, it has not always been the success that it is now. The property was first managed by Sir Rocco Forte's hotel company but after an unsuccessful period, the agreement was terminated. Morale was at an all-time low, direction and leadership non-existent, and this was one week before the arrival of Plácido Domingo. To change the atmosphere, negativity, and morale there was only one solution. A total of 140 hotel employees were interviewed by the new owners to establish and understand the reasons behind the emotions, lack of confidence, and poor morale; in short, address the issues. Each employee was asked what he or she wanted to achieve in the hotel to be happy and enjoy what they were doing, and who they preferred to work with in each department.

After four days of interviewing 128 employees and 12 departmental heads, the core issue was found to be lack of communication. Only departmental heads knew of the celebrities who were arriving, and they were all given front row seats at the concerts of Sting, Carlos Santana, Plácido Domingo, Lady Gaga, and many others. In essence, departmental heads and managers put themselves above the rest. There was clearly one rule for departmental heads/managers and another rule for the very hard-working, dedicated, and passionate staff. This resulted in the instant dismissal of nine departmental heads, starting with the General Manager and ending with the spa manager. The change in atmosphere was instantaneous, they worked as a team and the front row tickets became lottery tickets. In 2013, the Augustine won the prestigious 'World Luxury Hotel' award in recognition of the unsurpassed facilities and services. It is crucial for managers to understand the issues as well as the origin of the issues. Behind the door in each of GE's meeting rooms around the globe, there is a framed statement: 'Problems do not exist, only issues'.

CASE STUDY 2 Grays of Westminster

Gray Levitt, one of the cofounders, took on the challenge of a lifetime to become a Nikon-only camera dealer – most people would have said that he was mad. At the time of his founding Grays of Westminster, in almost every high street in the United Kingdom, one would find a Jessops camera dealership. One could purchase any brand of cameras, lenses, videography equipment, lighting equipment, and chemicals for the dark room, from 187 stores. Jessops went bankrupt in July 2013, but Grays of Westminster still flourishes. When Gray Levitt first opened the door of number 40 Churton Street in Pimlico, London, he had the most amazing phrase: 'Good morning, the answer is yes – how can we help you?' Thirty years on, in 2015, Grays of Westminster was awarded its own Coat of Arms by Robert Noel, first Herald of Lancaster. The motto: 'lead in order to serve'.

At the awards ceremony, the President of Nikon, Mr. Kazuo Ushida, had this to say: 'Grays of Westminster represents a timeless partnership and I am honoured to be able to celebrate the 30th anniversary and to be part of the journey through history'. At the ceremony a 207-page book was published with the title 'Grays of Westminster – the legend and the legacy', by Gillian Greenwood (2015). Greenwood said, 'as I stepped through the doors at Grays of Westminster … for the first time, I knew I had arrived somewhere special' (Greenwood, 2015).

In most cases, success or failure is often caused by individuals. In March 2022, Grays of Westminster was awarded the prestigious Platinum Good Service Award. At the time of writing, it has received 37 domestic and international awards. Gray Levitt is the individual who, together with a tremendously successful team behind him, has served royalty, nobility, and world-famous photographers. Today, Grays of Westminster serves nearly half a million customers worldwide each year and ships internationally. As an individual, Gray has become a legend in the world of photography.

References

Aaker, D. A. (1996), 'Measuring brand equity across products and markets', *California Management Review*, Vol 38, No. 3, Spring, 102–120.

Cheales, P. (1994), *I was your customer*, Sandton, South Africa, Waterman.

CIPD (2021), Evaluating Learning and Development. [Online]. Available from: www.cipd.co.uk/knowledge/fundamentals/people/development/evaluating-learning-factsheet#gref

Daisley, B. (2019), *The Joy of Work*, London, Penguin Random House.

Frei, F. and Morriss A. (2020), *Unleashed, The unapologetic leader's guide to empowering everyone around you*. New York, HBR press.

Gates, M. (2019), *Moment of lift: How empowering women changes the world*, London, Bluebird.

Greenwoog, G. (2015), *Grays of Westminster*, London, World Books.

Handy, C. (2016), *The second curve*, New York, Random House.

Kapferer, J.N. and Bastien, V. (2012), *The luxury strategy: Break the rules of marketing to build luxury brands*, London, Kogan page.

Laddha, A. & Naresh, S. (2022), Creating the EVP Pillars for the New Era of Work. *People Matters*. 4th April 2022.

Lewis, C. and Malgren, P. (2019), *The leadership lab*, London, Kogan Page.

Light, L. (2020), *Harley Davidson Adore Your Core*. [online]. Available from: www.forbes.com/sites/larrylight/2020/10/29/harley-davidson-adore-your-core/?sh=829b7e6121c1

Nagendra, K. M., Radha, S., Naidu, C. G. (2013), 'Enhanced Industrial Employability Through New Vocational Training Framework with Attitude-Skill-Knowledge (ASK) Model', *IUP Journal of Management Research*, July 2013, Vol. 12. No. 3, 45–54.

O'Farrell, I. (2021), *The manager's dilemma*, Washington USA, Kindle Direct Publishing.

Statista (2019), Average spend on learning and development per employee worldwide 2008-2020 (online) Available from: www.statista.com/statistics/738519/workplace-training-spending-per-employee/

SECTION 2

Luxury Products

CHAPTER 4

Legal protection for luxury goods and the counterfeiting challenge

Nkechi Amobi

4.1 INTRODUCTION

Intellectual Property Rights (IPRs) confer legal ownership to creators of novel intangible products, which encompasses human intellectual endeavour. Different types of IPR regulate how these products are used and provide remedies for unjustified interferences. IPRs generally grant monopoly or anti-copying rights. It is often said that IPR is an important element in trade transactions because it can boost the economic growth of nations and drive innovation, as well as encourage research and development (R&D). Research indicates that between 2014 and 2016, IPR-intensive industries generated 45% of GDP in the European Union (EU), worth 6.6. trillion euros, and 43% of GDP in the UK, worth over 1 trillion euros (EPO EUIPO, 2019). According to a joint report by the U.S. Patent and Trademark Office (USPTO), and the Economic and Statistics Administration, IPR-intensive industries contributed roughly 38% to the United States GDP, worth 6 trillion USD in 2016.

Luxury goods industries rely on strong IPR frameworks for the protection of their products and services, to affirm the originality and exclusivity of their products, and to secure long-term investment in their innovations. In 2018, the global luxury industry was estimated to have grown by 5%, generating over 1.2 trillion euros (Bain & Company, 2018). At a national level, the UK luxury industry was worth 48 billion GBP to the nation's economy between 2013 and 2017 (Walpol Economic Impact Study, 2019).

It is therefore unsurprising that the global luxury industry, which represents a significant percentage of global trade, is, unfortunately, targeted by the counterfeit goods industry. 'Counterfeit' refers to inferior items, manufactured to imitate branded products; counterfeiters operate in the grey market. Many counterfeit products infringe on the IPRs of luxury brand owners. The validity of this claim is backed up by a joint EU Intellectual Property Office (EUIPO) and OECD Report, which indicates that sales in counterfeits represent over 3% of global trade, grossing up to 509 billion USD. This chapter examines the relevance of IPRs to luxury goods industries, by

DOI: 10.4324/9781003015826-6

investigating how successful they are in securing monopoly or anti-copying rights for luxury goods. The discussion will focus on the four main IPRs, and the legal emphasis will be on EU and UK laws. The UK, as a former member of the block, has similar IPR laws to those of the EU, which are premised on standard international provisions.

4.2 IPR AND LUXURY BRANDS

Luxury brands invest in various forms of IPRs to gain rights *in personam.* These rights give them different layers of anti-copying or monopolistic rights, which they can assign, mortgage or license to third parties. The relevant IPRs for the luxury goods focused on in this chapter include trademark, copyright, design right and patent. Many of these laws are not automatically granted but must be applied for and paid for. Depending on the category of right, the application process can be expensive and cumbersome. It is worth noting that IPRs are generally subject to territorial restriction; their holders are required to file for protection in as many countries as possible, to prevent infringement. Although IPRs are useful tools for the protection of intellectual creativity, they are sometimes used by luxury brands to appropriate aspects of the cultural heritage of indigenous communities for commercial gains. This is evidenced by the Mexican government's allegation of plagiarism against the luxury brand Carolina Herrera, for appropriating elements of the cultural heritage of the indigenous communities of Tenango de Doria and Saltillo, in its Resort 2020 collection (Sádaba, 2020).

4.3 PATENT

As an intellectual property tool, patent grants monopolistic rights to the holder. Under the provisions of section 1(2) of the *UK Patent Act 1977*, it is awarded on products or processes deemed to be 'novel', 'inventive' and 'non-obvious'. Patent is relevant to different industries, including the luxury industry. It not only encourages creativity but can be used as a capitalist tool to create scarcity. Irrespective of the substantive examination to which patent applications are subjected, and the cost it entails, it is only valid for twenty years, after which time the knowledge falls into public domain. It can cost up to 5000 GBP to file a UK patent application, which is limited in territorial coverage. As it pertains to luxury goods, patent protects the 'novel' knowledge behind the functionality of products such as watches and automobiles. Patented luxury goods boost the global economy, as demonstrated by the global market value of the luxury watch industry, which in 2020 was in excess of 6.98 billion USD, and the automobile industry, estimated at 550 billion euros. The usefulness and economic worth of patent in the luxury watch industry cannot be overstated. In 2019, Patek Philippe sold its Grandmaster Chime Ref 6300A-010 watch, which holds a patent for its reversing mechanism, at an auction in Germany for 31.19 million USD. The 2018 UK Intellectual Property Office (UKIPO) report revealed that the luxury car maker, Jaguar Land Rover (JLR), held over 200 patents in 2018 – the highest number of approved patents in the UK that year. Even though patent protects novel inventions, the counterfeit industry still poses an enormous challenge to luxury patented goods. Counterfeit products not only tarnish the reputation of luxury brands but are dangerous to the health and safety of consumers.

4.4 COPYRIGHT

Copyright protects literary, artistic, musical, and dramatic works that are original or derivative. It is automatically awarded on qualifying works and lasts throughout the author's lifetime plus an additional twenty-five to seventy years, depending on the category of work. Copyright grants the holder an anti-copying right. In the UK, the *Copyright, Design Patent Act 1988* (CDPA*)* protects this area of intangible property and is premised on the provisions of international legislations such as the *Berne Convention for the Protection of Literary and Artistic Works (1886).* For copyright protection to apply in the UK, the work must fall within one of the subsections provided under the CDPA.

Theoretically, the category of copyright relevant to luxury goods is artistic works, which, under s.3–4 of the CDPA, comprises works that demonstrate graphic and artistic craftsmanship. Nevertheless, the correlation between copyright and luxury goods is blurred. To illustrate: in *Shirin Guild v Eskandar Ltd (2001),* the UK judiciary rejected an argument by the plaintiff that his garment was protectable under the provisions of the CPDA as a work of artistic craftsmanship. In opposition to this, in *Response Clothing Ltd v the Edinburgh Woollen Mills Ltd (2020),* the court held that the plaintiff's garment, which was a jacquard fabric, qualified for copyright protection because it demonstrated artistic craftsmanship protectable under s.4 CDPA. The plaintiff, by weaving its wave design into the fabric instead of printing it on had demonstrated artistic skills in the eyes of the court, as opposed to the judgement in *Shirin Guild v Eskandar,* where the plaintiff asserted that merely by virtue of being an artist his garment qualified as a work of art under s.4 CDPA. Premised on the above judicial decisions, it is obvious that luxury garments – especially *haute couture* designs that display enough originality or artistic craftsmanship – will qualify for protection under the CDPA. Furthermore, since copyright protects literary and artistic work, drawings or sketches of luxury products can also be protected by copyright. Finally, the correlation between copyright and luxury automobiles is shown in the 2019 Italian General Court's landmark decision, which recognised the Ferrari 250 GTO as an industrial design, protectable as a work of art.

4.5 DESIGN

In the UK, design rights (registered or unregistered) protect only the aesthetics of a product. Registered design grants monopoly rights to the holder for a maximum of twenty-five years. Previously, in the UK, registered design was an underused IP tool, despite its direct and indirect annual economic contribution of over 200 billion GBP gross value added (GVA) to the UK economy. In the past decade, however, there has been an increased use of design registration. Therefore, although in 2011 there were fewer than 3500 registered designs in the UK, there were more than 24,400 registered designs granted in 2019 (UKIPO *Facts and Figures Report*, 2019). Prior to Brexit, UK registered design was under the harmonised designs laws, which included the *Registered Community Designs (RCD) (EC/Regulation No 6/2002)* and the UK *Registered Designs Acts 1949 (RDA, 1949)*. The RCD grants the holder a monopoly right across the EU for twenty-five years. Under the provisions of the RCD and RDA, to qualify for registration, the design must be novel and have individual character. For a design to be deemed novel with Individual character, a comparison is made between the existing design corpus available to the public at the time of design application, and the overall impression the later design makes on an informed user (*BMW v Premier Alloy Wheels & Ors (2020)*). The precedent set in *Magmatic Ltd v PMS International Ltd (2016)*, and reiterated in Shnuggle v Munchkin (2019) highlights important issues to consider when registering designs, and challenges faced by the judiciary when assessing infringement claims. It is worth noting the advantage of the RCD over the UK legislation for design protection, demonstrated by the CJEU's rejection of the defence of innocent infringement by Towerstone for allegedly infringing Jimmy Choo's RCD on its Ramona bag (*Jimmy Choo v Towerstone (2008)*). On the contrary, UK national laws provide an exemption for financial remedy to right holders if infringement was unintentional (s.24B RDA 1949 & s.233 CDPA 1988).

A design that has individual character is automatically protected as an unregistered design under s.213 of CDPA, and an unregistered community design (UCD) (*EC/Regulation 6/2002)*, for a period of fifteen and three years respectively. These laws protect different dimensions of the designs and give anti-copying rights to the holder. In the event of an infringement, the burden of proof rests upon the rights holders to prove that their designs were copied. However, as affirmed in *Karen Millen v Dunnes (2014)*, if the dispute relates to allegation of lack of individual character of the design then the burden of proof shifts to the alleged infringer to dispel. Indubitably, design right is an important IP tool for luxury goods as it differentiates a brand's product from those of its competitors. Any unjustifiable compromise of this would negatively affect investment in design creativity, and profit margins.

4.6 TRADEMARKS

A business can register, as its trademarkI), any distinctive sign (conventional or unconventional), to serve as an indicator of the origin of its goods or services. In addition to designating the commercial origin of products or services, TM also indicates the quality of goods or services, and is a medium for advertisement and investment in brand image. A registered trademark confers on the holder a monopolistic right, which can last for infinity. The UK *Trademarks Act 1994* (TMA) protects TM in the UK. This act is shaped by various international treaties such as the *Madrid Agreement 1981* and European Regulations & Directives, including the EU *Trademarks Regulation 2017 and Trademarks Directive 2015*. Trademark protects the brand image of products or services and is vital to the overall success of any company. It is ubiquitous – all too important and well used in the luxury sector. One of the most valuable luxury brands in the world, Louis Vuitton (LV), which has an estimated brand value of over 47 billion USD (Forbes, 2020), fosters its creativity through IPR protection. The brand manages over 19,000 IPRs, including trademarks, and is actively engaged in the global fight against counterfeiters and IP infringement. Trademark gives its holders offensive and defensive rights, which are immensely beneficial for luxury brand protection. For instance, in respect of goods or services, its defensive benefit prevents the subsequent registration, as a TM, of a sign that is identical or similar to an earlier mark. This defensive benefit stops the possibility of any confusion as to the origin of a product, due to similarities between an earlier and later trademark.

To determine whether or not consumers would be confused between two marks because of their similarity, the court adopts a global approach. It assesses the effect that factors such as visual, aural, and conceptual similarities between the competing marks might have on a hypothetical consumer. A hypothetical consumer is an average person, who is reasonably well informed with regard to the product or service area and who is circumspect but does not have the chance to make a direct comparison between the two marks. If this hypothetical consumer is confused by the two marks, then a likelihood of confusion will be established. This point is illustrated by the recent unsuccessful opposition claim by Christian Dior (CD) against Adele Savage's application to register the mark *'Pretty Savage'* as her trademark for goods in a class, which includes cosmetics and cleaning substances. CD brought its claim under the provisions of s.5 (4)(a) TMA 1994, arguing that the use of the name *'Pretty Savage'* would confuse consumers as to the origin of the applicant's product, or imply an economic connection between *'Sauvage'* by CD and *'Pretty Savage'* by Adele Savage. This argument was made by the claimant, premised on its earlier TM on *'Sauvage'*, a product in the same class of goods. The court rejected the opposition claim on the grounds that the goods of both undertakings were dissimilar and there were no grounds for direct confusion on the part of the average consumer.

The offensive benefit of TM that is relevant for luxury goods protection can be found within the EU *Trademarks Directive 2015*, which accords an earlier TM with reputation – an extended blocking power over a later TM. The issue here is not the likelihood of confusion about the origin or affiliation of goods emanating from either the earlier or later TM. Instead, the aim is to prevent the use of a mark similar or identical to an earlier TM if it accords the later mark with unmerited advantage, or if it potentietilldilutes or tarnishes the reputation of the earlier brand. It is irrelevant whether or not there is commonality between the commercial fields of both brands. To illustrate the above point, the European Court of Justice (CJEU) in *L'Oreal v Bellure (2010),* upheld L'Oreal's power to block the use of its TM by the defendant in its price comparative list of perfumes. In a 2018 case, DC Comics successfully prevented Superglide Bi-folds Ltd from using a sign similar to its iconic Superman 'S' logo, despite a lack of commonality between the services rendered by both marks. The court upheld the opposition claim on the grounds that it would accord the applicant an unmerited advantage, allowing it ride on the coattails of the already established reputation and image of DC Comics. By riding on the coattails of DC Comics, Superglide Bi-folds would not need to market their products aggressively to achieve prominence, since it would gain this from the opponent's substantial promotion of the mark. This section of the chapter has broadly discussed the characteristics and relevance of IPRs to luxury goods. Subsequent sections will examine UK IP law in the era of Brexit, and the challenges of counterfeits to the luxury goods industry.

4.6.1 Brexit and UK IPR Laws

As a result of Brexit, the *European Union Withdrawal Act 2018* repealed the *European Communities Act 1972* and converted existing applicable EU IPR laws into UK domestic laws. Although the substantive UK and EU IPRs presently remain the same, the impact of Brexit is noticeable in the areas of EU trademarks (EUTM) and registered and unregistered community designs (RCD) & (UCD). The EUTM, RCD and UCD no longer grant unitary rights across the EU to UK trademarks and designs. The UK Intellectual Property Office (UKIPO) was charged with creating a comparable system of national TM and registered designs, which automatically cloned all existing EUTM and RCD registrations from 1 January 2021. With respect to registered design and TM applications, the situation is slightly different. At the end of the Brexit transition period, applicants with pending TM and design applications were given a nine-month grace period to refile their applications, claiming priority from their pending EU applications. Finally, those who want to file an international application must designate the UK separately from the EU before they can receive protection in the UK.

4.6.2 Counterfeits and Luxury Goods

One could be forgiven for wondering why trade in global counterfeit products continues to soar, despite the existence of IPRs. Many intellectual property laws, especially those relating to TMs, are used by luxury brands to prevent the reproduction and sales of their products, especially the counterfeit versions. Irrespective of the existence of these laws, the counterfeit industry continues to boom as a result of globalisation and technological growth. Although the seamless movement of people, goods and services, and the growth of technology are benefits of living in a globalised twenty-first century, these benefits also enable the growth of the counterfeit industry. The sale of counterfeits is not just a national or even a regional business; it is a global phenomenon. Although illegal, it is an extremely lucrative business driven by high profit margins and low risk. The volume of international trade in counterfeit goods has reached 1.2 trillion USD, resulting in a loss of over 98 billion USD to the global luxury industry (*Global Brand Counterfeiting Report*, 2019).

The effect of counterfeit products on the EU Organisation for Economic Cooperation and Development (OECD) market is just as dire. Between

2016 and 2019, 6.8% of imports into the EU were fake goods, accounting for approximately 121 billion USD (*Status Report on IPR Infringement*, 2020). Counterfeits have a devastating effect on luxury brands. They present reputational risk, affect brands' bottom-lines and overall consumer satisfaction, and lead to loss of jobs and government revenues. Once luxury goods become common, their retail value is impaired, and this adversely affects R&D, marketing, and advertising resources invested in creating such goods. Just under half of luxury counterfeit products originate from East Asian countries and are sold through online platforms such as eBay, Instagram, Facebook, Amazon, and AliExpress. They are transported primarily by sea, via free trade zones. A recent study shows that the luxury industry has lost over 30.3 billion USD on sales of counterfeits through online platforms (*Trends in Trade in Counterfeit and Pirated Goods*, 2019). There have been several initiatives – global, regional and national – set up to curb the activities of counterfeiters. For instance, the Alibaba Anti-Counterfeiting Alliance (AACA), in partnership with over 130 brands, share industry knowledge and monitor counterfeiting activities. In 2018, through the activities of the AACA, 524 manufacturing and distribution locations of counterfeit products were shut down. At the European level, the EU publishes a *Counterfeit and Piracy Watch List,* which identifies online and physical marketplaces outside the region, through which EU citizens access counterfeit products. This initiative is important, since judicial precedents at both UK and EU levels illustrate that third parties bear no liability in IP infringement if they are unaware that counterfeit products are stored or transmitted through their platforms (*L'Oréal v eBay (2009); Google France SARL & Google Inc. v Louis Vuitton Malletier SA (C-236/08); Cartier International AG & Ors v British Broadcasting Ltd & Ors (2014)*). In spite of the above, the decision of the court, in *Coty Germany GmbH v Amazon (C-567/18),* that luxury brands can prevent the sale of their products on platforms such as Amazon where necessary to prevent diluting the exclusivity of their brand, represents a small victory for luxury brands.

EUROPOL, INTERPOL, and other local authorities such as Trading Standard agencies, Police Intellectual Property Crime Units (PIPCU), and the UK Anti-Counterfeit Group (ACG), have been working in coordination, where possible, to curb and tilize counterfeiters. In conclusion, it is clear that counterfeits continue to be a challenge to luxury goods and, although the industry continues to grow and to tilize IPRs to protect its products, sales in counterfeit remain a real challenge to it.

Seminar exercises

Discussion topics:

1. Carry out research into two of the following types of intellectual property rights for group discussion: trademark, copyright, design right, and patent. Share back with the class.
2. Outline two challenges posed by the counterfeit industry to luxury patented goods and share back in class discussion.

Group exercises:

1. Imitation is said to be the highest form of flattery, although this is not so for the luxury industry. International trade in counterfeit goods reached £1.31 trillion in 2020 and this number is growing. The majority of counterfeit 'luxury' goods seized are sunglasses, watches, and leather goods. According to the Global Brand Counterfeiting Report 2018, the most Imitated brands are Chanel, Louis Vuitton, Prada, Fendi, Gucci, and Dior. Carry out research and prepare a case on how luxury brands can challenge the counterfeit market. Report back to the class (Source: World Trade Review, 2020).
2. Select a luxury brand of your choice and create a presentation to address the following:
    *   How has the brand been impacted by the counterfeit market?
    *   How might the brand address the issue?

Source: World Trade Review (2020) Counterfeit luxury goods. [online]. Available from: www.worldtrademarkreview.com/anti-counterfeiting/counterfeit-lux ury-goods

References

Bain & Company (2018). Personal Luxury Goods Market Delivers Positive Growth in 2018 to Reach €260 Billion- A Trend That is Expected To Continue Through 2025. www.bain.com/about/media-center/press-releases/2018/fall-luxury-goods-market-study/ (accessed 13 January 2021)

Bainbridge, D (2018). *Intellectual Property.* Tenth Edition. Pearson BMW v Premier Alloy Wheels & Ors (2020). EWHC 2094

D' Arpizio, C et al. (2019). Eight Themes That are Rewriting the Future of Luxury Goods. www.bain.com/insights/eight-themes-that-are-rewriting-the-future-of-luxury-goods/ (accessed 18 October 2020)

EPO-EUIPO Study (2019). Intellectual Property Rights Strongly Benefits the UK Economy. https://pressreleases.responsesource.com/news/98454/intellectual-property-rights-strongly-benefit-the-uk-economy-epo-euipo-study/ (accessed 21 September 2020)

EUIPO/OECD (2019). Trends in Trade in Counterfeit and Pirated Goods www.oecd.org/corruption-integrity/reports/trends-in-trade-in-counterfeit-and-pirated-goods-g2g9f533-en.html (accessed 14 June 2020)

EUIPO Report (2020). Status Report on IPR Infringement, Why IPRs are important, IPR infringement, and the fight against counterfeiting and piracy: Executive Summary, June 2020 https://euipo.europa.eu/tunnelweb/secure/webdav/guest/document_library/observatory/documents/reports/2020_Status_Report_on_IPR_infringement/2020_Status_Report_on_IPR_infringement_exec_en.pdf (accessed 27 July 2020)

Forbes (2020). Louis Vuitton. www.forbes.com/companies/louis-vuitton/#b12abb96dbe7 (accessed 23 December 2020)

Jimmy Choo v Towerstone (2008). E.C.C 20.

Karen Millen v Dunnes (2014). C-345/13.

L'Oreal v Bellure (2010). EWCA Civ 535.

Magmatic Ltd v PMS International Ltd (2016). UKSC 12.

Response Clothing Ltd v the Edinburgh Woollen Mills Ltd (2020). EWHC 148 (IPEC).

Sádaba, T., LaFata, V., Torres, A. (2020). Cultural Appropriation in the Digital Context: A Comparative Study Between Two Fashion Cases. In: Nah, FH., Siau, K. (eds) *HCI in Business, Government and Organizations. HCII 2020. Lecture Notes in Computer Science()*, vol 12204. Springer, Cham. https://doi.org/10.1007/978-3-030-50341-3_38

Shnuggle v Munchkins (2019). EWHC 3149 (IPEC).

Silverman, I (2014). Copyright and Fashion: A UK Perspective (WIPO Magazine) www.wipo.int/wipo_magazine/en/2014/03/article_0007.html%20 (accessed 1st October 2020)

Walpole Report (2019). Economic Contribution to the UK and Policy Recommendation High End Cultural & Creative Industries. www.thewalpole.co.uk/wp-content/uploads/2019/06/Economic-and-financial-contribution-of-high-end-creative-and-cultural-industries-to-the-UK-economy.pdf (accessed 12 August 2020)

World Trade Review (2020). Counterfeit Luxury Goods. www.worldtrademarkreview.com/anti-counterfeiting/counterfeit-luxury-goods (accessed 21 August 2020)

CHAPTER 5

The case for the wine experience

John Harrison

5.1 INTRODUCTION

The case for the 'Wine Experience' finds its roots in France, the country which has set the standard for the world and has the monopoly on 'luxury' wines (Cardebat & Figuet, 2006). Three areas in particular are the focus of this chapter: Bordeaux, Burgundy, and Champagne. These three regions are at the top of the list for fine wines and, although there are many other excellent wine regions in France, these three are dominant in producing 'much sought after wines' (Paul, 2002). This, of course, raises issues among many major producers in the rest of the world, who produce some superb wines. The Romans cultivated vines in France; they were in the Rhone Valley in 60 BC and active in the Bordeaux region by the first century AD. The area became well known for its wines, which were distributed to Roman soldiers and citizens in Gaul and Britain (*Wine Cellar Insider*). If you look at a map of France and look for Bordeaux in the south-west of the country you will see the Gironde estuary, which meets the Atlantic Ocean. The Gironde is fed by two rivers – the Garonne, which flows from the south-west, and the Dordogne, from the south-east. They join the Gironde just north of Bordeaux, and then flow north-west from what looks like an inverted 'Y', the Garonne on the left branch and the Dordogne on the right. The land between these two rivers is known as the Entre-Deux-Mers, and the surrounding area, affectionately known as the Left Bank and the Right Bank, creates one of the world's largest wine growing areas and produces the world's most sought after wines (Forster, 1961).

In these fine wine regions, very strict rules govern grape growing and wine production, and also what products can be called. Champagne is a case in point. To be allowed the 'Champagne' label, the wine must be made entirely in the tightly defined Champagne region of north-east France, with Reims and Epernay its major centres (Lehning, 2005). This is about *terroir* and concerns the soil and unique environmental factors of a particular area, as well as the microenvironment of the region. It is the basis of what the French

DOI: 10.4324/9781003015826-7

call *Appellation d'Origine Contrôlée* (AOC), which means 'controlled designation of origin'. The certifications and the process are controlled overall by an organisation called the Institut national de l'origine et de la qualité (INAO). AOCs apply to regions whose grapes are expected to reflect similar *terroir* (qualities) in their subsequent wines (Farmer, 2014). French wines fall into four groupings: *Vin De Table*, is everyday wine, with no indication of where the grapes come from; *Vin de Pays* or 'country wine' is identified by the origin of the grapes, and wines are also tasted before they gain their designation; *Vin Délimité de Qualité Supérieure* (VDQS) referred to wines that were originally tasted before they gained their designation, but this category was phased out in 2011; *Appellation d'Origine Contrôlée* (AOC) is the highest level where tasting is undertaken (*Sedimentality Anon*).

Restrictions specify certain grapes that can be used in an AOC, along with important variables relating to the methods used in the wine-making process and its subsequent storage. All the particular variables are of concern to the AOC system and are what make types and styles of wines unique. AOCs also serve as a guide for wine buyers; in understanding AOCs one gains the knowledge about what exactly is being bought. Other European wine producing countries have followed France, with regulatory bodies based on the AOC principle. This chapter will bring together aspects of the world of wine, with an emphasis on luxury experiences. 'Experience' is becoming a significant concept generally, and particularly in the world of luxury. Both wine and food are very complex issues and, to a great degree, much of the experience comes down to individual perception.

5.2 THE STARTING POINT

Experiencing wine, of course, is about cultivation and also about economics. There is a vast range of wine, from the very cheap to the eye-wateringly expensive. Generally, the price of wine is an important indication of quality when there are few other clues available prior to purchase. Accordingly, the quality of wine is often referred to, but rarely defined. One argument claims there is no way to determine quality, other than examining the purpose the wine will serve, and its value for money. One can categorise the methods of classifying and assessing wine quality as either intrinsic or extrinsic. Intrinsic quality relates to the wine-in-the-glass or, in other words, to what is tasted. Extrinsic classification methods make use of factors extraneous to the wine in an attempt to establish its quality (Charters, 2003). The world's highest acclaimed tasting expert has been, and probably still is, Robert M Parker Jnr. from Maryland, USA. Although he is now retired, his reach and influence have been global, and his scoring of fine wines has had a huge effect on the price (Jefford, 2020).

What is in the price of a bottle of wine? Are price and quality in direct relationship? The answer is 'not necessarily'. Within the world of luxury products, 'heritage' is a well-used term and the world of wine is no exception (Wiedmann et al., 2012). Whatever affects the price, heritage is certainly used to advantage in the world of wine, particularly in terms of wines from the previously mentioned regions. It applies very much to Old World wines, although New World wines are also getting in on the act with huge improvements. Geographic regions have always been an index of quality, and the provenance of a wine is guaranteed by the appellation system in France and by similar organisations in other European countries (Lepré et al., 2011). To generalise without being too simplistic, New World nations have far more relaxed rules and fewer restrictions than the European wine growing nations. Kapferer & Bastien (2012), make the point that Old World wines will not be able to remain relevant if they do not suppress their self-imposed limitations. Their production laws do not encourage supplier concentration, which is a big part of their heritage. Robinson (2019) highlights the fact that the progression of time now sees wines that have sold themselves as luxury products, such as LVMH portfolio stable mates Château Cheval Blanc and Château d'Yquem, working hard to forge links directly with end buyers rather than continuing to rely on Bordeaux's many-linked distribution chain. Château Latour opted out of the annual *en primeur* Bordeaux tastings and sales, an annual tasting ritual that takes place each spring in Bordeaux. It is a historic way for buyers of the most desired Bordeaux wines to purchase them a few years before they are bottled and released on the market and, as they would hope, increase in price. This originated in the eighteenth century and the present system was established in the 1980s, involving tastings by experts, who give ratings to the wines (*Le Blog*, 2020).

The luxury French wines emanating from the Bordeaux region are sold through *negociants,* a method of selling wine started by the Dutch in Bordeaux, dating back to the early 1600s, and mentioned by Kapferer (2012). The Bordeaux system remains unique and is one of the reasons why wine from this region has become some of the most important. As the top châteaux only sold their wine through the *negociants*, Bordeaux became the only wine producing area that did not need any direct interaction between customers and the château and its owners (*Wine Cellar Insider*).

5.3 BORDEAUX – THE LEFT BANK

In 1855 the *Exposition Universelle* took place in Paris. It was a great exhibition where France set out to sell itself to the world. One outcome was the birth of the Bordeaux classification (Barbe & Bouzdine, 2013). This system classified the vineyards of the Médoc and Haut-Médoc, and the areas at the extremity of the region – AOC Pessac-Léognan, Graves with AOC Barsac, and AOC Sauternes – the latter two mostly famous for sweet white wines. There are exceptions, however; Château Haut-Brion, one of the five Premier Crus, is to be found in Pessac, rather than Haut-Médoc. This region has also produced the only Premier Cru Supérieur, from Château d'Yquem, Sauternes. The classification system looked to the châteaux in the Médoc and Haut-Médoc, the region on the Left bank of the Gironde north of the City of Bordeaux. The Gironde Chamber of Commerce, headed by the president, Duffour-Dubergier, ordered the official 1855 classification. These châteaux have maintained their position to this day, as the Premier Cru first growth.

That doesn't mean they have kept their position easily; there have been good and bad seasons, as well as two world wars. There have also been changes in ownership of the châteaux over the years. The first growth Premiers Crus are: Château Lafite Rothschild AOC Pauillac; Château Margaux AOC Margaux; Château Latour AOC Pauillac; Château Haut-Brion AOC Pessac; Château Mouton Rothschild; and AOC Pauillac (which was not in the original group but was elevated to Premier Cru in 1973). The list also included châteaux in Barsac and Sauterne, with a total of eleven sweet white wines from this AOC, and fifteen overall with the Premier Cru classification. The only one with the highest of all classifications, Premier Cru Supérieur, was Château d'Yquem AOC Sauternes, which still maintains its position.

5.3.1 Classification of Red Wines of the Left Bank

There is more to Bordeaux than just the Haut-Médoc, and there is more to the Médoc than just the Premier Cru. The Médoc Classification of 1855 gave First Growths (Premiers Crus), Second Growths (Deuxièmes Crus), Third Growths (Troisièmes Crus), Fourth Growths (Quatrièmes Crus), and Fifth Growths (Cinquièmes Crus). In February 2020 there was a return to the Cru Bourgeois. According to Jane Anson, it was said to have been founded in the thirteenth century. Others claimed it began in the fifteenth century, but it certainly rose after the French Revolution. It is hoped it will give lasting power and sustainability to a category of wines, which, in many ways, are the backbone of the entire Bordeaux system – great quality, reasonably priced claret. (Anson, 2020). It is early days yet, but it represents a distinct revival for the Bordeaux system.

5.3.2 The white wines of the Gironde

These are Premier Cru Supérieur, First Growths (Premiers Crus), and Second Growths (Deuxièmes Crus). With the exception of the one Premier Cru Supérieur, there are only two classifications. In other words, the classification First Growth (Premier Cru) designates the wine as A+, and Second Growth (Deuxième Cru) as A- (*Wine Cellar Insider*).

5.4 BORDEAUX – THE RIGHT BANK

The Right Bank is the other region of Bordeaux that is on the north bank of the Dordogne. What is the difference? It has been said that the big difference is that Right Bank wine producers get their hands dirty. The Left Bank, of course, has the great châteaux, whereas on the Right Bank, the term 'château' is more likely to be a figure of speech than an architectural description, and the owner lives on the premises rather than in Paris, according to Margaret Rand (*Decanter*, 2008). The right bank did not fall into the 1855 classification but had to wait one hundred years; Saint-Émilion was first classified in 1955. However, unlike the 1855 classification, which was set in stone, Saint-Émilion's was a more flexible classification. It was updated in 1969, 1986, and

1996. The Right Bank has risen in stature, and in many ways rivals the Grand Cru of the Left Bank, with the appellations of Saint-Émilion and Pomerol producing some of the world's most sought-after wines. The Pomerol Appellation d'Origine Contrôlée (AOC) produces one of the Bordeaux 'stars' – the most famous Petrus, which is probably one of the most expensive wines in the world (Shepard, 2016). Further to this, and perhaps one of the ironies, is that Pomerol does not have a classification system like all the other AOCs in the Left Bank and Right Bank. Petrus ranks alongside the Premiers Crus of the Left Bank. For marketing people, the classification system has been, and still is, a major marketing tool for these wines (Hall & Mitchell, 2007). In a sense, Petrus has proved that you can reach the top without the classification and be one of the most rare and expensive wines in the world.

The difference between Left Bank and Right Bank is, in many ways, the *terroir*. The Left Bank has gravelly rock deposits and limestone sub-soil; the Right Bank has limestone closer to the surface and less gravel. The different *terroirs* quite simply make use of different grapes. The Left Bank is largely Cabernet Sauvignon supported by Merlot; the Right Bank tends to be more Merlot supported by Cabernet Sauvignon. Left Bank wines are higher in tannins; those of the Right Bank are generally much smoother (Bell, 2016). The rest is down to the climate and weather conditions, with frost, hail and strong winds being major problems affecting the method of growing the vines, and the whole process of turning grapes into wine. Added to this are diseases such as mildew and pests – phylloxera aphid being the worst. The most serious outbreak, in the middle of the nineteenth century, very nearly decimated the French wine industry and many other European growers. Today, there is massive growth in organic growing and management of the estates in general, all of which contributes to the price of a bottle of wine.

5.5 GENERAL PROCESS AND STORAGE

The production of wine is an agricultural process, and the vines also need a great deal of human tender loving care – a combination of tradition and the synthesis of science and state of the art techniques. As with many agricultural processes, the soil must be prepared and today, with the growth in organic farming, a great deal of thought is given to sustainable agriculture. In the northern hemisphere, the grape harvest is normally completed in October, after which the whole cycle starts again. As with all fruit growing, the vine is dormant at the beginning of the winter, after harvest. The ground needs preparation and vines need protection from winter frosts. Pruning takes place from January/February and in March the vines start to wake up. In April, the buds start sprouting and need to be supported. During May, the vines still need protection from spring frosts and must be treated to prevent any disease. In June the flowers appear on the vine, and in July pruning and trimming takes place, continuing into August, if needed. September, harvest usually begins, although heavy rain, hail and strong winds can be problems. In October, the harvest ends and the next cycle begins. The yield needs to be limited through the pruning during growth to produce the quality. This is the basic process, but there are many issues that growers must watch for at this crucial time, not the least of which is the maturity of the grapes.

After harvest, the grapes are crushed and the juices allowed to ferment. The processes vary from this point, for red wine, rosé, white wine and sparkling wines. When fermentation stops, the natural yeast has been exhausted with the natural sugars and becomes alcohol. Red wine has a period of maceration and fermentation. In this process, the grape solids add all the constituent colouring to the grape juice. There are slight variations in this part of the process in the different AOCs. Then the pressed juice is run off and separated from the solids. There is a final fermentation and clarification, to remove fine particles, then 'racking' to remove the lees, or spent yeast. This is done by pouring the liquid from one barrel into another. Then the wine needs to mature – generally in oak barrels. Storage time can vary greatly prior to final bottling, where temperature control is hugely important. After final bottling the process continues with correct storage and temperature control, and with a timescale until the wine is mature. Times can vary according to the wine, but generally this is the process. All of the stages can have huge effects on the final result.

5.6 SOME OF THE GREAT WINES FROM THIS REGION

Producing wine isn't just about the château; it is about the particular year where all the points that affect the wine throughout the process come together to create what the experts would term a 'great wine'. Great wines, of course, command eye-watering prices and, for many who can afford them, such prices indicate wines that are not just for drinking, but also for laying down as an investment (Aytac et al., 2016). This will be looked at later in the chapter. The Médoc, the area we call the Left Bank, splits itself into two AOCs – Médoc and Haut-Médoc. Just to add confusion, Haut-Médoc splits further into six commune AOCs within which are some extremely prestigious Châteaux: Château Mouton Rothschild Pauillac AOC; Château Lafite Rothschild Pauillac AOC; Château Latour AOC Pauillac; Château Margaux; Margaux AOC; and Château Haut-Brion Pessac AOC, which is to the south of the City of Bordeaux. Even further south is the Premier Cru Supérieur Château d'Yquem Sauternes AOC. Although Haut-Médoc is about prestige, the prestige winemakers also produce less prestigious offerings, which they market under different labels, and you will find affordable wines in most of the AOCs.

The Right Bank has already been mentioned, but added to Petrus are Lafleur and Le Pin in Pomerol, and Saint-Émilion, with Ausone, Cheval Blanc, and Pavie. These are the great wines of Bordeaux.

5.7 BURGUNDY

Burgundy is another area of French viniculture with a great heritage (Chapuis, 2017). It is about a fifth of the size of Bordeaux and is spread out down the eastern side of France from Chablis, its most northerly point, to Lyon in the south. It is a region that many people drive past on their way south to the Côte d'Azur. It is complex in the sense that there are essentially five separate areas under the Burgundy AOC, starting with Chablis, and Yonne, which is actually closer to the Côte de l'Aube in the Champagne region. The predominant grape varieties in the area are Pinot Noir, Chardonnay, and Gamay.

Further south is Dijon and the Côte D'Or, which actually splits into two AOCs – Côte Nuit, at the northern end, and Côte De Beaune. Côte Nuit is predominantly red wine, offering twenty-two Grands Crus. Côte De Beaune produces both red and white wine, with at least seven classified as Grand Cru. Most of the *climats* in these two AOCs are quite small. Their history is due to Napoleonic law, which stated that land passed on after the death of its owner had to be shared directly among all offspring. Côte De Challonais can put forward several impressive Premier Crus, and the experts also declare that good wine can be bought there at affordable prices. The Maconnais area produces both red and white wines. Depending on which critique you read, the wines are very reliable, but seldom exciting (Simon, 1994). Beyond Maconnais is the well-known AOC, Beaujolais, at the southern extremity of the Burgundy region. It is the largest wine growing area of Burgundy, extending to the outskirts of Lyon. The bulk of the wines, including the famous Beaujolais Nouveau, tend to come from the southern part of the area. In Beaujolais the dominant grape is the Gamay. Beaujolais also produces the high-quality Beaujolais crus. Unlike Bordeaux the name 'château' does not appear often; instead in Burgundy you will see the word '*climat*', which refers to a plot of land. You will also see the word '*clos*' which refers to a vineyard. There are châteaux in Burgundy, but again, unlike Bordeaux, they are generally farms. Some of the great *domaines* of Burgundy are Domaine de la Romanée-Conti, Domaine Leroy, Domaine Dujac, Domaine Georges Roumier, Domaine Rousseau, and Domaine du Comte Liger-Belair.

5.8 CHAMPAGNE

Champagne is the most esteemed bottle of 'fizz' in the world, used to celebrate all manner of events. The tradition of drinking champagne to accompany celebrations originated in the Royal courts of Europe (Guy, 2003). It became popular in the UK in the mid-nineteenth century with the younger elite. Today, it has several competitors in the market, but Champagne is still unique and protected by the use of the term *Méthode Champenoise*, which cannot be applied to any wine from outside the Champagne region. The Champagne region, 90 miles east of Paris, is the most northerly wine-growing area in France. It does not take long to reach it by car from the Channel Ports. The area extends southwards along the Vallée de la Marne and its main centres are Reims, Epernay, Bouzy, Avize, and Troyes. The sub regions of Champagne are the Montagne de Reims, Vallée de la Marne, Vallée de la Vesle, Vallée de l'Arde, Côte des Blancs, Côte des Bar, Côte de Sezanne, Côte de l'Aube, and Troyes. The greatest activity is concentrated in Reims and Epernay.

There are no great temperature variations from one season to the next and the climate is generally cool. Often rain and misty mornings make the region somewhat dull, with June, July, and August the sunniest months. Champagne has only half the number of hours of sunshine annually, compared with Bordeaux. Frost is an ever-present danger to vines, and particularly so in the Champagne region. Very strictly, the grapes for making Champagne must be Pinot Noir, Pinot Meunière, and Chardonnay. Most Champagne is a blend of these three grape varieties, which are grown in a rich topsoil with a chalk sub soil (WSET, 1991). As an aside, the grape harvest is a major experience for many people, not just for the local Champagnois. Picking the grapes carefully is hard work and time is of the essence, but people travel from all over the world to help pick the grapes and enjoy the street parties in the villages.

Once picked, the grapes are taken for pressing. At this stage, the process is the same as for any other wine. They are pressed very carefully to extract, in this case, clear, almost colourless juice, for the first fermentation. It is increasingly common for this to take place in thermostatically controlled stainless steel vats, although several producers still use wooden vats. Artificial yeast is added to the natural yeast to control the fermentation process. Fermentation lasts for three to seven days and produces around 70 percent of the alcohol. Then the blending process creates the style of the house, in terms of the quality and the particular character, which need to be replicated year after year. The outcome is the *cuvée*. The process does not stop there; next is the *prise de mousse* or, in other words, putting the 'fizz' into the Champagne, during the second fermentation. The *mousse* is the foam on the top of the Champagne when it is poured, and the 'fizz' is*etillantllant*, which the 'mousse' forms on the top for a very short period (*Comité Champagne*). The wine is next placed in thick heavy bottles with metal tops, a mixture of yeast and sugar is added, and it is stored in very dark cool cellars. This is the stage when carbon dioxide is produced, and the Champagne takes on its characteristic bubbles. The process takes about four or five weeks. Again, following strict rules, the Champagne must be stored in cool cellars for a minimum of fifteen months after bottling. Wines classified as vintage are stored in these conditions for a minimum of three years. In a process known as *remuage*, the bottles are stored at an angle with the bottom of the bottles uppermost, and this allows the dead yeast to find its way down into the neck of the bottle.

For around two to three of those months, the bottles are turned. This is either done by hand or modern equipment does the work automatically. This concentrates all the dead yeast deposits in the neck of the bottle. Finally, the residue is removed by freezing the neck of the bottles containing the sediment, using a liquid refrigerant. Then the bottles are opened and the Champagne, under pressure, disgorges the frozen sediment from the bottle. The pressure in a bottle of champagne is the same as that in a tyre of a London bus (Cooper, 2010). A small amount of a mixture of old Champagne and cane sugar, known as 'dosage', is now poured quickly into the open bottles, which are then corked and secured with small wire cages. This process affects the style of the finished product and determines whether it is Brut Nature, Extra Brut, Brut, Extra Sec (Extra Dry), Sec (Dry), Demi-Sec (Medium Dry), or Doux (Sweet). So, who are the big players in the Champagne world? The 'big brands', in name, though not always in output, are Moët & Chandon,

Veuve Clicquot, Dom Pérignon, Nicolas Feuillatte, G.H. Mumm, Taittinger, Pol Roger, Bollinger, Pommery, Piper-Heidsieck, Louis Roederer (Cristal), Perrier-Jouet, Krug, Armand de Brignac, Canard-Duchêne, Ruinart, Billecart-Salmon, and Lanson (Charters & Spielmann, 2014).

It is not the intention of this study to look at all of the French wine producing areas of the country; the regions selected are because of the nature of the particular wines and the issue of luxury, there are many excellent wines from other regions of France. Other European countries such as Italy and Spain are producing some fantastic wines, and certainly many of those wines rival the French wines. Many of the most valuable wines, however, emanate from the regions covered in this chapter. Further reading will be recommended.

5.9 CAN NEW WORLD WINES SURPASS THOSE OF THE OLD WORLD?

The New World regions are the USA, Australia, New Zealand, Argentina, Chile, and now China and India. The first five are the most prominent in British markets, but in the last two years India has made an appearance. In 1976, the Judgement of Paris was held. British wine writer, Stephen Spurrier, was then a young wine merchant working in Paris. He and his colleague, Patricia Gallagher, had heard that some interesting wines were being made in California and decided to draw attention to them in France. Perhaps a California tasting, scheduled to coincide with the bicentennial of American independence, would garner some useful publicity for their business. The Napa Valley wines were up against eight of the finest French wines. He organised the fateful blind tasting of California and top French wines on 24 May 1976 (Robinson, 2016). The outcome was conclusive and caused huge embarrassment for the tasters and an outcry in France when the news broke that, in the blind tasting, California wines in both red and white categories had gained the top accolades. For France, this was a national disaster and forced the resignation of two of the French tasting judges from their positions as heads of the appellation contrôlée authority and of Paris's restaurant association. Spurrier was disowned by the French wine establishment and physically ejected from one Burgundian cellar (Robinson, 2016).

5.10 INVESTING IN FINE WINES

Wine has become one of the top investments in the world and, literally, a liquid asset that can spread investment portfolios. In a portfolio of financial planning, wine is an alternative investment, which has an established track record for achieving solid income and has performed better than financial markets over the long term (Fogarty, 2012). As the world grows, there are more people looking for alternative investments, particularly with the growth of wealth in Asia. Wine investment is an unregulated market and therefore, if you plan to invest, you need to do some research. There are reliable wine investment companies in the world but also unscrupulous operators. Wine investment requires research to find such reliable companies and, remember, they all charge for their services. Philippe Masset and Jean-Philippe Weisskopf of the École hôtelière de Lausanne studied the profitability of wine as an investment during the financial crisis. They found that adding wine to a portfolio boosted returns, as well as risk:

> We find that fine wine yields higher returns and has a lower volatility compared to stocks, especially in times of economic crises. Forming portfolios for typical investors and taking risk aversion, different financial assets and various wine indices into consideration we confirm that the addition of wine to a portfolio as a separate asset-class is beneficial for private investor.

Most wine investment companies tend to say that you do not need to be an expert in wine to invest in it, but it is well worth having some knowledge of the subject (Masset & Weisskopf, 2010). Investment companies will deal with all expert issues and discuss the money you plan to invest. Expert collectors are a different matter; they are probably connoisseurs of fine wines and know what they are talking about. There are obviously different ways of buying wine. One obvious way is by auction. People sell collections, and there are many companies that hold wine auctions. The large companies, Christie's, Sotheby's, and Bonham's, for example, regularly hold major wine auctions, particularly for high-end fine wines. All three companies operate internationally. Of course, they charge buyers a twenty percent commission, to which is added a vendor's commission of ten percent. Naturally the auction house will conduct a strict authenticity and condition check of all consignments received, but this admittedly, is a very difficult call.

Returning to *en premieur*, which was mentioned earlier, is another way of investing in wine. April is traditionally the month when *en premieur* wine sales take place. It is all about buying wines before they have left the barrel; the bottling will follow in several years' time. A main point of buying *en premieur* is that the wine might be, but is not necessarily, cheaper than it would be once it is bottled and finally released. The Bordeaux *en premieur* is a huge gathering of merchants, traders, brokers, and experts, who go through the process of critically assessing the vintage of the previous year. The process starts with the châteaux and the *négociants*. The *negociants* have a historic place in this procedure, as they take over the continuing process by buying the wine from the châteaux in advance, and the growers receive money in advance to cover their costs. The *négociants* are, in a way, bankers to the châteaux; they go through the process as follows. The *négociants* and other respected experts assess the quality of the wine. The majority of wines are sold through *négociants,* who generally sell on to international merchants. London, for example, is a major home of some very internationally respected wine merchants. Investors and wine connoisseurs buy through these wine merchants. Wines purchased *en primeur* are normally purchased excluding duty and VAT. When the wine arrives in the UK, for example, it is automatically delivered to, and stored in, a bonded warehouse. Needless to say, if you choose to store the wine at home you must pay duty on the wine. The purchaser can alternatively leave the wine in the bonded warehouse, which will be temperature controlled. Naturally, there are storage fees. When you decide to take delivery of the wine, if you are in the UK, you are required to pay the prevailing rate of UK duty and VAT. If you are in another country, the laws of that country will apply. Wine sold *en premieur* does not just apply to Bordeaux; it is also undertaken, for example, in Burgundy, Rhone, Tuscany, and Piedmont.

5.11 LONDON INTERNATIONAL VINTNERS EXCHANGE (LIV-EX)

> The London International Vintner's Exchange is now in its twentieth year, having been founded in 2002 by two former stock brokers, James Miles and Justin Gibb, and ten members. The membership has now grown to 400 members worldwide. The aim of the exchange is to make fine wine trading more transparent, efficient and safe for the benefit of its members and the global market as a whole. As Liv-Ex states, the main focus is on Bordeaux, with highest volume of trade being the wines from this region. There has also been market growth in the other regions of France, such as Burgundy, Champagne and Rhone, as well as in Italian, German, Spanish, Portuguese and New World wines, which have grown as investment wines. Liv-Ex is only available to professional wine buyers and sellers. Private buyers need to purchase cases through a reputable wine merchant or through a wine fund.
>
> Liv-Ex, 2021

What does Liv-Ex do? It trades in fine wines worldwide, regularly publishes weekly and monthly market updates, and Liv-ex Indices, of which there are five categories: Fine Wine 50 Index, Fine Wine 100 Index, Bordeaux 500 Index, Fine Wine 1000 Index, California 50 Index, and Port 50 Index (Liv-Ex, 2021).

5.12 FRAUD AND COUNTERFEIT WINES

Returning to unscrupulous operators, there is one step beyond that: fraudulent operators. 'Buyers fear they will be left with nothing but a bad taste in their mouths after their wine goes missing' (Byers, 2020). In a case of what looks like a fraudster selling wine for investment from a company that has gone into administration, wine worth £11.5 million, and at least £10 million worth of fine Haut-Médoc wine cannot be found. It was supposedly being kept in a bonded warehouse. In a news article, police warned of the growth in fraudsters promoting investment in wine, along with gold, silver, diamonds, and art (Byers, 2020). The next step is actually counterfeiting fine wines; one of the biggest scams has been in the USA. In 2014, Rudy Kurniawan was sentenced to ten years imprisonment for one of the biggest fine wine forgeries. When the FBI raided his house in Los Angeles, they found a complete wine counterfeiting operation, particularly of Bordeaux and Burgundy wines. In 2013, after turning the Los Angeles house he shared with his mother into a 'wine factory', Kurniawan was convicted of making and selling hundreds of fake fine wines and fooling wealthy collectors. It is estimated that his wines sold for tens of millions of dollars and experts believe that not all of them have been located (Mercer, 2017).

The eye watering prices mentioned earlier in the chapter have naturally encouraged the growth of such fraud and forgery. Whatever has created the growth in fraud and the counterfeiting of fine wines, inflation is one of the problems. It has increased the price of fine wines five-fold. Furthermore, the practice is highly lucrative and difficult to detect. French wine, particularly from the Bordeaux and Burgundy regions, is a major focus. The punishment for masquerading and forging fine wines carries a two-year prison sentence. In the USA, however, Kurniawan was given a somewhat heavier sentence. The USA has produced another major personality in the world of fine wine in Maureen Downey, who helped put Kurniawan behind bars. She is one of the world's leading 'wine detectives' and highlights the three main types of counterfeiting wine – the re-fill, the re-creation, and the 'unicorn' – and how empty bottles of fine wine are routinely sold in plain sight on eBay, a practice, she says, that 'breaks my heart' (Barrie, 2017).

5.13 MARKETING FINE WINES

Those marketing luxury make use of the word 'heritage', and fine wines are no exception. Wine is a complex product with strong links to the Christian faith, to cultural influences, and to aristocracy and royalty, yet is also a peasant's drink. Finally, it is a fashion item and commodity all in one (Hall & Mitchell, 2007). The 1855 Classification has been a huge marketing tool. Since its inception, the Left Bank Médoc classification has only been adjusted once, and that was in 1973. After many years of trying to gain First Growth (Premier Cru) status, Château Mouton Rothschild was finally raised to the status. It has been mentioned by several wine critics that the 1855 classification bears no resemblance to the châteaux of today, in terms of the *terroir*. Most of the estates have bought and sold land over the years and certainly ownership has changed, all of which has changed things since 1855. According to Lewin (2014), the châteaux at the time were going through a rough time financially, because of poor vintages, so the chance to be part of the classification was probably a heaven-sent opportunity. Lewin goes on to point out, that the wines produced then would hardly be recognised today, and he adds the fact that those wines would have been drunk within about two years – a far cry from the vintage process in today's market. There are other issues also highlighted; the most interesting is that the classification was undertaken by brokers, who dealt with the châteaux and very quickly came up with a system based on price over a period of time, and not on *terroir*.

By today's standards, the classification might look quite different, particularly if the Right Bank Saint-Émillion and Pomerol were to be included. They were not included at the time because they did not come under the Bordeaux Chamber of Commerce. In 1961, there was a move in France to change the classification but that collapsed after a leak to the press prior to the announcement. For many years, the wine world has raised this issue: that the classification is outdated and does not represent reality. The debate is likely to continue. It might be exposing itself with the fact that several Third Growth and Fifth Growth wines of Bordeaux are commanding prices of at least Second Growth wines, and Right Bank wines are continually maintaining Premier Cru status and prices. This could be an indication that the market is becoming the benchmark (*The Wine Cellar*).

The marketing of fine wines is very much dependent on maintaining 'brand'. Very few wines are advertised in the way other consumer products are. An exception is probably the Casillero del Diablo, a mass market wine from Chile established over 100 years ago, which uses sponsorship as a promotional tool, particularly on television. According to recent Nielsen data, Casillero del Diablo has become one of the top-selling wine brands in the UK retail market, overtaking competitor Blossom Hill. The analyst's latest results show total sales of Casillero del Diablo in the off-trade reached £139.9 million in value in the 12 months to 15 June 2019 (*Vinex*, 2019). Good reviews are a marketing tool in themselves.

Leyland Pitt (2017) stated: 'Fine wine buying director for the prestigious wine importer, Berry Brothers & Rudd, has said of [wine critic Robert Parker], "Nobody sells wine like Robert Parker. If he turns around and says 2012 is the worst vintage I've tasted, nobody will buy it, but if he says it's the best, everybody will"'. This highlights quite a simple fundamental of niche marketing. So, why would a region with centuries old traditions embrace social media platforms? All the work is being undertaken by the *negociants*. When I ask him about his 'big' insight, Lewin says rather emphatically, '95% of Bordeaux's châteaux aren't dynamic enough on digital'. 'If there is one conclusion I can draw it's that a lot of the smaller brands are strong on social media and many of the big brands or big châteaux are weak' (Lewin, 2014). Robinson (2016) wrote: 'We're still obsessed with figuring out how to have conversations with generations Y, Z, and Alpha – and in the process, we're probably missing out on the conversations we should be having with the overwhelmingly large group of consumers currently over 50 years of age'.

The top châteaux on social media were Château Margaux, Château Cheval Blanc, Château Lafite Rothschild, and Château D'Yquem. Much depends on *which* social media, but these châteaux were, to date, the top of the list for the widest use of social media generally, according to www.amustreadbog.com. Classification is still firmly with us and reinforces the Premiers Crus, which are in an admirable position; however, they need to produce excellent vintages to maintain their standard. The classification has kept them exclusive in the luxury world, and they have received good scores from the experts. This doesn't always happen year after year. Being the sparkling wine that it is, Champagne appeals to almost everyone for very special occasions, and it has been able to maintain luxury status. Moreover, some cuvees have been successful in the masstige class.

The masstige strategy is also applied by many other luxury brands. They are trading down by extending their product range with masstige products that are more accessible to middle-class consumers (Kapferer & Bastien, 2012). Therefore, they make themselves affordable to the middle classes in society, at the same time maintaining elements of prestige. They have undertaken this quite well by generally producing non-vintage champagnes. The main difference between vintage and non-vintage Champagne is not that vintage is old, but that it is made from the grapes of only one year's harvest, whereas non-vintage Champagne is a blend of different years' harvests. Brands such as Moët & Chandon and Veuve Clicquot are good examples of masstige products. According to its annual report, LVMH (parent company of these two brands) sold almost 60 million bottles of champagne in 2012. Masstige brands cut back on some luxury characteristics, such as price, rarity, and extraordinariness, to make luxury-like products accessible to middle-class consumers (Heine & Petersen, 2015).

In the UK, just looking at rivals Sainsbury and Tesco supermarkets and their range of Champagnes, we see some veritable brands on sale: Moët et Chandon, Veuve Clicquot, Champagne Bollinger, and Mumm. This is just a sample from two leading UK supermarkets. Other luxury brands use a similar strategy to create affordable luxury, which is incompatible with exclusiveness; it can, however, be very good for cash flow, while keeping the aura of luxury as much as possible.

Champagne has been involved for many years in high profile sports. Mumm (owned by Pernod Ricard), for example, has been involved as one of the sponsors for international sailing events, such as the Admiral's Cup, the Vendée Globe, the Hermes GH Mumm Regatta, and the Skandia Cowes Regatta, and has been Official Champagne for Formula One motor racing (Hall & Mitchell, 2007). Moët et Chandon (owned by LVMH) has sponsored London Fashion Week, which has aesthetic appeal. Polo, as an elite sport, has found champagne sponsors for many of its clubs and events. However, Champagne sales have fallen in France, although more expensive Champagne is being drunk. The UK is also seeing a fall in sales of champagne, which is being replaced by other sparkling wine alternatives. Sales of the premium French bubbly fell by 28% in 2019 (Goodly, 2019).

5.14 WINE TOURISM

Wine grapes do not seem to thrive in ugly places. From the stately glory of Bordeaux to the majesty of Stellenbosch and from the rugged valleys of Barossa to beautiful Napa, the places where wine grapes are grown, and wine is made, are among the most scenic in the world. This has made wine tourism and wine experiences a huge business, which contributes significantly to national economies above and beyond the sales of its products.

We need to know more about the intricacies of wine tourism and the staging of wine experiences (Pitt, 2017). Wine tourism, part of the wine experience, is defined by wine tastings, visits to wineries, holidays in wine regions, and wine festivals. Wine tourism is a major attraction in the USA, Australia, France, and Italy – major wine countries where wine tourism is embedded as a tourism strategy (O'Neill & Palmer, 2004). The big starters in wine tourism have been the New World wineries of the USA's Napa Valley, Australia's Barossa Valley, and South Africa's Stellenbosch. For these areas, wine tourism has become a tremendous force and, in some specific cases, now accounts for greater profits than the retail sale of the wine itself. The Old World of wine has a very different history. After growing over hundreds of years and establishing reputations as premier producers, destinations like Spain, Portugal, France, and Italy have not experienced the same dependence on tourism as the New World has. Instead, Old World locations have developed extensive networks of wine dealers to whom they sell their wines, many of which still remain (Glennen, 2017).

It is true to say that European wine producers are responding to wine tourism as a revenue earner and a tool in their marketing portfolio. Tourists today increasingly look for more than a standard bland tour. Not every wine tourist is the same. Not every wine tourist wants the same kind of experiences. Wine tourism implies that wine producers in a destination 'intentionally use services as the stage, and goods as props, to engage individual customers in a way that creates a memorable event' (Karlson & Karlson, 2017). They identify four different types of tours. There is 'Open Door' wine tourism, which they see as simply receiving people for wine tastings and cellar visits, and 'Edutainment' (education and entertainment), which as an experience is more complex than just a visit, as it can involve visitors in activities such as harvesting or blending sessions. 'Disneyland' Wine Tourism – and the authors apologise for the terminology – aims for big budget joint projects with other tourist businesses. Finally, there is 'Eventification', including wine festivals, etc. (Karlson & Karlson, 2017). There is wine tourism in the Médoc. Visits to the châteaux must be made with formal guides and there is a smart-casual dress code, with no jeans and T-shirts allowed, very much in keeping with afternoon tea at the Ritz. Wine tastings are possible but, unlike in the Napa Valley or Barossa Valley, visitors do not buy wines at the châteaux. Visits are available in all the fine wine areas mentioned, and are certainly part of the experience, adding greatly to the knowledge of the wines. The city of Bordeaux has added experiences, particularly the Cité du Vin wine experience, which embraces the whole region and its wine.

5.15 WINE IS FOR DRINKING

You might think wine tasting is for the experts but, in fact, it is a practice you might appreciate having some knowledge about. From the earliest times, wine consumption was an occasion for intense social exchanges and conveyed a real sense of prestige. Wine can be described as a food for hierarchy, and helps in the hierarchisation of society (Demmossier, 2004). Restaurants generally charge quite high prices for wine; much depends also on the particular restaurant and its status. Invariably, in a high-class fine dining restaurant, once the menu has been decided, the sommelier will offer you the wine list and diplomatically guide you through particular wines that are a good pairing with your food. Diplomacy is an important skill, as well as a first-class knowledge of wine. Some guests will inevitably be connoisseurs who know what they want, and there will also be the less knowledgeable who will not want to be embarrassed – not only about their lack of knowledge, but perhaps their need to be careful about the price.

When you dine in a restaurant you follow the ritual of being presented the wine you have chosen to taste by the wine waiter, before the glasses are actually charged. As the designated host of the table your glass is presented with a small sample. The blame is on the restaurant for serving you the wrong wine, but on you too, for confirming it to be the right wine (Seal, 2017). The situation puts you firmly on the spot to make the decision. The decision-making might be the key to a good relationship, a promotion in your career, or to sealing an important deal. Money may be of no object to you, but even in this situation, you need value for money. It requires you first to swirl the wine gently around the glass, to aerate it and free the aroma. Then you place your nose over the glass, smell the bouquet, and then taste the wine. If it smells and tastes musty there might be something wrong with it, and you would tell the waiter, and ask for it to be replaced (Seal, 2007). It is worth considering the potential benefits of extending your knowledge in this area, as it is fascinating in its own right. High-class restaurants invariably employ a sommelier, whose responsibility will be the stock of wines, the purchase of those wines, and responsibility for the wine waiters. The sommelier is the wine ambassador for the establishment, as well as a connoisseur and a manager.

Unlike almost any other type of alimentary product, wine requires the use of all five senses to appreciate its qualities fully. It is one of the rare products for which the correct way to taste it has been codified through guides or literary works (Demmossier, 2004). Before tasting, consider the glasses you will use. This is important, as there are many glasses on the market, and there are unique glasses for particular wines. A common glass used for tasting is the Paris goblet. It has a broad base and a narrow top to increase the bouquet and is suitable for all light wines (WSET). For sparkling wines, a tall narrow flute glass is generally used. In this glass, the bubbles last longer and the narrow rim ensures the bouquet is not lost (Lepré et al., 2011). You can start by tasting with friends and colleagues in the home, perhaps by agreeing to taste wines from a particular region or country. For example, you could look at particular grape varietals. Some are more common around the world than others. Cabernet Sauvignon, for example, grows in just about every wine-producing country in the world. Merlot, Tempranillo, Chardonnay, Syrah, Sauvignon Blanc, and Pinot Noir can be a little more specific. Try one of these wines from different countries and consider the *terroir*. Does using the same grape, but with different variables, make for a standardised wine, or are they all quite different?

There is more than taste and bouquet to consider; there is also appearance – colour, clarity, and brilliance. For Champagne or other sparkling wine, you must also consider the effervescent, or *petillant* quality, and the *mousse*. Professionals discuss tasting notes. For a simple exercise, one can make use of the following: appearance (colour and clarity), aroma (impression and bouquet), taste (flavour and balance, dryness or sweetness, tannin and acidity), and the overall impact (length of flavour and quality). Think about the sensations you have as you go through this tasting process and record your impressions. If you make notes under the individual headings, you can discuss the notes with the group when tasting is complete. It might open a lot of discussion on several issues. How different were the wines, even though the common varietal was the basis of the content of each bottle? Where were they grown? Certainly soil, weather, altitude, the management of the vines, production processes, and, needless to say, the grapes themselves, all affect and either add or take away from the particular taste.

There is always the possibility of organising a more formal occasion in the home. Many companies offer wine tasting in the home with a professional expert. Most concierge companies, wine merchants, and at least one of the leading supermarkets in the UK will organise home wine tasting. The fees vary, obviously, depending on whether or not the tasting is combined with a selection of appropriate food.

5.16 FUTURE CONCERNS

The biggest concern expressed in reports on wine is climate change (Drappier et al., 2019). It shows the effects on wine growing, with the northern hemisphere showing increased warming, which can change the grape varieties quite considerably and bring on earlier harvests (Mozell & Thach, 2014). During a blind tasting, one way to deduce a wine's origins is to assess the fruit's character. If the fruit notes in a red wine taste very ripe, or even jammy, it's likely from a warm climate. If it tastes tart or delicate, like a freshly picked raspberry, the wine probably came from a cooler climate (Mowery, 2020). Many grape varietals produce quite different wine, depending on where they are grown. Warming climates are obviously starting to have an effect, which can be an advantage for wine growers in Britain and for potential growers in the world's more northern countries. We cannot generalise, but many wines are grown in microclimates, which vary from the general trend for several reasons. The general trend is that climate change can alter many of the characteristics of renowned wines, so growers will have to consider ways to change how things are done. Of major concern are water shortages in some wine areas of Australia and South Africa, major fires in California, Oregon, and Washington State, and extreme temperatures in parts of Australia. Other concerns are coastal flooding caused by rising water levels, leading to higher salinity levels in the soil. Bordeaux Haut-Médoc could be particularly prone to this in the future. Warming can also raise the number of insects, which can be a danger to the vines. As the problems grow, many apply to all forms of agriculture. This presents a huge danger to viniculture and to the future of wines.

The COVID-19 pandemic has had an almost instant impact on shopping habits around the world. Many have turned to wine retailing websites, especially to those operators who can deliver, and without long delays. Examples of all these trends can be seen in the news. In the UK, for example, Majestic has experienced a surge in online wine orders big enough to bring down its website. Berry Bros & Rudd had its biggest single day of web-based sales in its history, and this historic UK wine merchant was one of the first to invest seriously in digital drinks retailing (Schmitt, 2020). Beyond this, there is the 2020 grape harvest to consider. There have been mixed reports from the Southern Hemisphere, where the harvest comes in the early months of the year, but COVID-19 has taken its toll. The Northern Hemisphere has its harvests still to come, but many of the wine cellars are full of unsold wine, largely caused by the closure of restaurants and hotels during the pandemic.

5.17 Summary

This chapter has given a glimpse of the place of fine wines in the world, and their place in terms of lifestyle. It has shown that wine is not only a social drink to enjoy with friends and family, but also a possible investment to complement any portfolio. The case study identifies a thriving local wine bar where social relationships are strengthened and knowledge is gained through a common enjoyment of wine. The world of wine, however, does not exist in its own bubble; it is very much part of the wider world and is affected by major international issues. As of writing, in 2020, the world has been hit by a virus, which has had a major impact on the populations of many nations. It has also affected wine production and sales and, as in many other areas, buying habits have changed. It highlights the nature of wine as a product that is actually quite difficult to market. It could be argued that the châteaux of Bordeaux and Burgundy have such strong brands that they market themselves, but even they have to work hard to maintain their standards and meet the expectations of the market.

Wine is very much a product that relies on what wine experts say about it. This doesn't apply only to fine wines; all wines gain from the positive comments of the experts. Most of the quality weekend newspapers in the UK and other countries feature the recommended wines of the week, with comments about them and information about where to buy them. This chapter has identified some of the difficulties in getting wines into premier positions in the market and has highlighted the growth of counterfeit wine, and the difficulties of eradicating it. A key issue raised in the chapter is that the standards for wine have been established in France, but that there is competition from other wine growing areas of the world. Arguably, California has a place after the 'Paris decision' of 1976. In terms of wine investment, should investors be looking to newer areas outside the classic regions? Is Champagne still the luxury drink it was, and have other sparkling wines claimed their place in the market?

CASE STUDY Old Butcher's Wine Cellar

The village of Cookham is situated in the north-eastern corner of the county of Berkshire in the Thames Valley, UK. The village is famous as the home of the artist Sir Stanley Spencer, and the author Kenneth Grahame, who lived at 'The Mount' in Cookham Dean as a child, is said to have been inspired by the River Thames at Cookham to write *The Wind in the Willows*. The *Telegraph* stated that Cookham was the second most expensive village in Britain in 2011. Driving into Cookham is like arriving in the quintessential English village. Its close proximity to royal Windsor Castle, the meandering river Thames and London, makes this village very special. In the High Street of this idyllic location you will find the Old Butcher's Wine Cellar (OBWC). It is a family-owned business and independent wine shop, run by Paul and Angela Stratford, who have been in the wine trade since the early 1970s. Paul Stratford was one of the first people to bring Australian and New World wines to the UK market. For many years, he and his wife Angela ran one of the largest agency companies in the UK, nationally distributing wine from all over the world. Their experience during this time means they continue to be among the leading specialists in the UK market.

How it came about was quite by accident. In 1986, while Paul was delivering wine to a customer in Cookham, he walked down the high street and saw the shop was for sale. It was an original Cookham property, and in a very derelict state. The rest, as you might say, is history. Paul and Angela bought the property and, in 1988, after extensive restoration, the building was transformed into the Old Butcher's Wine Cellar. Over the years, the business has successfully developed into essentially three parts, the retail wine shop, the wine bar, and the wine club. The 'Old Butcher's' name came from the original seventeenth-century premises – the village butcher and abattoir, which supplied locals with fresh meat, poultry, and game. It is now a Grade II listed building. In terms of demographics, Cookham is ideally placed and the wine shop is in a very good location. The general statistics on social and occupational grades show that Cookham has 20% more high and intermediate managerial, administrative, or professional households than the national average. Cookham also has a higher rate of home ownership – either outright or with a mortgage – than the national average, which suggests it is a relatively affluent area. All of these facts can be very good for the business. The business has built up a good clientele and following in the area, and the brand has developed as a lifestyle brand with the well supported wine bar.

The wine bar has also helped in other ways. Originally the company offered free wine tastings; however, intuition took over. The owners believed that the tasters were feeling like they were expected to buy, and the last thing the business wanted was pressurised sales. The wine bar was established so people could come and buy wines in a social way, with no pressure, and discuss and taste wine informally, amongst other things. This led to the development of the wine club, which has now spread its wings nationally and sells wines with different wine plans for its members. It has a presence on both Facebook and Instagram with a reasonable following. Something is posted at least once a week, but Paul is aware that they could do more in this area. Working as an independent against the big companies, and building up the brand, has come about through patience, hard work, and an eye for something unique. As well as running the business, the owners spend time at wine fairs around the world, to meet growers. They constantly review their stock and keep their eyes open for exciting new additions to their range of around 500 wines, spirits, and liqueurs. These are wines you won't find piled high in your local supermarket, but individual wines from interesting and independent producers. Prices range from £10 to £200 per bottle. Serious collectors generally deal with companies such as Berry Bros & Rudd, or one of the other top British wine merchants.

It can be hard to find and build relationships with good suppliers. There is always the need to be looking for something new, while also maintaining old relationships that are valuable. Many of the suppliers are small independent growers who operate with better care and attention, have organic operations, and produce wines with lower alcohol levels, which are certainly a major part of a growing trend. This, of course, benefits the growing British wine industry, as higher alcohol levels generally come from the warmer climates with more sun during the day. Sourcing is also a matter of recognising quality and knowing the customers, while pricing the wines is a matter of integrity. One of the key issues for the business is trying to predict where the public's taste and drinking patterns are going. Predicting wine trends is a tough call, according to Chris Mercer of *Decanter Magazine*. For OBWC, much will depend on the wine bar evenings where two-way discussions are taking place. Customers can learn more generally about wine and OBWC can pick up the trends and influences from them. This has also built good customer relations for business and personal contacts. OBWC, for example, asks questions about Sauvignon Blancs from New Zealand. Which has been a good seller? Which is good on taste and flavour but not so good in its finish? What will take over from NZ Sauvignon Blanc? Rosé wines have had a rapid growth in popularity and are now being drunk all the year round. There is also a feeling that there is movement back to more European wines.

New World wines, particularly high-quality wines from Napa Valley, California, are harder to come by, simply because of smaller output, and because sales are largely in the US market. The mass brands are in most of the UK supermarkets, E&J Gallo being one of the largest. Wines from Australia, NZ, Chile, Argentina, and South Africa are also popular in UK markets, as a visit to any wine retailer will show you.

Seminar exercises

Discussion topics:

1. 'It is clear that where there is alcohol, there is almost always a dedicated environment in which to drink it, and that every culture creates its own, highly distinctive public drinking places'. Discuss this statement with reference to OBWC.
2. An issue for the owner of OBWC was predicting the trends in wine for the next year. Using the Internet, look at the trends in wines sales of white, red, rosé, and sparkling wines.
3. 'Generally, with wine, price is an important clue to quality when there are few other clues available prior to purchase'. Discuss this statement and consider the influence of wine experts.

Further group discussion:

A) We are now seeing wines that have sold themselves as luxury products, such as LVMH portfolio stable mates Château Cheval Blanc and Château d'Yquem, working hard to forge links directly with end buyers, rather than continuing to rely on Bordeaux's many linked distribution chains. Château Latour opted out of the annual *en primeur* Bordeaux tastings and sales, an annual ritual that takes place each spring in Bordeaux.

What are the advantages and disadvantages of following this as a strategy?

B) Consider the 'masstige strategy' of several of the champagne houses. They are making themselves affordable to the middle classes in society and at the same time maintaining elements of prestige. Discuss the advantages and disadvantages of this strategy in the current market.
C) Think about 'some of the great *domaines* of Burgundy'. All of these domaines produce extremely expensive fine wines, but one has produced a bottle of wine that sold at auction for a staggering price of $558,000. Using the Internet, identify the *domaine*.
D) Take any of the châteaux or *domaines* and identify some of their wines, e.g. Châteaux Margaux 2012, and follow the prices on the Liv-Ex. Are they a good investment?
E) Use your library and Internet resources to discover further information on Bordeaux wines and the AOCs. Do you believe that the AOCs restrict creativity in wine production, or do they enhance the product?

References

Anson, J (2020). Behind the 14 new Cru Bourgeois Exceptionnel estates. *Decanter*. September 2020. Future Publishing Ltd; London, UK.

Aytac, B, Hoang, T & Mandou, C (2016). Wine: To drink or invest in? a study of wine as an investment asset in French portfolios. *Research in International Business and Finance*. 36. Pp 591–614.

Barbe, P & Bouzdine, T (2013). *Bordeaux Wines Classifications: Scope And Limits*. [Online]. Available from: www.wine-economics.org/wp-content/uploads/2013/07/Barbe_Bouzdine.pdf

Barrie, S (June 2017). *The Wine Detectives*. BBC Radio 4; UK.

Bell, E (July 2016). *The Differences Between Left Bank and Right Bank Bordeaux*. [online]. Available from: https://vinepair.com/articles/the-differences-between-right-and-left-bank-bordeaux/

Byers, D (2020). The Ten Million Pound Investment Hangover. *The Times*. 27 June 2020. Times Newspapers; UK.

Cardebat, J & Figuet, J (2006). What explains Bordeaux wine prices? *Applied Economics Letters*. 11, 5. Pp 293–296.

Chapuis, C (2017). *Sustainable Viticulture: The Vines and Wines of Burgundy*. Taylor and Francis.

Charters, S (2003). *PhD Thesis: Perceptions of Wine Quality*. Edith Cowan University; Perth, WA, Australia.

Charters, S & Spielmann, N (2014). Characteristics of strong territorial brands: The case of champagne. *Journal of Business Research*. 67, 7. Pp 1461–1467.

Cooper, R (2010). *The Wine Year*. Merrell Publishers Ltd; London, UK.

Demmossier, M in Sloan, D et al (2004). *Culinary Taste*. Butterworth Heinemann; Oxford, UK.

Drappier, J, Thibon, C, Rabot, A & Geny-Denis, L (2019). Relationship between wine composition and temperature: Impact on Bordeaux wine typicity in the context of global warming. *Critical Reviews in Food Science and Nutrition*. 59, 1. Pp 14–30.

Farmer, E (2014). Codifying consensus and constructing boundaries: setting the limits of *Appellation d'origine contrôlée* Protection in Bordeaux, France. *PoLAR*. 37, 1. pp 126–144.

Fogarty, J (2012). Wine investment and portfolio diversification gains. *Journal of Wine Economics*. 5, 1.

Forster, R (1961). The noble wine producers of the Bordelais in the eighteenth century. The Economic *History Review*. 14, 1. Pp 18–33.

Glennen, C (2017). *The New World of Wine Tourism*. [Online]. Available from: www.businessdestinations. com/featured/the-new-world-of-wine-tourism/

Goodly, S (2019). UK sales of champagne and sparkling wine lose their fizz in past year. *Guardian*. 30 December 2019.

Guy, K (2003). When Champagne became French: wine and the making of a national identity. John Hopkins University Press; Maryland, United States.

Hall, M & Mitchell, R (2007). *Wine Marketing: A Practical Guide*. Butterworth Heinemann; Oxford, UK.

Heine, K & Espinoza Petersen, F (2015). *Wine Brands*. [Online]. Available from: www.europeanbusinessreview. com/marketing-lessons-luxury-wine-brands-teach-us-about-authenticity-and-prestige/

Jefford, A (2020). Robert M Parker Jnr. Decanter Hall of Fame. *Decanter*. August 2020. Future Publishing Ltd; London, UK.

Kapferer & Bastien (2012). *The Luxury Strategy*. 2nd Edition. Kogan Page; London, UK.

Karlson, P & Karlson, B (2017). *Four successful types of wine tourism*. [Online]. Available from: www.forbes. com/sites/karlsson/2017/07/21/the-four-successful-types-of-wine-tourism

Le Blog. i Deal wine (2020). *Bordeaux's en primeur | What is it?* [Online}. Available from: www.idealwine.info/4931-2/

Lehning, J (2005). When champagne became French: wine and the making of a national identity. *Journal of Interdisciplinary History*. 35, 4. Pp 648–649.

Lepré, G et al. (2011). *Larousse Wine: The Definitive Reference*. Hamlyn; London (Copyright Larousse; Paris).

Lewin B. (2014). The 1855 Classification: on the mark or marketing ploy? *Decanter*. December 2014. Future Publishing Ltd; London, UK.

Liv-Ex (2021). *London International Vintners Exchange*. [online]. Available from: www.liv-ex.com/

Masset, P & Weisskopf, JP (2010). Raise your Glass: Wine Investment and the Financial Crisis. [Online]. Available from: https://papers.ssrn.com/sol3/papers.cfm?abstract_id=1457906

Mercer, D (2017). Fake DRC Prosecutor demands prison for alleged gang member. *Decanter*. January 2017. Future Publishing Ltd; London, UK.

Mowery, L (2020). How climate change impacts wine. [Online]. Available from: www.winemag.com/2020/05/12/how-climate-change-impacts-wine/

Mozell, M & Thach, L (2014). The impact of climate change on the global wine industry: challenges & solutions. *Wine Economics and Policy*. 3, 2. Pp 81–89.

O'Neill & Palmer (2004). *Wine production and tourism*. [Online]. Available from: www.researchgate.net/publication/258130426_Wine_Production_and_Tourism

Paul, H (2002). *Science, Vine and Wine in Modern France*. Oxford University Press; Oxford, UK.

Pitt, L (2017). Ten reasons why wine is a magical marketing product. *Journal of Wine Research*. Published online. 30 October 2017.

Rand, M (2008). Bordeaux: Right Bank vs Left Bank. *Decanter*. August 2008. Future Publishing Ltd; London, UK.

Robinson, J (2016). *That Paris Judgment 40 Years on*. [online]. Available from: www.jancisrobinson.com/articles/that-paris-judgment-40-years-on

Robinson, J (2019). Bourdeaux 2019 Guide. [Online}. Available from: www.jancisrobinson.com/articles/bordeaux-2019-guide.

Schmitt, P (2020). Producer Views COVID19 Wine Market 'With a Smile and a Tear'. [Online]. Available from: www.thedrinksbusiness.com/2020/04/.

Seal, L (2017). *Taste Wine in the Restaurant*. [Online] Available from: www.decanter.com/learn/taste-wine-in-the-restaurant-36494

Shepard, G (2016). *Neuroenology: How the Brain Creates the Taste of Wine*. Columbia University Press; New York.

Simon, J (1994). *Discovering Wine*. Mitchel Beazley; London, UK.

Vinex (2019). *Vinex*. [Online]. Available from: https://en.vinex.market/articles/2019/07/10/casillerodediablo

Wiedmann, K, Hennigs, N, Schmidt, S & Wustefeld, T (2012). The perceived value of brand heritage and brand luxury managing the effect on brand strength. In Diamantopoulos, A., Fritz, W. and Hildebrandt, L. (Eds.), *Quantitative Marketing and Marketing Management – Marketing Models and Methods in Theory and Practice*, Wiesbaden: Springer Gabler, Pp. 563–583.

Wine & Spirit Education Trust (1991). *Introducing Wines and Spirits and Associated Beverages*. WSET; London, UK.

CHAPTER 6

Luxury and sustainability

Eleonora Cattaneo

6.1 INTRODUCTION

Until fairly recently, luxury and sustainability were considered incompatible. The purchase of luxury products was seen as the main cause of the widening gap between the rich and the poor – something irrational and unnecessary, and hence, largely unsustainable (Kapferer, 2010). In several studies, luxury is declared to be the polar opposite of sustainability since it is superfluous, conspicuous, and excessive, as well as devoid of any utilitarian use (Guercini & Ranfagni, 2013, Beckham & Voyer 2014). The luxury industry seeks maximum gross margins and, as a result, luxury providers do not emphasise cost reduction, but rather they focus on value creation, with the aim of making the buyer feel like a celebrity. This focus on quality over cost is maintained along the entire value chain, beginning with the selection of high-end production materials and continuing through the phases of production, selling, servicing, and branding. In contrast, sustainable development focuses on values such as parsimony, moderate consumption, and equality, which privilege economy over high quality. Historically, the luxury industry was not particularly focused on sustainability or corporate social responsibility. 'Conflict diamonds', stones mined in African war zones, often by forced labour with proceeds used to fund armed rebel movements, have plagued the luxury jewellery sector. Fashion and accessories were found to have been produced in sweatshop conditions (The Fashion Law, 2019).

The industry's response was that the preservation of physical and biological resources had always been at the heart of all true luxury brands (Kapferer, 2010). It had to be so, for failing to acknowledge the scarcity of these resources would mean not only their disappearance, but also the end of the businesses in question, and, in some cases, even of century-long traditions (Kapferer, 2010). They argued that through their limited production, strict control of demand and supply, limited use of machinery and preservation of craftsmanship, as well as the development of products expected

DOI: 10.4324/9781003015826-8

to last a lifetime, unlike mass market brands, luxury brands supported rather than undermined sustainability. However, as observed by Mauer (2014), 'as far as the preservation of precious resources is concerned, if luxury was not exploiting their use, there would be no need of preserving them either'.

In a survey published by www.salon.com in 2014, consumers ranked the luxury industry last in a list of product categories associated with a sustainable agenda, below both the financial and petrochemical sectors. As recently as 2018, Burberry burned unsold merchandise worth millions of dollars (Paton, 2018). Other luxury brands including Richemont and Louis Vuitton, have also been known to destroy unsold watches and handbags to avoid resale at reduced prices. In the last decade, consumers have expressed a growing concern with environmental issues (Mauer, 2014), with a specific focus on decreasing natural resource availability and biodiversity. Mauer (2014) argued that sustainability significantly influenced consumer decisions, although 58% of the respondents surveyed claimed that the non-sustainable nature of a luxury product would not stop them from purchasing it if they liked it, confirming that in the eyes of luxury consumers, sustainability was still secondary to product attractiveness (Mauer, 2014).

6.2 A CHANGE IN PACE

Consumer preferences are steadily moving towards a sustainable luxury industry. Leather alternatives, such as synthetic fibres, are at the core of consumer preferences. Arnett (2019) argues that some objections to leather may be associated with taste rather than ethical concerns. Nonetheless, the price for real leather products continues to dwindle. In a recent report, Deloitte (2020) found that young affluent consumers are more conscious of the impact of their buying behaviour. Their purchasing decisions are more likely to be influenced by a brand's ability to promote environmental and social values. Engaging with and buying from socially conscious brands is a key trend among many millennial and Gen Z consumers. A Nielsen study showed that under-40s prefer products from brands that are sustainable or socially conscious (Oakes, 2020). Furthermore, the study determined that 81% of millennials who purchase from luxury brands expect them to prove their commitment to sustainability (Oakes, 2020). It is important to underline that the opinions of the younger generations are crucial for luxury brands; according to Business of Fashion, by 2025 Gen Z members and millennials will together claim 45 percent of the luxury market. A 2017 Futurecast report stated that 60% of Gen Z members say they will support brands that take a stand on social causes such as human rights and inclusion. A 2019 Facebook study found that 68% of Gen Z-ers 'expect brands to contribute to society', while a McKinsey report from the same year said that nine in ten 'believe companies have a responsibility to address environmental and social issues'. There is increasingly strong demand from these key consumers for luxury brands to contribute positively to conserving the environment; therefore, a key concern is whether they can re-establish themselves to be consistent with consumer demands and build sustainable luxury, after decades of using animal products and destroying unsold goods.

6.3 THE BIRTH OF A SUSTAINABILITY CULTURE IN THE LUXURY CONTEXT

In 2001, when Stella McCartney launched her fashion brand in a joint venture with the Gucci Group (now Kering Group), she promoted a cruelty-free and ethical philosophy and stood against the use of leather, fur, skins, and feathers, in her catwalks and collections. The brand manifesto was followed by an action plan affecting every business decision and strongly differentiated the brand at the time. The fashion brand barred the use of leather, fur, and feathers on runways and in the manufacture of merchandise (Aviram, 2020). Stella McCartney products are currently manufactured using innovative materials based on vegetable leather, sustainable viscose and recycled fibers, such as the Falabella handbag in vegetable leather, or the KOBA vegetable fur.

In more recent years, a growing number of luxury brands have eliminated animal fur from collections as public outcry has become more insistent, opting instead for synthetics. The Kering Group announced that in the Autumn 2022 collections, animal fur will not be used in any kind of product created by the group's 13 fashion brands. In 2021, Prada launched a collection of accessories and ready-to-wear, named Prada Re-Nylon, with products made of regenerated nylon. This was developed by recycling textile fibre waste as well as plastic waste, collected from oceans and landfills. Gucci has a sustainability agenda called Gucci Equilibrium, which commits the brand to implementing a 'Culture of Sustainability' in every area of its business activities. Unlike faux fur, leather alternatives have yet to gain traction in luxury fashion. Vegan leather made up just two percent of women's leather goods produced by luxury brands, led by Stella McCartney in 2021. However, across the industry, interest is on the rise; according to Lyst, searches for vegan leather increased by 54 percent in 2021. Since 2020, the amount of apparel in UK stores described as vegan increased 180 percent. Veja launched a biodegradable, vegan version of its popular V-10 sneaker using leather-like corn starch waste in October 2021, responding to customer demand for a shoe made from non-animal products. Sales of brands known for using vegan leather, including Nanushka and Awake, are increasing rapidly.

Sustainability is also relevant beyond personal luxury and is being embraced across industries. The 76.6 metre Piriou explorer yacht, Yersin, has been classified as a Bureau Veritas Clean Ship, constructed from 95% recyclable materials, including recyclable resin decks that substituted wood for a more sustainable alternative. Luxury car brands, such as Bentley, have announced sustainability projects that embrace the entire production process. Sustainability has also given rise to organisations and associations with the objective of supporting eco-friendly manufacturing. Positive Luxury is an organisation established in 2011, with the aim of engaging luxury brands in environmental projects. It created the Butterfly Mark as an accredited certification for brands which meet specific sustainability standards and has a community of over 150 global members, from Dior Couture to Krug and IWC. The Butterfly Mark certification is built around an ESG+ framework (Environmental, Social, Governance, and Innovation). Each brand is given 'positive actions' according to its activity or vertical, turnover, and the location of its operations and supply chain.

The Fashion Pact, a worldwide federation of luxury brands launched in 2019 with the commitment to act across three pillars of environmental urgency: addressing global warming, restoring biodiversity, and protecting the oceans (Farra, 2019). The signatories represent one third of the fashion industry in 2022 and have made a commitment to implement Science Based Targets for Climate, to achieve net-zero carbon impact by 2050, and generate new revenue and long-term competitive advantage for the group. François-Henri Pinault, CEO of Kering, the second largest luxury group in the world, recently reaffirmed his conviction that an approach based on sustainability would show that fashion's long-held values of competition and exclusivity simply aren't conducive to serious change. Instead, he believes brands should be sharing ideas and sources (and, in Kering's case, working with suppliers to bring down the costs of new technologies to make them accessible to mid- and small-sized brands). 'Sustainability is no longer a differentiation point for a business. It is a licence to operate' (Luxury Society, 2022).

6.4 THE CIRCULAR ECONOMY

One of the features of the circular economy is rental and resale. Platforms offering pre-owned luxury products for sale or rental, are being backed by luxury brands who want to be part of this innovative business model. The traditional luxury model built around owning a product for life or 'looking after it for the next generation',[1] is now being replaced by brands with 'reuse-recycle', encouraging customers to return old items in exchange for a gift credit for their next purchase. Stella McCartney launched a partnership with The RealReal resale platform in 2017, offering a $100 credit to consumers consigning her products on the platform. Kering, and Tiger Global Management, invested €178 million in the Paris-based resale company Vestiaire Collective in 2021. Luxury rental and re-sale platform, My Wardrobe HQ, partnered with Burberry in 2021, to launch the British heritage brand's first womenswear rental and resale offering in the UK. Peer-to-peer options are also emerging, platforms that own no inventory but simply facilitate the rental transaction between peers, taking a commission on both sides. Pre-owned luxury is now a real and deeply rooted trend, especially among younger customers. Rather than ignoring it, our wish is to seize this opportunity to enhance the value we offer our customers and influence the future of our industry towards more innovative and more sustainable practices. This fits naturally with our entrepreneurial spirit, our pioneering sustainability strategy, and our modern vision of luxury.

The COVID-19 pandemic boosted this growth, as an increasing number of customers adopted new ways of shopping, both socially and digitally, with the trend also continuing post-lockdowns. In a global survey (BCG, 2020), 62% of respondents said they would buy more from online resale platforms, as well as from luxury labels, that partner with second-hand marketplaces. Some luxury brands are also adopting cradle-to-cradle inputs.[2] Certified materials are biodegradable and sourced from farms that meet animal welfare and land management requirements. Energy used in production is mainly renewable, using co-generation or hydroelectric plants and chemicals used in dyeing processes have a low environmental impact. The Italian firm Botto Giuseppe was the first to develop sustainable and ethically produced cashmere, followed by silk and wool products which are cradle-to-cradle certified. Prada eyewear also uses cradle-to-cradle inputs for frames and hinges, which are made with bio-plastics or polymers derived from castor oil.

6.5 INVESTING IN SUSTAINABILITY

Historically, investments in sustainability were evaluated narrowly, looking simply at the financial returns. There is now growing evidence that by focusing on 'people and the planet', greater long-term value can be generated. Global investors are demanding that the companies they invest in incorporate, track, and report environmental, social and governance (ESG) performance. A Deutsche Bank Research report found that the use of new materials and higher material recycling or upcycling would have a 'net-net neutral effect on gross margin as the benefits are likely to be mitigated by higher costs' for a luxury brand (Deutsche Bank, 2021). In 2012, Kering published its first environmental profit and loss report (EP&L), which measures and quantifies its environmental impact (much like a traditional financial report).

CASE STUDY 1 Soneva Resorts

The Soneva Group's earliest 'green' projects were first launched 20 years ago when they invested in a desalinating plant and eliminated plastic bottled water, at the Namoona resort in the Maldives. Today, Soneva has implemented a wide range of eco-friendly policies. Soneva Namoona now provides funding, expertise, and coordination for a waste management system that cleans up local islands and promotes the abolition of single-use plastics in the Maldives. The resort also invests in social projects encouraging local children to learn about the ocean and become responsible stewards for their environment. The Soneva Group has also developed a 'waste-to-wealth programme' to tackle issues innovatively. This aims to change the perception of waste by showing that it is a resource that can be recycled productively but also used in items for resort operations. Soneva recycles 90% of solid waste and generates around $400,000 in revenue from waste output. The group has created a glass studio, where waste glass can be reused to create works of art and resort guests can watch artists create objects, learn the art of glass blowing in special courses, and design their own creations. Soneva produces its own drinking water, one of the first hospitality brands in the world to ban branded bottled water. A percentage of revenues from Soneva Water funds over 500 clean water projects in more than 50 countries, providing clean water to over 750,000 people via charities such as Water Charity and Thirst Aid. Soneva has policy of excluding endangered species from restaurant menus and only fish caught sustainably are served. Menus are developed with a sustainability rating of all food products included. The embedded CO_2 in some of the ingredients, such as beef, is monitored in order to select the best suppliers through farming method and geographical location.

Most of Soneva's fixtures, fittings, and operating equipment are produced by local artisans. Soap and shampoo are in ceramic dispensers, allowing Soneva to support local traders as well as to avoid disposable packaging. Many of the fabrics used are hand-woven by women in rural communities, allowing them to work locally without having to leave their families. Each of the Soneva hotels has a designated Sustainability Officer, who collects and reports performance data on all resort activities and equipment that emit greenhouse gases. In addition to monitoring its own emissions, Soneva also collects data on emissions from activities that occur outside the resort property, but which can be directly attributed to the activities of the resort – such as emissions from the transport of goods and the air travel of hosts and guests.

CASE STUDY 2 Prada

In 1984, Prada first introduced a nylon backpack which was made from heavyweight, industrial nylon, redefining the traditional luxury leather item. 'Suddenly nylon started to look more intriguing to me than couture fabrics', Miuccia Prada commented. 'I decided to introduce it to the catwalk, and it challenged, even changed, the traditional and conservative idea of luxury. I am still obsessed with it' (Vogue, 2019). Nylon accounts for 20% of the world's fibre production, with over three and a half million tons produced each year. As nylon is made from petroleum, it has a negative environmental footprint and one of its by-products is nitrous oxide, a greenhouse gas 300 times more potent than carbon dioxide. Nylon, as all synthetic fibres, is not biodegradable and takes between 30 and 40 years to decompose. As it biodegrades, it produces minute fragments that can enter the ground and contaminate aquifers, water courses, basins, and soil. Fragmentation into microplastics has become a pressing issue as a result of the widespread usage of low-quality nylon yarn that rapidly breaks down, often when a garment is machine-washed. These microplastics are also formed during the manufacturing process, when the processed polymer compound is immersed in water for various phases of chilling and dyeing, becoming saturated with chemicals and plastic molecules.

Aquafil is a company which recovers nylon waste, such as fishing nets that can no longer be used, or textile production scraps normally marked for disposal, and turns them into a new yarn which has the same characteristics as that made of virgin raw material. The yarn is branded Econyl and is used in new products, from apparel to interiors.

The resulting fabric is water-repellent, lightweight, resistant to stains and soiling, and can undergo the regeneration procedure an indefinite number of times. As a result, Prada Re-Nylon was launched in 2019, with a capsule collection of bags for men and women. The following year, the product line was expanded into Prada ready-to-wear, accessories, and footwear. Prada's collection of recycled nylon bags are composed of the same shapes as the triangular Prada logo. However, it has been adapted from an upside-down triangle enclosing the company name and Milan (the city where it is based), to a triangular arrow to express the potential for endless recycling. '[The logo is] a unique interpretation of the Prada triangular logo that emphasises a bucking of the traditional, age-old linear supply chain into a cyclical one, focused on renewal', said the company (Vogue, 2019).

Seminar exercises

Discussion topics:

1. 'Fur and leather alternatives will never properly replace the authentic product'. Discuss.
2. How can a brand incorporate resale without diluting perceptions of exclusivity? Thinking of your own relationship with luxury brands, what is your perception of 'pre-owned' items?
3. Several luxury brands are still far behind on their environmental footprint, but this has not impacted sales or reputation significantly. Why is this the case?
4. Identify the benefits of using cradle-to-cradle certified raw materials for a luxury brand.

Group exercises:

1. Select a luxury brand of your choice which has committed to sustainable practices and create a presentation to address the following:
   • How has the brand implemented sustainability?
   • What was the identified need to move towards sustainability?
   • How does the brand communicate its sustainable practices?
2. Carry out research into two of the following trends: plant-based leather alternatives, environmental P&L or peer-to-peer luxury rental platforms. For each, do the following:
   • explain the concept
   • provide an example of how a brand has used it successfully
   • report the associated advantages from implementing the initiative.
3. Choose a luxury brand in a specific industry. Carry out research to identify the following:
   • highlight how they have migrated from traditional to a sustainable business model
   • highlight some characteristics of the customers that led the brand to adopt a new approach.

Notes

1 Patek Philippe generations campaign
2 Cradle-to-cradle products can be recycled (upcycled), imitating nature's cycle with all ingredients/components either recycled or returned to the earth, directly or indirectly through food, as a completely safe, nontoxic, and biodegradable nutrient.

References

Arnett, G (2019). Brands are phasing out fur. Could leather be next? Retrieved 8 September 2021 www.voguebusiness.com/sustainability/fur-leather-luxury-poll-peta

Aviram, D (2020). How sustainable is Stella McCartney? Retrieved 8 September 2021 https://luxiders.com/how-sustainable-is-stella-mccartney/

BCG (2020) True Luxury Global Consumer Insight, https://www.bcg.com/it-it/press/24giugno2020-true-luxury-global-consumer-insight

Beckham, D, & Voyer, B G (2014). Can sustainability be luxurious? A mixed-method investigation of implicit and explicit attitudes towards sustainable luxury consumption. *Advances in Consumer Research*, 42, 245–250.

Deloitte (2020). Global powers of luxury goods. Retrieved 7 September 2021 www2.deloitte.com/content/dam/Deloitte/ve/Documents/consumer-business/Luxury-Goods-2020.pdf

Deutsche Bank (2021). Towards net zero emission www.db.com/files/documents/Towards-net-zero-emissions.pdf

Farra, E (2019). At the Copenhagen Fashion Summit, Kering's François-Henri Pinault shares a radical new vision of sustainability. Retrieved 7 September 2021 www.vogue.com/article/francois-henri-pinault-kering-sustainability-vision

The Fashion Law (2019). Luxury Fashion brands and their "made in Italy" accessories at the center of sweatshop scandal in Naples. [Online]. Available from: https://www.thefashionlaw.com/luxury-fashion-brands-and-their-made-in-italy-accessories-at-the-center-of-sweatshop-scandal-in-naples/

Guercini, S, & Ranfagni, S (2013). Sustainability and luxury: The Italian case of a supply chain based on native wools. *Journal of Corporate Citizenship*, 2013 (52), 76–89.

Kapferer, J N (2010). All that glitters is not green: The challenge of sustainable luxury. *The European Business Review*, 2, 40–45.

Mauer, E (2014). Is green the new black?: sustainable luxury : challenge or strategic opportunity for the luxury sector, *Bibliothèque numérique RERO DOC*, ID :10670/1.b8piuu.

Oakes, J (2020). Sustainable Luxury: Millennials buy into socially conscious brands. Retrieved September 8, 2021 https://luxe.digital/business/digital-luxury-trends/millennials-buy-sustainable-luxury/

Paton, E (2018). Burberry, after provoking an uproar, will stop burning unsold merchandise. Retrieved September 8, 2021 www.seattletimes.com/business/burberry-after-provoking-an-uproar-will-stop-burning-unsold-merchandise/

Positive Luxury (2019). 2021 predictions report: business in the time of COVID. [online]. Available: https://www.positiveluxury.com/content/uploads/2021/12/Positive-Luxury-2021-Predictions-Report-Business-in-the-Time-of-Covid-.pdf

Vogue (2019). Prada's re-nylon project turns your favorite backpack into a sustainable accessory. Retrieved 8 September 2021 www.vogue.com/article/prada-re-nylon-sustainable-nylon-econyl

Digital Business

CHAPTER 7

Social media marketing in luxury brand management

Steve Mancour

7.1 INTRODUCTION

Social media is one of the most important aspects of modern marketing and should be considered vital to any brand management strategy (Vinerean, 2017). In today's digital world, social media should be combined with other channels (i.e. SEO/SEM, websites, and Public Relations), to enable and reinforce awareness and conversions (Appel et al., 2020). One of the primary considerations for social media marketing to the luxury sector is the product or service, and where it falls on the luxury spectrum. Luxury brands span a vast array of goods and services that range from socks to private jets and yachts. The more costly the item, the less influence that social media marketing has on the consumer, but it does have an effect in almost all cases. Human nature makes people more risk adverse than pleasure seeking. For this reason, the perceived risk associated with spending on high-ticket items carries more weight than the potential benefit, even if they have equal merit. If the associated costs are relatively low, it is easier to justify spending more on a luxurious bottle of vodka, or an item of expensive clothing, than on a luxury car. If the purchase is lost or destroyed, the loss of a lower-cost item is felt less keenly. This is one of the primary reasons that high-ticket items (whether luxury or not), often involve multi-step funnels to persuade consumers to purchase (Dierks, 2017).

The market for a luxury brand of vodka, for example, is significantly larger than, and has a greater pool of potential consumers, than luxury cars, therefore, their consumers can be more easily reached and are more readily persuaded to purchase. With lower value luxury goods and services, there is also a much higher potential for repeat purchases, incentives, and multi-buy offers (Jain, 2020). Conversely, higher-ticket luxury markets are increasingly smaller as the price climbs, due to the decreasing financial ability (or creditworthiness) of consumers to purchase. In marketing luxury brands through social media, you are feeding the aspiration of consumers to belong to one of

DOI: 10.4324/9781003015826-10

these more elite and exclusive groups by association (Nwanko et al., 2014). Social media provides the path to convey to potential customers the signals that they require to be influenced into action (Stephen, 2016). This chapter discusses a range of topics relating to social media marketing in luxury brand management, including advertising advantage, social proof, influencers, and super fans. The chapter also discusses some challenges.

7.2 ADVERTISING ADVANTAGE AND SOCIAL PROOF

The most significant advantage for brands advertising today is the ability to meet potential consumers where they feel safe and secure. Social networks provide a digital tribe or village where users can consider your product or service, discuss it with others, and eventually be persuaded into action (Bolotaeva & Cata, 2011). What that action is, whether conversion, advocacy, or denigration, is greatly dependent on marketers, such as brand managers, and how they use this primary marketing tool. A primary signal that consumers gain from social media is social proof (Sanak-Kosmowska et al., 2021). As people become aware of a product or service, they will inevitably discuss it in various social networks with those they consider peers, much like discussing new discoveries might have been around campfires in ancient history, or with local friends before social media was made available via the Internet. Social network 'friends' are simply our digital tribe. In social networks, having the input and discussion of new discoveries allows group analysis, and will significantly influence the confidence that someone has in deciding the merit, value, and confidence of the product or service (Amblee & Bui, 2012). Positive experiences that are promoted within these networks will have a confirmation effect on others in the group, even if their participation is merely passive. Negative experiences will have an even worse effect because of the risk aversion mentioned previously. Human nature will compound this with something called *confirmation bias*, where a positive (or particularly a negative) impression, will subconsciously push potential consumers further in the direction they are moving (Shin et al., 2021). This is one of the reasons that it is vital to monitor, and counter negative experiences, particularly in luxury brands, because so much effort is invested in building the brand name, reputation, and persona. Luxury brand reputations can take significant time, energy, and money to build, and can be ruined easily and quickly if not carefully nurtured and maintained. The most effective ways to do this are through social media and public relations (Kumar, 2020). These two channels include overlapping areas such as product/service support, answering questions posed on social networks, and defusing potential reputation-damaging information (and dis-information).

7.3 INFLUENCERS AND SUPER-FANS

One of the more recent, evolutionary changes to marketing on social networks was the advent of the influencer. Influencers are people who have developed their own following on social networks and can influence large numbers of people through their own private channels by advocating something (Freberg et al., 2011). As these influencers grow their audience in size, they can command increasing fees for persuading their large audiences to take action. Influencers for luxury brands should be chosen with care because of the reputational risk of choosing controversial or divisive personalities. The choice of who to approach when sponsoring these influencers should reflect the brand image, brand persona, and market segments that the brand is targeting (Lim et al., 2017).

Super-fans are another recent development that are increasingly being used by brands, including luxury brands (Hensel & Deis, 2010). These people are those that have an especially strong connection to the brand and are ardent advocates for everything involving the brand. They often defend or advocate the brand in groups, or with friends on social networks, and do this with no remuneration or incentive. They are advocates for various reasons and can often be rewarded for their actions by being given products for free, by being given discounts, or by gaining some insight into future events or product updates. They can even be invited to participate in brand marketing plans in some way, as a 'thank you' for their positive participation and advocacy. It is not always necessary to involve or reward these advocates as they're already sold on the brand and are often happy to continue to support it. Apple computer is an example of a luxury brand that has an extraordinarily high number of super-fans. The same care should be exercised when involving a super-fan, or brand ambassador, as choosing an influencer. There should be definite tangible benefits to involving them, and a very limited downside, because if they feel snubbed or neglected after being given some attention, the advocacy can sometimes be turned in the opposite direction. The influencer is often being paid in some way and is less likely to speak negatively about the brand because it may harm future sponsorships. A super-fan doesn't have this consideration, just a love of the brand.

7.4 TROLL TROUBLES

Trolls are no longer the stuff of fairy tales; they are the scourge of the Internet. Like 'spam' was adopted by the online world as a name for unsolicited (and unwanted) emails, trolls are people (both known and anonymous), that purposefully create negative experiences on the Internet. Sometimes they are simply people that are bored and trying to elicit a negative reaction to entertain themselves. Other times it may be someone with a malicious intent. The Internet can provide many ways for such people to be listed as anonymous, choose a pseudonym, or even operate openly using their own name, because of the nature of being physically distant from the object of their negativity. In such cases, they consider these attacks and provocative statements to be free of consequences for themselves but inflicting negative consequences on their victims (Birkbak, 2018).

Luxury brands have to deal with trolls on social media through both preparation and post-incident actions. The best practice on social networks is to moderate forums (super-fans can sometimes be used for this) and to search actively for, and counter, the statements made on open, unmoderated networks. It is important that when making counter statements on these unmoderated social networks, the responses are not emotional but conciliatory and reasonable. Trolls are trying to elicit a negative reaction from the brand. Providing a negative or emotional response will only damage the brand image and reward the troll with what they sought, which will only encourage more attacks. Be polite. Asking the troll for a neutral explanation of their issue and offering a reasonable solution will make the brand look stable, accommodating, and magnanimous; it will also expose the troll for the attention-seeker they are.

7.5 SOCIAL CONVERSATIONS, FEEDBACK, AND CROWDSOURCING

Social media has changed the nature of marketing in many ways. It has shifted the conversation from a one-way monologue being broadcast to a wide and random audience at sometimes eye-watering costs, to a more conversational dialogue that can be personalised to groups, to segments, and increasingly to individuals (Ohajionu & Mathews, 2015). One of the primary benefits of social media is the amount of information that brands can gather on their customers (Gangadharbatla et al., 2014). Social media networks offer a much more bespoke picture of the individual, so they can be much more influential by understanding their likes, dislikes, and motivations. Various social networks offer thousands of data points on every customer which allows you to understand what works better for different groups. One of the great benefits of social media marketing is the ability to test and to pivot to what works best. Brands advertising on social media can easily track the ad response from links embedded in the ad and engage in split testing on both their website sales funnel and on their social media advertisements, to see which fuels more conversions (Felt, 2016).

Involving your potential customers can be a great way to leverage word of mouth and brand participation at a much lower cost than normal advertising. Harnessing your audience to promote your brand, like Burberry's 'Art of the Trench' campaign, where people were invited to upload a picture of themselves in a Burberry's trench coat, is a great example (Bunz, 2009). However, luxury brands should look at the potential ways that this can backfire when considering whether to do this for their brand.

Taking the vodka example above, there only needs to be an incident with children or drink drivers participating in the promotion to swiftly turn the campaign negative. In such cases, if proceeding with a well thought out crowdsourcing campaign, it is best to plan mitigation strategies. These might be things such as disclaimers not to do this whilst driving or operating heavy equipment, or that they shouldn't be done by children, or by advocating responsible drinking. Doing a cost-benefits analysis, and brainstorming worst-case scenarios and mitigation plans, is a valuable exercise in deciding whether the proposed crowdsourcing idea is worth pursuing.

7.6 PANDEMIC PARADIGM

The recent COVID-19 pandemic lasted for two years before it was manageable and has shifted consumer habits because of the numerous lockdowns (Sheth, 2020). Even the Internet behemoth Google had issues with different search activity and had to make significant adjustments to their algorithms to compensate. Online activity has increased exponentially, beginning with frantic and prolonged searches for toilet paper. This shift represents an opportunity for marketers to use this vastly expanded online audience to help their ad spend in social networks to be much more efficient and trackable. It also allows the brand conversations to be more easily monitored and guided.

Luxury industries are cyclical, increasing and decreasing potential customer bases, depending on the economy and industry. Brand managers and marketers for luxury brands should bear this cyclical rhythm in mind when planning campaigns in social media. It can be helpful to see what the current discussions are about and find a way to make the brand relevant to the conversation. Less is more. Focus on fewer but higher quality social media aspects that reflect a more exclusive and richer feel. Stretching your brand image over too much space hints at desperation and non-exclusivity. Focus on more timeless, less trendy posts that are not controversial and won't come back to bite you. In other words, it is better to have two or three high-quality social media campaigns, rather than poor-quality ones on five or six networks. People will make judgments about the quality of your interactions and make valuations on the luxury brand based on that. Poor quality interactions will reflect poorly on the brand and brand image.

Seminar exercises

Discussion topics:

1. Discuss how social media has changed the way brands market to consumers, and what advantages/disadvantages this entails.
2. Different social media networks appear to specialise in one type of group or another. List the social media entities you know and describe the basis of their membership and who might be reached by your luxury brand through different interactions. Think about your experiences with these social media networks. Do any companies' interactions stand out to you as particularly good or especially compelling to their brand?
3. When using social media for a luxury brand, what are some of the things that you have to consider when planning a campaign? Choose a luxury product and list the considerations for a social media campaign. Is it for awareness, sales or reputation management? Do any of the considerations seem better or worse in consideration to the luxury brand you've chosen? List the best and worst ones and describe the reasons for your choices.
4. Describe what luxury brands you've seen in social media and whether they made a good or bad impression. What made the brand stand out? Did their social media presence give the impression of luxury? Why or why not?

References

Amblee, N & Bui, T (2012) Harnessing the influence of social proof in online shopping: The effect of electronic word of mouth on sales of digital microproducts. *International Journal of Electronic Commerce*. 16, 2. Pp. 91–114.

Appel, G, Grewal, L, Hadi, R & Stephen, A (2020) The future of social media in marketing. *Journal of the Academy of Marketing Science*. 48. Pp. 79–95.

Birkbak, A (2018) Into the wild online: learning from internet trolls. *First Monday*. 23, 5. https://doi.org/10.5210/fm.v22i5.8297

Bolotaeva, V & Cata, T (2011) Marketing opportunities with social networks. *Journal of Internet Social Networking and Virtual Communities*. DOI: 10.5171/2011.409860

Bunz, M. (2009). Burberry checks out crowdsourcing with The Art of the Trench. *The Guardian online, 9*.

Dierks, A (2017) Empirical application of a re-modelled brand purchase funnel. In Dierks, A (Ed) Remodelling the brand purchase funnel. Springer. Pp. 199–274.

Felt, M (2016) Social media and the social sciences: How researchers employ Big Data analytics. *Big Data & Society*. January – June Edition. Pp. 1–15.

Freberg, K, Graham, K, McGaughey, K & Freberg, L (2011) Who are the social media influencers? A study of public perceptions of personality. *Public Relations Review*. 36, 1. Pp. 90–92.

Gangadharbatla, H, Bright, L & Logan, K (2014) Social media and news gathering: Tapping into the millennial mindset. *The Journey of Social Media in Society*. 3, 1. Pp. 45–63.

Hensel, K & Deis, M (2010) Using social media to increase advertising and improve marketing. *The Entrepreneurial Executive*. 15. Pp. 87–97.

Jain, S (2020) Role of conspicuous value in luxury purchase intention. *Marketing Intelligence & Planning*. 39, 2. Pp. 169–185

Kumar, A (2020) Luxury Brands on Social Media Platforms. In Goyal, M & Eilu, E (Eds) *Digital Media and Wireless Communications in Developing Nations*. Taylor and Francis.

Lim, X, Radzol, A, Cheah, H & Wong, M (2017) The impact of social media influencers on purchase intention and the mediation effect of customer attitude. *Asian Journal of Business Research*. 7, 2. Pp. 19–36.

Nwanko, S, Hamelin, N & Khaled, M (2014) Consumer values, motivations and purchase intention for luxury goods. *Journal of Retailing and Consumer Services*. 21, 5. Pp. 735–744.

Ohajionu, U & Mathews, S (2015) Advertising on social media and benefits to brands. *Journal of Social Sciences and Humanities*. 10, 2. Pp. 335–351.

Sanak-Kosmowska, K, Mruk, H Tilbury, J & Aldridge, M (2021) *Evaluating Social Media Marketing: Social Proof and Online Buyer Behaviour* Routledge.

Sheth, M (2020) Impact of Covid-19 on consumer behavior. *Journal of Business Research*. 117. Pp. 280–283.

Shin, E, Chung, T & Damhorts (2021) Are negative and positive reviews regarding apparel fit influential? *Journal of Fashion Marketing and Management*. 25, 1. Pp. 63–79.

Stephen, A (2016) The role of digital and social media marketing in consumer behaviour. *Current Opinion in Psychology*. Vol 10. Pp. 17–21.

Vinerean, S (2017) Importance of Strategic Social Media Marketing. *Expert Journal of Marketing*. 5, 1. Pp. 28–35.

CHAPTER 8

Digital marketing and analytics for luxury brands

Sylvie Studente and Bhavini Desai

8.1 INTRODUCTION

Digital marketing is often defined as an umbrella term for the marketing of products and/or services using digital technologies to deliver value to customers (Kannan & Hongshuang, 2017). In this age of globalisation, it has become extremely important for brands to be able to make their offerings stand out, get closer and better connected with all of their business entities and most importantly, with their customers (Kannan & Hongshuang, 2017). Activities such as customer communication through to product distribution are supported by a combination of both traditional and digital media channels. Traditionally, brands used a variety of offline channels, such as advertising, PR, direct mail, exhibitions, merchandising, etc., to communicate with their customers. Digital marketing involves a number of technologies, including, but not mutually exclusive to, social media, email, websites, mobile, display advertising, search engine marketing, search engine optimisation, e-commerce, social media marketing, and analytics (Chaffey & Ellis-Chadwick, 2019; Bala, & Verma, 2018). The flow of information across both traditional and digital channels, could be perceived as a web of communication between customers and opinion leaders, built around the brand, and the consequences for marketing practices have been transformative (Shah & Murthi, 2020). It is important for brands to facilitate these communications, and in doing so, keep close to their customers.

Changes in consumer behaviour have become evident due to digital consumption becoming an increasing aspect of consumers' everyday lives (e.g. Bardhi & Eckhardt, 2017; Belk, 2013; Fritze et al., 2020). Changes in consumer behaviour, and preferences for mobile and digital platforms, has driven businesses to respond by redeveloping their marketing strategies to incorporate digital channels (Tiago & Verissimo, 2014; Durmaz, & Efendioglu, 2016). Scholars report numerous advantages of the shift from traditional to digital driven marketing models; the focus on relationship-based interaction with consumers, benefits to be garnered from segmentation and personalised

DOI: 10.4324/9781003015826-11

content, extended market reach, co-creation of content with consumers, multi-channels of communication and the ability to measure marketing success via analytics (Yasmin, et al., 2015; Kayumovich & Annauradovna, 2020; Chaffey & Ellis-Chadwick, 2019). Although many businesses across multiple industries have embraced this new way of marketing, there has been some resistance from luxury brands (Castello & Khelladi, 2016).

According to Beverland (2004), a luxury brand is based on trends, culture, history, product integrity, commercialisation, and support. The production of luxury goods is sometimes guided by multi-brand strategies in large companies, that do not always take into account what is a priority for their consumers. However, due to the diversity in demographic, psychological, and behavioural aspects of millennials and new age customers of today, luxury brands have had to evolve and reinvent themselves and their marketing means, to satisfy consumer needs and fulfil their business strategies. This may be through brand awareness, consumer interaction, or purchase motivations (Kapferer & Bastien, 2012).

This chapter will introduce the debate surrounding digital marketing for luxury brands and considers current trends in digital marketing. This chapter will be specifically centred around how consumers of today have shaped different marketing approaches and the types of digital channels that businesses use to communicate with customers. The chapter will conclude with detail on integrated marketing communications. Throughout the readings contained within, this chapter will be supported by activities, discussion points, and the cases of luxury brands Burberry and Gucci.

8.2 DIGITAL MARKETING FOR LUXURY: THE DEBATE

Vigneron & Johnson (2004) define luxury products as 'goods whose use or display brings along respect for their possessor, beyond all functionality'. 'Luxury' is generally associated with characteristics such as relative inaccessibility, wealth, and exclusivity (Kapferer, 2015; Brun et al., 2008; Ko et al., 2017; Wirtz et al., 2020). 'Luxury' also provides consumers with the emotional benefits of prestige and status (Wu et al., 2012; Grossman & Shapiro, 1988; Han et al., 2010). These characteristics and emotional benefits lose their meaning if a luxury good becomes widely available (Kapferer & Bastien, 2012). It is this notion of 'exclusivity' which led to initial reluctance by luxury brands to engage with digital strategies (Okonkwo, 2009; Castellano & Khelladi, 2016; Heine & Berghaus, 2014). Remaining exclusive and retaining an aura of exclusivity has proven challenging for luxury brands in the digital age (Blasco-Arcas et al., 2016; Baker et al., 2018). The perception at the time was that luxury consumers would not buy expensive products online as wider accessibility to luxury products would detract from the notion of 'exclusivity' (Dauriz et al., 2014; Baker, et al. 2018). The traditional perspective was that digital strategies used by generic brands would not be suitable for luxury brands as this would not be compatible with the characteristics associated with luxury products (Dion & Arnould, 2011; Kapferer & Bastien, 2012; Bjørn-Andersen & Hansen, 2011). This continues to be an ongoing area of debate today, and it is reported that many luxury fashion brands in particular are still reluctant to adopt digital marketing initiatives due to the 'uniqueness of luxury fashion value proposition' (Pini & Quaquarelli, 2018; Oliveira & Fernandez, 2020).

8.2.1 Trends

The perceptions towards the adoption of digital strategies has evolved over recent years within the luxury industry; however, this has been slow in comparison to other sectors (Rios, 2016). Studies within the area have reported success cases, where well-known luxury brands have moved towards digital strategies resulting in online sales growth exceeding physical store sales (D'Arpizio et al., 2019; Mu et al., 2020). Other scholars have reported positive effects on brand, value, and relationship equity through the use of social media marketing for luxury brands (e.g. Kim & Ko, 2012). Those luxury brands who have embraced digital strategy have demonstrated that luxury consumers are willing to purchase luxury goods online. Key elements of success to this include the use of analytics to monitor consumer behaviour, developing a strong mobile presence, and effective approaches towards social media campaigns (Dauriz et al., 2014). Companies such as Burberry have embraced digital marketing to tap into younger consumers. The success of such an approach is supported by research, which indicates that millennials are the most 'digitally influenced' luxury consumers (i.e. Bailis, 2017). In 2019, Forbes estimated that millennials, and younger digital native cohorts, accounted for one-third of luxury customers, and are expected to exceed 50 per cent by 2024, thus radically changing luxury markets. Generation Z consumers are most likely to shop online using a range of devices (Lee, 2018). Given that the luxury online market is expected to grow by 25% by 2025 (Mu et al., 2020), the importance of these target consumer groups should not be ignored by luxury brands. Building on these developments, we argue that luxury brands cannot continue to resist the advance of digitisation but rather must find ways to adapt to it.

8.2.2 Burberry: a success story

Burberry is today considered one of the most internationally esteemed fashion houses (Straker & Wrigley, 2016; Clark, 2012). This has been possible through their adoption of a strong digital media strategy. Embracing digital technology enabled Burberry to turnaround from a struggling company to the success it is today through targeting younger customers (Phan et al., 2011). Specifically, Burberry developed a digital marketing strategy to target millennials and in doing so the company drives brand awareness through user generated content, via social media (Kim & Mar, 2019). An example of this is Burberry's 'Art of the Trench' campaign, in which followers were encouraged to post pictures of themselves wearing the iconic trench coat. The campaign was launched in 2009, since which Burberry's online sales have surged by 50% year-on-year (Choi et al., 2014). This not only enabled Burberry to attract younger consumers, but also enabled them to rejuvenate the brand and increase brand awareness (Liu et al., 2019; Phan et al., 2011). The case of Burberry is an effective demonstration that engaging with customers via digital channels can lead to benefits in increased brand awareness through a lot of earned media, growth, and revenue (Chaffey & Ellis-Chadwick, 2019).

8.2.3 The current situation

Companies such as Burberry, Gucci, and Net-A-Porter, have successfully demonstrated that a strong digital strategy can provide effective channels for building relationships with customers (Straker & Wrigley, 2016). However, despite this, there still exists resistance from other luxury brands to integrate digital models, through fear of diluting perceptions of exclusivity associated with luxury goods (Mekonnen & Larner, 2018; Sherman, 2009; Kapferer & Bastien, 2012). Current trend information indicates that whilst digital technologies have contributed to overall growth, and attained positive responses from consumers, over 40% of luxury brands are still not selling their goods online (Mu et al., 2020). Currently, there still exists debate in the area surrounding the use of digital marketing within the luxury sector, and the adaption process within it continues to lag behind in relation to other sectors (Rios, 2016).

8.3 TYPES OF DIGITAL MEDIA CHANNELS

Brands use a variety of different media channels as part of their communication and marketing strategies (Dall' Olmo Riley and Lacroix, 2003). These channels can be used to encourage the audience to visit a brand's website, to participate in brand campaigns and purchase products (Chaffey & Ellis-Chadwick, 2019). In this section we will consider the following digital media channels: search engine marketing (SEM), affiliate marketing, social media marketing (SMM) and e-commerce.

8.3.1 Search engine marketing (SEM)

Search engine marketing (SEM) is used to promote a brand and its products to an organisation's website via search engines (Knezevi & Vidas-Bubanja, 2010; Green, 2003). Research within the area reports that 37% of purchase decisions are influenced by search engine results (Abou Nabout et al., 2012). However, there is much debate regarding which approach towards SEM is most effective (Dou et al., 2010). There are two key approaches that can be used in search engine marketing, paid-search marketing (also known as pay-per-click or PPC) and search engine optimisation (SEO). Paid-search marketing is a type of online advertising where brands pay a fee to search engines to have an advert displayed with prominence to organic search results (Ghose & Yang, 2009). Not only does PPC ensure prominence on the first page of results, but the brand does not pay until the advertising link is clicked (Mordkovich & Mordkovich, 2007). This online marketing approach has a number of reported advantages, including generating good leads due to being placed top in search engine results quickly (Yang et al., 2015), and the tendency of buyers to trust links placed in the sponsored section of search engine results (Sen, 2014). However, with all marketing approaches there are challenges to consider, for example, PPC might not be cost effective in terms of customer lifetime value for some brands (Chaffey & Ellis-Chadwick, 2019).

Search Engine Optimisation (SEO) is used to produce 'organic' search engine results using keywords to improve a website's ranking (Davis, 2006). There are reported advantages to this approach. Unlike PPC, SEO does not require a fee to be paid; however, for SEO to be effective it is important to ensure that all webpages within a site be optimised, which may require ongoing investment into development (Jones, 2008). SEO listing results may take a longer time to be achieved than PPC (Chaffey & Ellis-Chadwick, 2019). Whilst both approaches can improve search engine listings (Fiorini & Lipsky, 2012), numerous scholars report that PPC is the most popular approach (i.e. Bhandari, 2017; Kritzinger & Weideman, 2013; Sen, 2014)

8.3.2 Affiliate marketing

Affiliate marketing is a commission-based partnership between a merchant and an affiliate (partner), where affiliates are paid a commission for the referral of customers to their website (Dwivedi, et al., 2017). This means that goods are not only sold through the merchant's own website, but also potentially through numerous affiliate websites (Bowie, 2014; Bandyopadhyay et al., 2009). The amount of commission paid to affiliates tends to be based on a percentage of the product sale price (Brown, 2009). Essentially 'affiliate marketing' can be considered as a link between the merchant and the customer (Haq, 2012). The concept of affiliate marketing arose in 1996, when Amazon began to offer other websites (affiliates) commission on sales they generated through referring customers to their website (Goldschmidt et al., 2003). There are reported advantages to this approach; affiliation can lead to increased search engine visibility (Janssen & Van Heck, 2007), it also enables merchants to reach additional audiences (Brown, 2009), and it can provide the option to commence online marketing communications (Vladimíra, 2013). However, there are challenges to consider, for example, possible affiliate programme management fees (Chaffey & Ellis-Chadwick, 2019).

8.3.3 Social media marketing (SMM)

Tuten & Solomon (2015) define social media marketing (SMM) as 'the utilisation of social media technologies, channels, and software to create, communicate, deliver and exchange offerings that have value for an organization's stakeholders'. Many brands are making use of SMM to maintain brand loyalty with customers (Erdogmus & Cicek; 2012), to foster relationships with customers (Vries et al., 2012), extend audience reach (Pereira et al., 2014) and to increase purchasing behaviour and overall engagement with the brand (Lipsman et al., 2012). Many brands are tapping into the potential of SMM in order to drive their marketing campaigns by connecting to consumers (Tafesse & Wien, 2017; Neti, 2011). Due to millennials and Generation Z being the most mobile-savvy target groups, Facebook, YouTube, and LinkedIn have experienced a huge surge in their usage (Lin & Lu, 2011). The most popular social media platform continues to be Facebook; in 2014, the number of daily active Facebook users was reported to be 1.5 billion (Ashley & Tuten, 2014).

Marketers have recognised the opportunity to use SSM for engagement, driving lead generation, and encouraging consumers to share content, thereby involving the consumer in the marketing process (Evans, 2010). Essentially, the use of social media in marketing has shifted the role of consumers from that of passive recipients of information, to co-creators of brand content. An example of this is the 'Art of the Trench' campaign, run by Burberry, in which brand followers were encouraged to post pictures of themselves on social media wearing the iconic Burberry trench coat. This campaign generated brand awareness and engagement through earned media, and in-turn, led to a surge in sales by 50% (Choi et al., 2014). The most crucial influence here, is that SMM provides a vital and essential role in linking brands directly to consumers and potentials.

The use of brand pages also enables businesses to foster a sense of community with consumers by interacting with them on a frequent basis (Zaglia, 2013). However, the most effective strategy would be to consider the most appropriate social media platforms used by the target audience and to establish a social presence across these different platforms (Ling et al., 2005). This point is emphasised in a study conducted by Erdogmus & Cicek (2012), who report that there is a positive effect on brand loyalty through SMM, when brands make use of different social media platforms, the content is relevant to the consumer and SMM is used to promote campaigns advantageous to the consumer. This final concept is reinforced by Lin et al. (2011), who state that customer engagement and participation with a brand campaign can be increased through the use of incentives. There are numerous reported advantages of using SMM, as well as challenges to be considered (refer to Table 8.1).

The key point here, is that the application of social media platforms in marketing must be purposefully considered and applied, in order to reap the benefits of enhancing consumer engagement and sales (Pereira et al., 2014). Additionally, it is imperative that brands view SSM as an essential of a wider marketing strategy (Chaffey & Ellis-Chadwick, 2019).

8.3.4 E-commerce

E-commerce is the electronic exchange of goods, services, and payments online through which transactions are undertaken electronically (Turban, 2002). Sanyala & Hisamb (2019) define the four main types of e-commerce as business-to-consumer (B2C), business-to-business (B2B), consumer-to-consumer (C2C), and consumer-to-business (C2B). Due to the popularity of mobile devices, mobile e-commerce (or m-commerce) is becoming increasingly popular (Tarasewich et al., 2002). M-commerce functions in the same

TABLE 8.1 Advantages and challenges of SMM	
Advantages of SMM	**Challenges of SMM**
Allows brands to connect directly to consumers (Tafesse & Wien, 2017).	Any negative 'word of mouth' can damage brand reputation, as consumers tend to trust user-generated contact over brand-generated content (Gensler et al., 2013).
Can lead to increased engagement with consumers (Evans, 2010).	Decisions centred around the types of content to include in order to engage consumers can be challenging (Erdogmus & Cicek, 2012).
Has the potential to increase sales generation (Choi et al., 2014).	Using the most appropriate social media platforms suitable to the target audience needs to be carefully considered (Ling et al., 2005).
Can increase customer loyalty (Erdogmus & Cicek, 2012).	There may be instances where consumers do not wish to interact with brands, which can present a challenge to engagement (Chaffey & Chadwick-Ellis, 2019).
Can increase brand awareness (Bilgin, 2018).	
Increased audience reach and traffic (Pereira et al., 2014).	
Generating sales leads (Evans, 2010).	
Possible rise in search engine rankings (Yang et al., 2015b).	
Increase in consumer purchasing behaviours (Lipsman et al., 2012).	

way as general e-commerce, the only difference being that it is conducted via mobile devices. The shift to e-commerce and m-commerce, has been driven by changes in consumer attitudes towards luxury goods, and the expectation for digital offerings (Deloitte (2017). Berridge (2018) states that the traditional 'bricks and mortar' store approach is not enough, and that omni-channel digital approaches including e-commerce need to be adopted to accommodate the demands of millennials and Generation Z.

There are many components to e-commerce, including online relationships with customers, suppliers, and strategic partners (Warkentin et al., 2001). E-commerce platforms comprises two components: a storefront, which is the customer-facing end, and the 'back end' functions, such as accounting, order management, inventory management, and customer services (Chaffey & Chadwick-Ellis, 2019). The storefront is the web-based aspect seen by the customer, whereas 'back end' functions are driven by databases. Both parts of the system work together in processing e-commerce transactions. Selecting the most suitable e-commerce platform for a business is very important and is dependent on the type of business and the back-end functions required (Lixandroiu & Maican, 2015). The most popular e-commerce platforms are reported to be Shopify, Magento, BigCommerce, Open Cart, and Presta Shop.

There are numerous reported benefits of e-commerce: gaining new customers through better search engine visibility (Sanyala & Hisamb, 2019), sales growth (Chang et al., 2003), keeping up with competitors (Daniel & Wilson, 2002), reaching customers over geographically dispersed locations (Isoraite & Miniotiene, 2018), the availability of products to customers (Khan, 2016), improved customer service (Syed Shah Alam et al., 2005), reduced operation costs (Senn, 2000), customer retention (Ratnasingam, 2002), efficient delivery of products (Shin, 2001), increased interactivity (Rayport & Jaworski, 2001), effective inventory control management (Doyle & Melanson, 2001), and market expansion (Zhuang & Lederer, 2014). However, in addition to these benefits, there are also challenges to consider. These challenges include the consumers' perceptions of risk, fraudulent activities, and web insecurity in making purchases online (McKnight et al., 2002). The concept of 'trust' is crucial in the area of e-commerce, and consumers are more likely to make online purchases if they trust the brand, as well as the e-commerce platform security (Corbitt, et al., 2003). In response to targeting younger consumer groups (e.g. millennials and Generation Z), and changes in consumer attitudes towards digital marketing, many luxury brands have embraced developing an online presence (Sunghee, 2013). Guercini et al. (2020) point out that there is still room for growth, as the e-commerce presence of luxury brands is stronger in developed markets than in developing ones. In 2014, it was reported that 4% of luxury sales were made online (Dauriz, et al., 2014). However, more recent research indicates that the value of e-commerce will grow to 70 billion euros by 2025 (Chaffey & Chadwick-Ellis, 2019). In light of these statistics, luxury brands who are still reluctant to embrace digital marketing and e-commerce risk losing out on potential sales growth (Berridge, 2018).

The impact of the COVID-19 pandemic has brought further challenges, especially for brands who have yet to integrate their e-commerce activities. Due to the closure of physical stores during the pandemic, sales within the luxury sector were down by 70% in comparison to the previous year (Fernandes, 2020). Furthermore, within the luxury sector, 20–30% of revenue is generated by international consumers, and this was affected due to a global ban on travel during the lockdown period. Therefore, it has become vital for luxury brands to embrace digital marketing and e-commerce, in order to engage with their customers and generate sales (Achille & Zipser, 2020).

8.4 INTEGRATED MARKETING COMMUNICATIONS (IMC)

8.4.1 Evolution of IMC

Marketing communications is a complex activity that is used by organisations to engage with their audiences using varying degrees of sophistication and success (Fill & Turnball, 2019). Although there is no universally agreed definition of 'marketing communications', the roots of the concept lie in the 4Ps framework defined by McCarthy (1960). This framework was associated with the purpose of promotion as an activity to persuade people to buy products and services. However, during that period, there was only one-way communication, following a push strategy (Brocato, 2010), and the perspective was short term. In a push strategy, suppliers 'push' their goods toward consumers. In the current times of digital business and globalisation, this has changed to pull where consumers 'pull' information or products that are suitable for their needs, and communications have changed to two- or even three-way. Monologues from brands to their customers have changed to dialogues between the two of them, and also a trialogue between brand and consumer, and consumer and consumer (Dann, 2012).

At a time like this, it is essential for brands to manage all their communication channels, and the data coming from it, to improve their positioning, engagement, and communications. Due to advanced technology and high penetration of the Internet, management of marketing communications has become even more challenging. They need to not only ensure the development of the business by promoting products, but also build the values and reputation of the company.

8.4.2 Purpose of IMC

Today, marketing communications have become an audience-centred activity that is used by organisations to fulfil a range of business objectives. Some such business objectives can be creating differentiation, increasing engagement or improving conversion (Chauhan et al., 2020). In order to differentiate themselves, brands need to create niches either through their offerings, positioning, or communication strategies. In order to increase engagement, brands need to reinforce messages by amending their communication and message strategies. Lastly, in order to improve conversions, brands need to be able to convince and persuade customers to buy their product or services. Brands interact with customers using a combination of tactics and touchpoints across multiple channels and media, both traditional and digital (Shah & Murthi, 2020). As consumer purchasing behaviour has changed as a result of the intervention of digital technologies and social media, the consumer decision-making model has become more complex (Shah & Shay, 2019).

This also means that consumers encounter not only traditional purchasing cues, but also a range of those that are new and digitally enhanced. Management of a multitude of touchpoints, and immense amounts of data, can prove to be very challenging for brands; a slip on either of these can prove very damaging for its reputation and positioning. In order to provide a seamless and positive consumer experience, it is important for brands to integrate all media communications, increase touchpoints to capture appropriate data, and most importantly be able to analyse, measure, and respond to consumer behaviour and expectations. The main aim of integrated marketing communication is to create coherence between tools, their effective functioning, and high performance (Tairova & Dustova, 2020).

8.4.3 IMC in luxury

This level of engagement and interaction generates immense amounts of data (also known as big data) (Finne & Grönroos, 2017). An appropriate IMC strategy that would enable management, analysis, and investigation of this big data would help in modifying consumer behaviour thus influencing their buying process (Chauhan et al., 2020). As luxury is a social construct (Roper et al., 2013), and 'intimately tied to the dynamics of living together' (Kapferer, 2010), we draw on the specifics of luxury services (Wirtz et al., 2020) to argue that understanding, and enhancing, the multiple interactions and the infusion of technology are vital for luxury brands to align their service encounters with evolving customer needs. Communication-in-use is a customer's integration and sense-making of all messages from any source which the customer perceives as communication. Whether company-driven or stemming from other sources, it will form value-in-use for him or her for a specific purpose (Finne & Grönroos, 2017). It is important for a brand to embark on this journey along with their customers to provide an omnichannel experience (Dahl et al., 2019). Thus, a multi-actor perspective represents an opportunity for luxury brands to engage its customers more. The intricacies of managing luxury service encounters (Dion & Borraz, 2017) mean that multi-actor interactions need to be carefully adapted to fit the luxury context. Hence, by adapting an IMC strategy, a luxury brand can get a better understanding of the behaviour and expectations of their customers, be able to have a focused marketing strategy to target their customers, and finally succeed in fulfilling their needs and demands.

8.4.4 Steps for IMC

SOSTAC stands for Situation Analysis, Objectives, Strategy, Tactics, Actions, and Control (Smith, 2015). It is a simple *aide-memoiré* used by thousands of professionals to produce all kinds of plans – for example, business, digital marketing, advertising, and even HR and health and safety plans. Digital Marketing plans need to align with overall brand goals and objectives and hence need to be a part of a broader business plan. In order to achieve this, it is proposed that an IMC plan also follows the SOSTAC model.

In the context of an IMC plan, for 'Situation Analysis', a brand would need to answer the question, 'where are we now?' In strategy planning, they would need to identify a brand's situation in terms of their positioning, reputation, customers, resources, and the existing marketing strategy. At the 'Objective' stage, the brand would need to identify and appoint a clear set of objectives to be fulfilled through the implementation of an IMC strategy. These can either be associated with the 5S's framework (Sell, Serve, Speak, Save or Sizzle), and/or with measurement of their key performance indicators (KPI) pyramid. These might be associated with measuring a return on investment (ROI), brand awareness, market share, engagement through inquiries to visitors, reviews, or conversions, ranging from leads to sales and revenue generation. Hence, the 'O' of SOSTAC deals with the questions of 'where are we going?'

The third component, 'Strategy', deals with the 'how do we get there?' aspect of an IMC plan. Strategy will lay out an execution plan for the fulfilment of objectives and give direction to all the subsequent tactics. Strategy helps identify and shape customer segmentation targets, marketing mix, channels, and messaging strategy. In regard to identifying the target audience, a brand would need to look at their demographic, psychographic, behavioural, and digital profiles (Clow & Baack, 2018). Demographic profiling can help target a specific age group. Psychographic segmentation can help in understanding customer's activities, interests, and opinions. Behavioural segmentation would provide an understanding of customer's reactiveness and responses to different kinds of marketing and messaging tactics. One of the most important aspects about marketing to the new age customer is the communication strategy and an understanding of their digital profile, both web and social media. The next stage in an IMC plan is identifying 'Tactics' which looks into execution. Here the focus is on laying out information about the marketing mix, communications mix, channel mix, and, more importantly, the analytical tools that will be used to integrate and analyse all relevant incoming data.

The 'Action' phase of an IMC plan is about scheduling and actually launching the plan. This is where all the components from the marketing, communication and channel mixes, and the analytical tools, will come alive and start functioning as one entity in order to fulfil brand objectives. During this phase, implementation and integration become interchangeable and are expected to work in complete cohesion in order to deliver on the goals. The Control phase is about accountability and action. All the actions and tactics executed in the previous phase will be measured at this stage to identify what, when, where, and how the campaign is going. This is where all the analytical tools used will start drawing metrics about the outcome of the campaign, also in real time. Since it is all happening in real time, it is first an indicator of how things are going and also an identifier of what needs to change. The benefit of being online is that the changes can be executed in real time; hence, even unfavourable feedback can be made favourable with proper data analytics, intervention, and execution plans at the control stage. For an IMC plan to be successful, all the components of SOSTAC need to be properly implemented, integrated, and analysed.

8.5 Chapter summary

In this chapter we introduced 'digital marketing' as an umbrella term for the marketing of products and/or services using digital technologies to deliver value to customers. In traditional marketing approaches brands used offline channels to communicate with consumers; however, changes in consumer behaviour, and preferences for mobile and digital platforms, has driven the need for marketing strategies to incorporate digital omni-channel approaches. This is especially important in accommodating the demand of millennial and Generation Z consumers. Despite many businesses embracing this new way of marketing, there still remains some resistance from luxury brands. This resistance is driven by fear of diluting perceptions of exclusivity associated with luxury goods. Additionally, the use of social media in marketing has shifted the role of consumers from that of passive recipients of information, to co-creators of brand content.

The impact of the COVID-19 pandemic has brought further challenges, especially for brands who are yet to integrate their e-commerce activities. Due to the closure of physical stores during the pandemic, sales within the luxury sector are reported to be down by 70% in comparison to the previous year. Additionally, the luxury online market is expected to grow 25% by 2025. Given the impact of COVID-19, changes in consumer behaviour, and the predicted growth of the luxury online market, brands can no longer continue to resist the advance of digitisation, but rather, must find ways to adapt to it.

CASE STUDY 1 How Burberry became a digitally innovative brand

Founded in 1856 in London, England, Burberry are best known for their signature trench coat. The first store opened in 1891, followed by their first international store opened in Paris in 1910. To date, the brand has more than 500 stores operating in over 50 countries. Over time the brand began to struggle and was not on par with its peers. In response to this, in 2006, CEO Adriana Ahrendts set out to rejuvenate the brand by targeting younger customers. The key objective was to be the first luxury brand to go fully digital to tap into the millennial consumer market.

In order to reach its target audience, the brand deployed a well-planned digital marketing strategy which paved the way for other luxury fashion brands in embracing 'digital'. During their various campaigns the brand deployed a number of social media platforms, including Facebook, Twitter, and Instagram. The brand used social media as a means to reach and connect with consumers in a number of ways – for example, live-streaming of catwalk shows, purchasing via social media, and encouraging customer engagement and interaction via Facebook and Twitter. The brand also made use of brand advocates during their various campaigns and used celebrity endorsement to enhance brand visibility by sharing images of celebrities wearing their products.

The first digital campaign 'Art of the Trench' was launched by Burberry in November 2009, where consumers were invited to post photographs of themselves wearing their own Burberry trench coats. The drive behind this campaign was to engage consumers in user-generated content and enhance brand loyalty, by establishing a relationship with younger customers. The brand's website is optimised for all platforms and offers e-commerce, live chat, and a call-back facility via their website. Their 'flagship' store is based in Regent Street in London and the layout mimics that of their online store within their website. Between 2006 and 2014, under CEO Ahrendts, Burberry was transformed from a struggling brand to one of the most digitally innovative brands worldwide. Today 60% of their marketing budget is dedicated to digital marketing.

CASE STUDY 2 How Gucci increased sales via e-commerce

The Gucci Group is a multi-brand luxury company who launched a digital marketing initiative in 2010, which included an e-commerce platform. The platform not only enabled personalised user experiences but also supported multiple languages and currencies. By 2017, the company reported that there was a 17% boost in sales, 50% of which were attained via their e-commerce platform (Milnes, 2016). This increased the company's revenue to 3.5 billion USD which has since risen. Currently, the company's online sales account for 100 million unique visitors per day. Their existing e-commerce site is accessible in 28 countries worldwide and via eight languages, and offers benefits such as customer service, free returns, social media, video content, and a store locator option (Finocchiaro, 2017).

During the COVID-19 pandemic it was reported that 'organic' sales decreased by 44% over three months, whilst e-commerce sales increased by 72% (Bloomberg, 2020). In these unprecedented times it is becoming increasing important for luxury brands to tap into the benefits of e-commerce in order to survive. To do this, brands must follow current consumer preferences in terms of targeting the demands of millennial and Generation Z consumers.

Seminar exercises

Discussion topics:

1. Discuss the advantages of the shift from traditional to digital-driven marketing models in response to changes in consumer behaviour.
2. How can a brand incorporate digital models without diluting perceptions of exclusivity? Thinking of your own relationship with luxury brands, in what ways have you engaged with brands online that have made you feel valued as an individual consumer?
3. Brands use a variety of different media channels as part of their communication strategies. Reflect on your own experience and give an example where a brand has used different media channels to encourage you to visit their website, participate in a digital campaign and purchase a product.
4. Identify the need and benefits of an integrated marketing communications strategy for a luxury brand in the digital sphere.

Group exercises:

1. Select a luxury brand of your choice and create a presentation to address the following:
   - How has the brand moved to a digital-driven marketing model?
   - What was the identified need to move towards a digital marketing model?
   - How does the brand use technology to build relationships with consumers?
   - What have been the reported outcomes of incorporating digital technologies?

2. Carry out research into two of the following digital media channels: search engine marketing (SEM), affiliate marketing, social media marketing (SMM) and e-commerce. For each explain the following:
   - explain the concept of the digital channel
   - provide an example of how a company has used the channel successfully
   - report the associated advantages from implementing the digital channel.

3. Choose a luxury brand in a specific industry. Carry out research to identify the following:
   - highlight how they have migrated from a traditional to digital sphere
   - highlight some characteristics of the new age digital customers of luxury, and hence, the channels and messages used as a part of the IMC strategy to reach, engage, and convert them.

References

Abou Nabout, N, Skiera, B, Stepanchuk, T & Geratmeier, E (2012) An analysis of the profitability of fee-based compensation plans for search engine marketing. *International Journal of Research in Marketing.* 29. Pp. 68–80.

Achille, A, Zipser, D (2020) *A Perspective for the Luxury Goods Industry During and After Coronavirus.* McKinsey Report. [online]. Available from: https://www.mckinsey.com/industries/retail/our-insights/a-perspective-for-the-luxury-goods-industry-during-and-after-coronavirus

Ashley, C & Tuten, T (2014) Creative strategies in social media marketing: An exploratory study of branded social content and consumer engagement. *Psychology & Marketing.* 32, 1. Pp. 15–27.

Bailis, R (2017) Which brands are reaching luxury millennial shoppers online? *Internet Retailer.* [Online]. Available from: from www.digitalcommerce360.com/2017/03/22/which-brands-are-reaching-luxury-millennial-shoppers-online/

Baker, J, Ashill, N, Amer, N, & Diab, E (2018) The Internet dilemma: An exploratory study of luxury firms' usage of internet-based technologies. *Journal of Retailing and Consumer Services.* 41. Pp. 37–47.

Bala, M & Verma, D (2018). A critical review of digital marketing. *International Journal of Management, IT & Engineering.* 8, 10. Pp. 321–339.

Bandyopadhyay, S, Wolfe, J & and Kini, R (2009) A critical review of online affiliate models. *Journal of Academy of Business and Economics*. 9, 4. Pp. 141–147.

Bardhi, F, & Eckhardt, G (2017) Liquid consumption. *Journal of Consumer Research*. 44, 3. Pp. 582–597.

Belk, R (2013) Extended self in a digital world. *Journal of Consumer Research*. 40, 3. Pp. 477–500.

Berridge, H (2018) A practical look at the challenges luxury fashion brands face in the wake of digitalization: is it time that luxury fashion brands learn to love e-commerce platforms? *Journal of Intellectual Property Law & Practice*. 13, 11. Pp. 901–909.

Beverland, M (2004) Uncovering 'theories in use': Building luxury wine brands. *European Journal of Marketing*. 38, 3 and 4. Pp. 446–466.

Bhandari, R (2017) Pay per click marketing strategies: A review of empirical evidence. *Journal of Industrial Distribution & Business*. 8, 6. Pp. 7–16.

Bilgin, Y (2018) The effect of social media marketing activities on brand awareness, brand image and brand loyalty. *Business & Management Studies: An International Journal of*. 6, 1. Pp. 128–144.

Bjorn-Andersen, N & Hansen, R (2011) The adoption of Web 2.0 by luxury fashion brands. *Proceedings of the International Conference on Service Management and Innovation with Information Technology*. University of Auckland.

Blasco-Arcas, L, Holmqvist, J, & Vignolles, A (2016) Brand contamination in social media: Consumers' negative influence on luxury brand perceptions: A structured abstract. In *Rediscovering the Essentiality of Marketing*. Cham: Springer. Pp. 265–269.

Bloomberg (2020) Gucci owner sees online leading recovery after sales plunge *The Japan Times*. [Online]. Available from: www.japantimes.co.jp/news/2020/07/29/business/corporate-business/gucci-online-sales-coronavirus/

Bowie, D (2014) Technology-driven online marketing performance measurement: Lessons from affiliate marketing. *International Journal of Online Marketing*. 4, 4. Pp. 1–16.

Brocato, D. (2010) *Push and Pull Marketing Strategies*. Wiley International Encyclopaedia of Marketing.

Brown, B (2009) *The Complete Guide to Affiliate Marketing on the Web*. Atlantic Publishing Group Inc; Ocala, Florida.

Brun, A, Caniato, F, Caridi, M, Castelli, C, Miragliotta, G, Ronchi, S, Sianesi, A & Spina, G (2008) Logistics and supply chain management in luxury fashion retail: Empirical investigation of Italian firms. *International Journal of Production Economics*. 114, 2. Pp. 554–570.

Castello, S & Khelladi, I (2016) Reputation, image, and social media as determinants of e-reputation: The case of digital native and luxury brands. *International Journal of Technology and Human Interaction*. 12, 4. Pp. 48–64.

Chaffey, D & Ellis-Chadwick, F (2019) *Digital Marketing: Strategy, Implementation and Practice*. Seventh Edition. Pearson; Harlow.

Chang, K, Jackson, J & Grover, V (2003) E-commerce and corporate strategy: an executive perspective. *Information and Management*. 40, 7. Pp. 663–675.

Chauhan, S, Thapar, N & Kumar'Ranjan, R (2020) Effect of marketing communications on the consumer decision making: A study of indian life insurance industry. *Sustainable Humanosphere*. 16, 1. Pp. 504–515.

Choi, S, Chai, S, Nam, Y, Yang, S & Protoppa, C (2014) Success factors for luxury e-commerce: Burberry's digital innovation process. *International Journal of Information Systems Management Research and Development*. 4, 1. Pp. 1–10.

Clark, N (2012) *Burberry Boosts Digital Approach with Interactive Campaign*. [Online]. Available from: www.campaignlive.co.uk/burberry-boosts-digital-approach-interactive-campaign/1134144

Clow, K & Baack, D (2018) *Integrated Advertising, Promotion, and Marketing Communications*, 8th Edition. Pearson; Harlow.

Corbitt, B, Thanasankit, T & Yi, H (2003) Trust and e-commerce: a study of consumer perceptions. *Electronic Commerce and Research Applications*. 2, 3 Pp. 203–215.

D'Arpizio, C, Levato, F, Prete, F, Del Fabbro, L, & de Montgolfier, J (2019) The future of Luxury: A look into tomorrow to understand today. *Bain and Company*. [Online] Available from: www.bain.com/insights/luxury-goods-worldwide-market-study-fall-winter-2018/

Dahl, A, Milne, G, & Peltier, J (2019) Digital health information seeking in an omni-channel environment: A shared decision-making and service-dominant logic perspective. *Journal of Business Research*. DOI: 10.1016/J.JBUSRES.2019.02.025

Dall' Olmo Riley, F, & Lacroix, C (2003) Luxury branding on the Internet: Lost opportunity or impossibility? *Marketing Intelligence & Planning*. 21, 2. Pp. 96–104.

Daniel, E, & Wilson, H (2002) Adoption intentions and benefits realised: A study of e-commerce in UK SMEs. *Journal of Small Business and Enterprise Development*. 9, 4. Pp. 331–348

Dann, G. (2012) Remodelling a changing language of tourism: From monologue to dialogue and trialogue. *Sociology*. DOI: 10.25145/JPASOS.2012.10.053.

Dauriz, L, Remy, N, & Sandri, N (2014) Luxury shopping in the digital age. Mckinsey and company. [online]. Available from www.mckinsey.com/industries/retail/our-insights/luxury-shopping-in-the-digital-age

Davis, H (2006) *Search Engine Optimization*. O'Reilly; Sebastopol, California.

Deloitte (2017) *Global Powers of Luxury Goods: The New Luxury Consumer*. Deloitte Report. Deloitte University; Diegem, Berkenlaan.

Dion, D & Arnould, E (2011) Retail Luxury Strategy: Assembling Charisma through Art and Magic. *Journal of Retailing*. 87. DOI: 10.1016/j.jretai.2011.09.001

Dion, D, & Borraz, S (2017) Managing status: How luxury brands shape class subjectivities in the service encounter. *Journal of Marketing*. 81, 5. Pp. 67–85.

Dou, W, Lim, K, Su, C, Zhou, N & Cui, N (2010) Brand positioning strategy using search engine marketing. *Management Information Systems Quarterly*. 34, 2. Pp. 261–279.

Doyle, T & Melanson, J (2001) B2B Web exchanges: easier hyped than done. *Journal of Business Strategy*. 22, 3. Pp. 11–13.

Durmaz, Y & Efendioglu, I (2016) Travel from traditional marketing to digital marketing. *Global Journal of Management and Business Research*. 16, 2. Pp. 34–40.

Dwivedi, Y, Rana, N & Alryalat, M (2017) Affiliate marketing: An overview and analysis of emerging literature. *The Marketing Review*. 17, 1. Pp. 33–50.

Erdogmus, E & Cicek, M (2012) The impact of social media marketing on brand loyalty. *Procedia: Social and Behavioural Sciences*. 58. Pp. 1353–1360.

Evans, D (2010) *Social Media Marketing: The Next Generation of Business Engagement*. Wiley; Indiana, Indianapolis.

Fernandes, N (2020) Economic effects of coronavirus outbreak (COVID-19) on the world economy. *Social Science Research Network*. [online]. Available from: http://dx.doi.org/10.2139/ssrn.3557504

Fill, C & Turnbull, S (2019) *Marketing communications: touchpoints, sharing and disruption*. Pearson; UK, Harlow.

Finne, Å. & Grönroos, C (2009) Rethinking marketing communication: From integrated marketing communication to relationship communication. *Journal of Marketing Communications*, 15, 2–3. Pp.179–195.

Finocchiaro, P (2017) Gucci pushes iPad engagement with remodelled ecommerce site. *Industry Dive*.

[Online]. Available from: www.retaild ive.com/ex/mobilecommercedaily/ gucci-pushes-ipad-engagement-with-remodeled-digital-commerce-site

Fiorini, P & Lipsky, L (2012) Search marketing traffic and performance models. *Computer Standards & Interfaces*. 34. Pp. 517–526.

Fritze, M, Marchand, A, Eisingerich, A, & Benkenstein, M (2020). Access-based services as substitutes for material possessions: The role of psychological ownership. *Journal of Service Research*.

Gensler, S, Völckner, F, Liu-Thompkins, Y & Wiertz, C (2013). Managing brands in the social media environment. *Journal of Interactive Marketing*. 27. Pp. 242–256.

Ghose, A & Yang, S (2009) An empirical analysis of search engine advertising: sponsored search in electronic markets. *Management Science*. 55, 10. Pp. 1605–1622.

Goldschmidt, S, Junghagen, S, & Harris, U (2003) *Strategic Affiliate Marketing*. EE Publishing; Cheltenham.

Green, D (2003) Search engine marketing: Why is benefits us all. *Business Information Review*. 20, 4. Pp. 195–202.

Grossman, G & Sharpiro, C (1988) foreign counterfeiting of status goods. *Quarterly Journal of Business Economics*. 103, 1. Pp. 79–100.

Guercini, S, Ranfagni, S & Runfola, A (2020) E-commerce internationalization for top luxury fashion brands: Some emerging strategic issues. *Journal of Management Development*.

Han, L, Nunes, J & Dreze, X (2010) Signalling Status with Luxury Goods: The Role of Brand Prominence. *Journal of Marketing*. 74. DOI: 10.1509/jmkg.74.4.15

Haq, Z (2012) Affiliate marketing programs: A study of consumer attitude towards affiliate marketing programs among Indian users. *International Journal of Research Studies in Management* 1, 1. Pp. 127–137.

Heine, K & Berghaus, B (2014) Luxury goes digital: How to tackle the digital luxury brand-consumer touchpoints. *Journal of Global Fashion Marketing*. 5, 3. Pp. 223–234.

Isoraite, M & Miniotiene, N (2018) Electronic commerce: theory and practice. *Integrated Journal of Business & Economics*. 2, 2. Pp. 73–79.

Janssen, D & Van Heck, E (2007) *How Will Online Affiliate Marketing Networks Impact Search Engine Rankings?* July. ERIM Report Series Reference No. ERS-2007-042-LIS

Jones, K. (2008) *Search Engine Optimization*. Wiley; Indiana.

Kannan, P & Hongshuang, A (2017) Digital marketing: A framework, review and research agenda. *International Journal of Research in Marketing*. 34, 1. Pp. 22–45.

Kapferer, J (2015) Kapferer on Luxury: How Luxury Brands Can Grow Yet Remain Rare. Kogan Press; London.

Kapferer, Jean (2010) All that glitters is not green: The challenge of sustainable luxury. *European Business Review*

Kapferer, J, & Bastien, V (2012) *The Luxury Strategy: Break the Rules of Marketing To Build Luxury Brands*. Logan Page Publishers; Philadelphia.

Kayumovich, K & Annauradovna, F (2020) The main convenience of internet marketing from traditional marketing. *Academy*. 1, 52.

Khan, A (2016) Electronic commerce: A study on benefits and challenges in an emerging economy. *Global Journal of Management and Business*. 6, 1.

Kim, A & Ko, E (2012) Do social media marketing activities enhance customer equity? Am empirical study of luxury fashion brands. *Journal of Business Research*. 65, 10. Pp. 1480–1486.

Kim, S & Mar, J (2019) A study on the digital transformation strategy of a fashion brand: Focused on the Burberry2 case. *The Research Journal of the Costume Culture*. 27, 5. Pp. 449–460.

Knezevi, B & Vidas-Bubanja, M (2010) Search engine marketing as a key factor for generating quality online visitors. *Proceedings of the 33rd International Convention MIPRO.* Pp. 1193–1196.

Ko, E, Costello, J & Taylor, C (2017) What is a luxury brand? A new definition and review of the literature. *Journal of Business Research.* 99. DOI: 10.1016/j.jbusres.2017.08.023

Kritzinger, W & Weideman, M (2013) Search engine optimization and pay-per-click marketing strategies. *Journal of Organisational Computing and Electronic Commerce.* 23, 3. Pp. 273–286.

Lee, C. (2018) Wise up: the biggest mistakes luxury brands are making with China's Gen Z. *Jing Daily.* [Online]. Available from https://jingdaily.com/luxury-brands-china-gen-z/

Lin, K & Lu, H (2011) Why people use social networking sites: An empirical study integrating network externalities and motivation theory. *Computers in Human Behaviour.* 27. Pp. 1152–116.

Ling, K, Beenen, G, Ludford, P, Wang, X, Chang, K, Cosley, D, Frankowski, D, Terveen, L, Rashid, A, Resnick, P. & Kraut, R (2005). Using social psychology to motivate contributions to online communities. *Journal of Computer-Mediated Communication.* 10, 4.

Lipsman, A, Mudd, G, Rich, M & Brunch, S (2012) The power of 'like': How brands reach (and influence) fans through social-media marketing. *Journal of Advertising Research.* 52, 1. Pp. 40–52.

Liu, X, Shin, H & Burns, C (2019) Examining the impact of luxury brand's social media marketing on customer engagement: Using big data analytics and natural language processing. *Journal of Business Research.* 35. Pp. 815–826.

Lixandroiu, R & Maican, C (2015) An analysis on choosing a proper ecommerce platform. *Proceedings of the International Conference on Risk in Contemporary Economy.* Pp. 54–9. Romania.

McCarthy, J (1960) Recursive functions of symbolic expressions and their computation by machine, Part I. *Communications of the ACM.* 3, 4. Pp. 184–195.

McKnight, D, Choudhury, V & Kacmar, C (2002) Developing and validating trust measures for e-commerce: an integrative typology. *Information Systems Research.* 13, 3. Pp. 227–359.

Mekonnen, A & Larner, L (2018) Exclusivity dared: Impact of digital marketing on luxury fashion brands. In Ilson Ozuem & Tiika Azemi (Eds.) *Digital Marketing Strategies for Fashion and Luxury Brands.* IGI Global; Hershey, Pennsylvania.

Milnes, H (2016) The digital strategy driving Gucci's growth. *Digiday.* [Online]. Available from: https://digiday.com/marketing/digital-strategy-driving-guccis-growth/

Mordkovich, B & Mordkovich, E (2007) *Pay-Per-Click Search Engine Marketing Handbook.* MordCom; New York

Mu, W, Lennon, S & Liu, W (2020) Top online luxury apparel and accessories retailers: What are they doing right? *Fashion and Textiles.* 7, 6.

Neti, S (2011) Social media and its role in marketing. *International Journal of Enterprise Computing and Business Systems.* 1, 2. Pp. 1–5.

Okonkwo, U (2009) Sustaining the luxury brand on the internet *Journal of Brand Management.* 16. Pp. 302–310.

Oliveira, M & Fernandez, T (2020) Luxury brands and social media: drivers and outcomes of consumer engagement on Instagram. *Journal of Strategic Marketing.* Pp. 1–19.

Pereira, H, de Fátima Salgueiro, M & Mateus, I (2014) Say yes to Facebook and get your customers involved! Relationships in a world of social networks. *Business Horizons.* 57. Pp. 695–702.

Phan, M, Thomas, R & Heine, K (2011) Social media and luxury brand management: The case of Burberry. *Journal of Global Fashion Marketing.* 2, 4. Pp. 213–222.

Pini, F & Quaquarelli, B. (2018) Organisational and marketing challenges in designing and implementing an omnichannel strategy for luxury fashion brands. In Ilson Ozuem & Tiika Azemi (Eds.) *Digital Marketing Strategies for Fashion and Luxury Brands*. IGI Global; Hershey, Pennsylvania.

Ratnasingam, P (2002) Perceived versus realised benefits in e-commerce adoption. *Malaysian Journal of Library & Information Science*. 7, 2. Pp. 57–68.

Rayport, J & Jaworski, B (2001) *E-commerce*. McGraw-Hill/Irwin; Boston, MA.

Rios, A (2016) The Impact of the Digital Revolution in the Development of Market and Communication Strategies for the Luxury Sector. *Central European Business Review*. 5. Pp. 17–36.

Roper, S, Caruana, R, Medway, D, & Murphy, P (2013). Constructing luxury brands Exploring the role of consumer discourse. *European Journal of Marketing*. 47, 3 & 4, Pp. 375–400.

Sanyala, S & Hisamb, M (2019) Factors Affecting Customer Satisfaction with Ecommerce Websites – An Omani Perspective. Proceedings of the *International Conference on Digitization*. Pp. 232–236. United Arab Emirates.

Sen, R (2014) Optimal search engine marketing strategy. *International Journal of Electronic Commerce*. 10. Pp. 9–25.

Senn, J (2000) Business-to-business ecommerce. *Information Systems Management*. Spring. Pp. 23–32.

Shah, D & Murthi, B (2020) Marketing in a data-driven digital world: Implications for the role and scope of marketing. *Journal of Business Research*. DOI: 10.1016/J.BUSRES.2020.06.062

Shah, D, & Shay, E (2019) How and why artificial intelligence, mixed reality and blockchain technologies will change marketing we know today. In A. Parvatiyar, & R. Sisodia (Eds). *Handbook of Advances in Marketing in an Era of Disruptions*. New Delhi; SAGE Publications.

Sherman, L (2009) Online Luxury Retail Remains Elusive. *Business Week*. November, p. 9.

Shin, N (2001) Strategies for competitive advantage in electronic commerce *Journal of Electronic Commerce Research*. 2, 4. Pp. 34–41.

Smith, P (2015) *The SOSTAC Guide to Your Perfect Digital Marketing Plan* PR Smith. http://www.prsmith.org/books

Straker, K & Wrigley, C (2016) Emotionally engaging customers in the digital age the case study of 'Burberry love'. *Journal of Fashion Marketing*. 20, 3. Pp. 276– 299.

Sunghee, K (2013) A classification of luxury fashion brands e-commerce sites. *Journal of Fashion Business*. 17, 6. Pp. 125–140.

Syed Shah Alam, A, Khatibi, A, Bin Ismail, H & Ahmad, I (2005) Perceived benefits of e-commerce adoption in the electronic manufacturing companies in Malaysia. *Journal of Social Sciences*. 1, 3. Pp. 188–193.

Tafesse, W & Wien, A (2017) A framework for categorizing social media posts. *Cogent Business & Management*. 4. Pp. 1–22.

Tairova, M, Giyazova, N & Dustova, A (2020) Goals and Objectives of Integrating Marketing Communications. *Economics*. 2. Pp. 5–7.

Tarasewich, P, Nickerson, R and Warkentin, M (2002) Issues in mobile e-commerce. *Communications of the Association for Information Systems*. 8, 3. Pp. 41–64.

Tiago, M & Verissimo, J (2014) Digital marketing and social media: Why bother? *Business Horizons* 57, 6. Pp. 703–708.

Turban, E. (2002) *Electronic Commerce 2002: A Managerial Perspective*. 2nd Edition. Prentice Hall; Hoboken, New Jersey, U.S.

Tuten, T & Solomon, M (2015) *Social Media Marketing* (2nd ed.) Sage; Thousand Oaks, CA

Vigneron, F, & Johnson, L (2004) Measuring perceptions of brand luxury. *The Journal of Brand Management.* 11, 6. Pp. 484–506.

Vladimíra, J (2013) Affiliate marketing in the context of online marketing. *Review of Applied Socio- Economic Research.* 5, 1. Pp. 106–111.

Vries, L, Genseler, S & Leeflang, P (2012) Popularity of brand posts on brand fan pages: An investigation of the effects of social media marketing. *Journal of Interactive Marketing.* 26, 2. Pp. 83–91.

Warkentin, M, Sugumaran, V & Bapna, R (2001) Intelligent agents for electronic commerce: trends and future impact on business models and markets. In S. Rahman and R. Bignall (Eds.) *Internet Commerce and Software Agents: Cases, Technologies and Opportunities.* Idea Group Publishing; Hershey, PA, Pp. 101–120.

Wirtz, J, Holmqvist, J, & Fritze, M (2020) Luxury services. *Journal of Service Management,* 31, 4. Pp. 665–691.

Wu, M, Chen, C & Chaney, I. (2012) Luxury brands in the digital age – the trust factor. In Wiedmann, K & Hennigs, N (Eds) *Luxury Marketing: A Challenge for*

Theory and Practice. Springer-Gabler; Wiesbaden. Pp. 207–219.

Yang, A, Carlson, J & Ross, W (2015) Brand engagement on social media: will firm's social media efforts influence search engine advertising effectiveness? *Journal of Marketing Management.* 32, 5. Pp. 526–557.

Yang, Z, Shi, Y, & Wang, B. (2015b) Search engine marketing, financing ability and firm performance in e-commerce. *Procedia Computer Science.* 55. Pp. 1106–1112.

Yasmin, A, Tasneem, S & Fatema, K (2015) Effectiveness of Digital Marketing in the Challenging Age: An Empirical Study. *International Journal of Management Science and Business Administration,* 1, 5. Pp. 69–80.

Zaglia, M (2013) Brand communities embedded in social networks. *Journal of Business Research.* 66. Pp. 216–223.

Zhuang, Y & Lederer, A (2014) An instrument for measuring the business benefits of ecommerce retailing. *International Journal of E-Commerce Retailing.* 7, 3. Pp. 65.

CHAPTER 9

The future of commerce with digital business

Patrice Seuwou and Vincent F. Adegoke

9.1 INTRODUCTION

In today's digital world, people are spending more money online, which has shifted business emphasis to digital sources of revenue and digital channels. The growth of the digital economy has made people more familiar with digital products and services, which has driven companies to seek new competitive advantages in the digital space. 'Business' may be understood as the organised efforts of enterprises to supply consumers with goods and services for a profit. Since the introduction of the Internet more than three decades ago, we have experienced the slow death of the high street market. Most businesses are now going online, and some are becoming digital businesses, with traditional businesses disappearing. A digital business could be defined as a business that uses technology to create new value in business models, customer experiences, and the internal capabilities that support its core operations. We are moving from brick and mortar to click and order. The term digital business includes both digital-only brands and traditional players that are transforming their businesses with digital technologies. Digital technologies have transformed entire industries and created challenges for numerous traditional business models (Lansiti & Lakhani, 2014). Established organisations that neglected the transformative power of digital technologies were dared by innovative digital start-ups, lost their competitiveness, or were driven out of business (Downes & Nunes, 2013; Hess, Matt, Benlian, & Wiesböck, 2016). For others, which have willingly embraced digital technologies, novel market opportunities have emerged and so far, unsolved problems have come within reach to be solved.

In this chapter, we'll explore some of the key components of digital businesses, why most businesses must go through the process of digitisation, change their business models, reinvent themselves or may have to disappear altogether. We will evaluate why it's so disruptive to traditional business models, and how to prepare for disruption in your industry. The remainder of the chapter is structured as follows: firstly, we explore the emergence of

DOI: 10.4324/9781003015826-12

e-commerce and the death of high street; secondly, we define the concept of Digital Business models; thirdly, we evaluate emerging technologies for competitive advantage; fourthly, we analyse how digital strategies could be used to help businesses thrive; and finally, we look at security concerns and possible cyber-attacks on businesses.

9.2 EMERGENCE OF E-COMMERCE

For most people in the UK, e-commerce is something we participate in daily, like making an online bill payment or purchasing from an online seller. In the past few decades, the evolution of e-commerce has been studied, and followed up, by several researchers and stakeholders in the field. E-commerce (also known as electronic commerce) is the buying and selling of products or services via the Internet. Despite being commonly thought of as a product of the late 1980s and early 1990s, the roots of the World Wide Web, much like e-commerce, lie in the 1960s and 1970s. With the 1969 introduction of Arpanet, the world's first network run on packet-switching technology, users were able to transmit large and complex amounts of data simultaneously. Developed and funded primarily by the Advanced Research Projects Agency (ARPA) and the United States Department of Defence, it was opened to university use in late 1969 for collaborative research and scientific purposes, a decision which, albeit accidentally, led to what many believe is the first e-commerce transaction.

The 1990s was a period of rapid technological advancement in many areas. However, it was the commercialisation of the Internet that led to the greatest expansion of capital growth the world had ever seen (Santos et al., 2017). Following the unprecedented investments in Internet-based companies in the late 1990s at the turn of the year 2000, the 'dotcom' bubble burst and shares crashed. In the UK, the episode dealt a heavy blow to the culture of individual share ownership. Equities entered a bear market after the bubble burst in 2001, which caused several Internet companies to go bust. In today's digital society, e-commerce is one of the most visible examples of the way in which information and communication technologies can contribute to economic growth. It can take many forms and involve different transactions, and with shopping behaviours changing, brands must be ready, flexible, and always on. There has been much talk about how Britain's high streets are entering their death throes, their inevitable decline accelerated by the overpowering threat of e-commerce (Hughes and Jackson, 2015). Many high street shops are closing mainly because most people are finding online shopping more convenient, as it saves time and the cost of transport, and is more efficient. With cities being complex entities and a product of economic, political, and social processes that evolve over time and across spatial entities, they are 'gradually transformed in a process of continual creative destruction and reconstruction' (Bryson, 1997, p. 1439, drawing on Harvey, 1978; Massey, 1984; Zukin, 1991). The number of shops in the United Kingdom has been decreasing for at least a century. A study in the 1920s estimated that there were 950,000 shops in the so-called nation of shopkeepers: 583,000 in 1950 and just over 300,000 shops in the UK by 1997. By then these were highly efficient businesses. Self-service meant they needed fewer staff per shop, even if that meant they had to introduce measures like rigid plastic packaging to protect fragile goods (McCrudden, 2019).

There are massive changes taking place in most countries of the West. They are all going through some level of transformation, and this can be seen within the retail sector, due to, for example, retail business innovation; pressures from consumers; technological innovation; and political intervention with the actions of occupiers, investors, and developers made within an economic and regulatory context (Bryson, 1997). This comes alongside changes in consumer spending and behaviour, and central and business financial restructuring.

9.3 DIGITAL BUSINESS MODELS

9.3.1 Defining a business model

Traditionally, managers and entrepreneurs faced a conflict between pursuing the company's main purpose, maximising profits, and achieving other purposes, such as generating positive social and/or environmental impact. These purposes conflicted because one usually came at the expense of the other. A business model describes the rationale of how an organisation creates, delivers, and captures value (Osterwalder & Pigneur, 2010). It depicts the way a company works, how a company intends to make money, or the logic by which it sustains itself financially.

Different companies can have similar offerings but different business models. In theory and practice, the term 'business model' is used for a broad range of informal and formal descriptions to represent core aspects of an organisation or business, including purpose, business process, target customers, offerings, strategies, infrastructures, organisational structures, sourcing, trading practices, and operational processes and policies, including culture.

9.3.2 The Business Model Canvas

The Business Model Canvas (BMC) is a strategic management tool to define and communicate a business idea or concept quickly and easily. It is a one-page document which works through the fundamental elements of a business or product, structuring an idea in a coherent way. Figure 9.1 below depicts the nine building blocks of the business model canvas.

These building blocks are further detailed below.

9.3.2.1 CUSTOMER SEGMENTS   This component answers the questions: 'For whom are we creating value? Who are our most important customers?' An organisation serves one or several customer segments:

- Mass market
- Niche market
- Segmented

FIGURE 9.1 The key Building blocks of the Business Model Canvas		
1. List the top three segments. Look for the segments that provide the most revenue.	2. What are your products and services? What is the job you get done for your customer?	3. List your top three revenue streams. If you do things for free, add them here too.
4. How do you communicate with your customer? How do you deliver the value proposition?	5. How does this show up and how do you maintain the relationship?	6. What do you do every day to run your business model?
7. The people, knowledge, means, and money you need to run your business.	8. List the partners that you can't do business without (not suppliers).	9. List your top costs by looking at activities and resources.

- Diversified
- Multi-sided platform

9.3.2.2 VALUE PROPOSITIONS   This component answers the questions: 'What value do we deliver to the customer? Which one of our customer's problems are we helping to solve? What bundles of products and services are we offering to each customer segment? Which customer needs are we satisfying?' It seeks to solve customer problems and satisfy customer needs with value propositions. Characteristics might include:

• Newness • Performance • Customisation • 'Getting the Job Done' • Design	• Brand/status • Price • Cost reduction • Risk reduction • Accessibility • Convenience/usability

9.3.2.3 DISTRIBUTION   CHANNELS This   component   answers   the questions: 'Through which channels do our customer segments want to be reached? How are we reaching them now? How are our channels integrated? Which ones work best? Which ones are most cost-efficient? How are we integrating them with customer routines?' Value propositions are delivered to customers through communication, distribution, and sales channels.

9.3.2.4 CHANNEL PHASES

1. Awareness – How do we raise awareness about our company's products and services?
2. Evaluation – How do we help customers evaluate our organisation's value proposition?
3. Purchase – How do we allow customers to purchase specific products and services?

4. Delivery – How do we deliver a value proposition to customers?
5. After sales – How do we provide post-purchase customer support?

9.3.2.5 CUSTOMER RELATIONSHIPS This component answers the questions: 'What type of relationship does each of our customer segments expect us to establish and maintain with them? Which ones have we established? How are they integrated with the rest of our business model? How costly are they?' Customer relationships are established and maintained with each customer segment. Examples might include: Personal Assistance, Dedicated Personal Assistance, Self-Service, Automated Services, Communities and Co-creation.

9.3.2.6 REVENUE STREAMS This component answers the questions: 'For what value are our customers really willing to pay? For what do they currently pay? How are they currently paying? How would they prefer to pay? How much does each revenue stream contribute to overall revenues?'

Types:	Fixed pricing	Dynamic pricing

• Asset sale
• Usage fee
• Subscription fees
• Lending/Renting/
  Leasing
• Licensing
• Brokerage fees
• Advertising
	• List price
	• Product feature
	  dependent
	• Customer segment
	  dependent
	• Volume dependent
		• Negotiation
		  (bargaining)
		• Yield management
		• Real-time-market

9.3.2.7 KEY RESOURCES This component answers the questions: 'What key resources do our value propositions – our distribution channels, customer relationships, revenue streams – require?' Key resources are the assets required to offer and deliver the previously described elements. Types of resources include: physical, intellectual (brand patents, copyrights, data), human, and financial. In terms of 'key activities', here we address the question, 'what are the most important activities?'

9.3.2.8 KEY PARTNERS This component answers the questions: 'Who are our key partners? Who are our key suppliers? Which key resources are we acquiring from partners? Which key activities do partners perform?' Some activities are outsourced, and some resources are acquired outside the enterprise. Motivations for partnerships might include: optimisation and economy, reduction of risk and uncertainty, and acquisition of resources and activities.

9.3.2.9 COST STRUCTURE This component answers the questions: 'What are the most important costs inherent in our business model? Which key resources are most expensive? Which key activities are most expensive?' The business model elements result in the cost structure. Here we ask ourselves if our business is: cost driven (leanest cost structure, low price value proposition, maximum automation, extensive outsourcing) or value driven (focused on value creation, premium value proposition). Sample characteristics here include: fixed costs (salaries, rents, utilities), variable costs, economies of scale, and economies of scope.

9.3.2.10 EXAMPLES OF BUSINESS MODEL INNOVATION   Well-known brands that are examples of business model innovation are:

- Uber: Taxi industry
- Netflix: TV industry
- Spotify: Music industry
- Amazon: Retail industry
- Airbnb: Hotel industry
- Tesla: Automobile industry
- Tinder: Online dating industry

The Business Model Canvas can be printed out on a large surface so that groups of people can jointly start sketching and discussing business model elements with post-it notes or board markers. It is a hands-on tool that fosters understanding, discussion, creativity, and analysis.

9.4 EMERGING TECHNOLOGIES FOR COMPETITIVE ADVANTAGE

9.4.1 Smart cities

A city is a large and permanent human ecosystem which provides a lot of services and opportunities to its citizens. Urban growth, and city population, are growing at a fast pace causing various issues to the environment, as well as the economic and social sustainability of cities (Bibri and Krogstie, 2017; Neirotti et al., 2014). Traffic congestion, poor urban infrastructure, health issues, energy shortages, educational challenges (Lee et al., 2013), inadequate housing, increasing crime rates, higher unemployment, ageing infrastructure, power thefts, issues in supply connections, insufficient power generations capacity, high power loss in transmission, frequent power breakdowns, and lack of real time data sharing are some of common concerns in existing cities, mostly in developing countries. Many cities are enhancing the quality and performance of urban services by being digitalised, intelligent, and smarter.

According to predictions in the literature, by the year 2026, the first city with more than 50,000 inhabitants and no traffic lights will be in existence. The policymakers and city authorities are exploring solutions to deliver the new services in an efficient, responsive, and sustainable manner for a large population. Many cities will connect services, utilities and roads to the Internet which will have a huge impact on future businesses. These smart cities will manage their energy, material flows, logistics, and traffic. Progressive cities, such as Singapore and Barcelona, are already implementing many new data-driven services, including intelligent parking solutions, smart rubbish collection, and intelligent lighting. Smart cities are continuously extending their network of sensor technology and working on their data platforms, which will be the core for connecting the different technology projects and adding future services based on data analytics and predictive modelling (Kumar et al., 2020).

9.4.2 Artificial intelligence (AI)

Digital financial inclusion is increasingly becoming central in the debate on how to ensure that people who are at the lower levels of the pyramid become financially active (Peric, 2015). Banks and non-bank institutions are coming together to widen financial access using digital financial approaches to include those who are financially excluded and the under-served populations (Peric, 2015). Banks and non-banking institutions are building on digital ways that were in use for years through the direct application of artificial intelligence (AI) to improve access even to the people who were previously served by the formal financial institutions (Alameda, 2020; Peric, 2015). The fourth industrial revolution is bringing changes in traditional businesses and the banking sector which was built in the industrial revolution and premised on paper and the physical distribution of cash (Alameda, 2020).

The term 'fintech' (or financial technologies) is used to describe different innovative business models that have great potential to transform the businesses and the financial services industry (Mamoshina et al., 2018). The fintech business model offers various financial products or services in an automated fashion through the wide use of the internet (Paul, 2019). Technologies that are driving industry 4.0 such as AI, machine learning, cognitive computing and distributed ledger technologies can be used to supplement fintech new entrants and traditional incumbents (Lopes and Pereira, 2019). Some other AI technologies that can be applied in the fintech sector to promote financial inclusion include audio processing, knowledge representation, speech to text, deep learning, expert systems, natural language processing, machine learning (ML), robotics, and symbolic logic (Paul, 2019). It is believed that the popularity of AI technologies boomed in 2011, when companies such as Google, Microsoft, IBM, and Facebook embarked on a massive investment in AI and machine learning to be applied in the commercial space. And this will play a very important role in future businesses, particularly in the developed world.

9.4.3 Robotic Process Automation (RPA)

RPA is the automation of services tasks that reproduce the work that humans do (van der Aalst, 2018). The automation is done with the help of software robots or AI workers that can perform, accurately, repetitive tasks. The task instructions are set by the developer using some form of screen recording and defining variables. These tasks include actions like logging into applications, copying, and pasting data, opening emails, and filling forms among others (Asquith & Horsman, 2019). Van der Aalst et al. (van der Aalst, 2018) state that 'RPA is an umbrella term for tools that operate on the user interface of other computer systems'. Although traditional forms of process automation (such as screen recording, scraping, and macros) also rely on the computer's user interface, RPA's core function is via element identification and not by screen coordinates (Asquith & Horsman, 2019) or Xpath selections. This, in most cases, provides a more intelligent interaction with the user interface.

Commercial vendors of RPA tools report a surge in demand since 2016 (van der Aalst, 2018) and we see some research in which these tools are used for automating digital forensics (Asquith & Horsman, 2019), auditing (Moffitt et al., 2018), and industry (Madakam, 2019). The advent of the fourth industrial revolution (Industry 4.0) is paving the way for new ways to automate mundane rules-based business processes, using RPA tools on information obtained from smart devices (Madakam, 2019). For business processes, RPA is the extrapolation of a human worker's repetitive tasks by a robot (where those tasks are done quickly and profitably). This aims to replace people by automation in an outside-in manner. Unlike traditional methods, RPA is not part of the information infrastructure but rather sits on top of it, implying a low level of intrusiveness (Enríquez, 2020), and possibly reducing costs. Some reports present a 30% to 50% decrease in operational costs of transactional activities within shared services with the use of RPA technologies (Williams & Allen, 2017).

9.4.4 Blockchain technology

Blockchain technology entered public awareness with its first application, the cryptocurrency bitcoin (Nakamoto, 2008), which was established in 2009 and currently exhibits a market capitalisation of more than 100 billion USD. In the last decade, blockchain technology has developed significantly and is now implemented in a wide range of scenarios, including Ethereum and Hyperledger Fabric, which allow distributed platforms to function with unprecedented versatility (Lockl et al., 2020). Consequently, many researchers and practitioners have realised that blockchain technology holds disruptive potential beyond its use in cryptocurrencies (Beck, 2018; Fridgen et al., 2018a; Labazova et al., 2019). Blockchain technology permits secure transactions to be made without the involvement of intermediaries, and is, therefore, appealing to individuals as well as to industry and the public sector. The reason for the interest in blockchain is that its central attributes provide security, anonymity, and data integrity, without any third-party organisation in control of the transactions, and therefore it creates interesting research areas, especially from the perspective of technical challenges and limitations. Overall, blockchain as a technology has the potential to change the way transactions are conducted in everyday life. In addition, the applications of blockchain are not limited to cryptocurrencies, for the technology could possibly be applied in various environments where some forms of transactions are done.

9.5 DIGITAL STRATEGY TO HELP THE BUSINESS THRIVE

9.5.1 What is 'Digital Strategy'?

Digital strategy is one those technology buzzwords that can be defined as a plan that employs digital initiatives to achieve organisational goals. It focuses on using technology to improve business performance, creating new products, or reimagining current processes. Therefore, it is used to digitally specify the direction an organisation will take to create new competitive advantages with the use of technology (Reyes, 2022). Porter asserted that strategy is the creation of a unique and valuable position, involving a different set of activities. It is about making trade-offs in competing. Therefore, the essence of strategy is choosing what not to do. Without trade-offs, there would be no need for choice and thus no need for strategy (Porter, 1996). According to Glueck and Jauch, strategy is a unified, comprehensive, and integrated plan designed to ensure that the basic long-term aims or objectives of the enterprises are met (Glueck & Jauch, 1989).

It is part of the contemporary tactics that are required to make dramatic changes to a business model that was no longer sustainable to remain competitive. Digital strategy, which is becoming the essence of business strategy, is a way to achieve the business goals and objectives through the implementation of digital initiatives with the advantages of information technology.

9.5.2 Hierarchy of strategic intent

Strategic intent refers to the purposes that the organisation endeavours to achieve or that indicate the organisation's long-term market position. These could be expressed in terms of hierarchy of strategic intent, as illustrated in Figure 9.2.

The components of the above model are defined in Table 9.1.

9.5.3 Digital strategy application in modern business

Digital strategy uses technology and related capabilities and organisational needs to create, or become, a digital business. This involves the use of

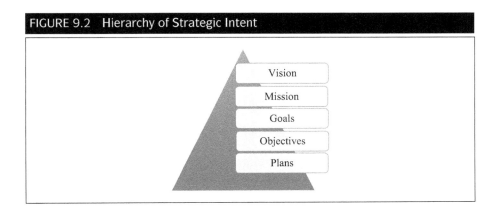

FIGURE 9.2   Hierarchy of Strategic Intent

Vision
Mission
Goals
Objectives
Plans

Table 9.1	Defining components of the Hierarchy of Strategic Intent Model
Component	**Description**
Vision	Refers to aspiration for the future position of the company. It is about the company's dream and base plan for the planning process that are expected to follow.
Mission	Defines the company's business, goals, and ways of achieving them, including the company's present scopes, activities, business niche, and focus.
Goals	Refers to the end results that the organisation is trying to achieve. It helps people to understand the direction that the organisation is heading in, and the purpose of heading there. It must be SMART: specific, measurable, achievable, realistic, and time-based.
Objectives	Refers to the operational definition of goals. The organisation's performance targets, results, and outcomes to accomplish.
Plans	Action plans regarding the performance of required functions to achieve the organisation's objectives and their priorities. It consists of competitive efforts and business approaches that are applied to satisfy customers and achieve organisational goals and objectives.

technology to improve efficiency, value, and innovation (Reyes, 2022). It is a crucial key component of the digital transformation process which ensures that technology is being implemented in a way that supports business models and objectives. Several establishments define great digital transformation strategies, but most digital transformation projects fail due to poor strategy execution (Correani, et al., 2020).

Digital transformation drives change in the areas of customer experience, operational processes and business models (Gobble, 2018). The way organisations get work done is changing rapidly with technology being integrated with businesses and liquid workforces. To remain contemporary, businesses need modern business strategy that is built on strategic and operational agility to thrive and grow, especially in today's apprehensive times (Lau, 2020). There have been seismic changes in what customers are buying and how they are buying it. Analysis of consumer behaviour and marketing strategy shows that 60% of consumers now focus on buying essential items, and 29% say that their shopping behaviours have changed forever. The ever-changing consumer behaviour means that 75% of consumers now prefer to receive brand communications via email or mobile, and a third prefer to start customer support interactions via phone or customer service representatives (Jarry, 2021).

The COVID-19 pandemic has forced a few businesses to rethink the marketing strategy of their products and services. This has resulted in a high rise in the use of advancing tools and application of real options to business strategy (Ferreira, 2013) in decision making. It is also used to meet real-time demand and delivery of goods and services to customers in e-commerce, digital marketing, supply chain marketing, and other contemporary businesses.

9.5.4 Building a digital strategy

Digital strategy involves the application of digital technologies to business models to accomplish new, differentiating business capabilities. Digital strategy is the future solution to maximise the business benefits of data assets and technology with focus on initiatives, innovation, and related areas Bharadwaj, et al., 2013; Evans, et al., 2008). The steps in building a digital strategy are as follows: establish your goals, formulate your strategy, set your objectives, set key performance indicators (KPIs), build a content plan, analyse and execute, and analyse and adjust.

9.5.4.1 THE CASE OF BLOCKBUSTER AND NETFLIX   Blockbuster had a compelling business model. Its value proposition was enabling consumers to watch movies in the comfort of their own homes with an extensive value delivery network. It also had an innovative barcode system to track customers and their fees. However, Blockbuster could have created novel films and presented premieres of films, but failed to keep itself alive due to its refusal to make changes to its core business models in the face of aggressive competition from Netflix, including a previous rejection of Netflix's partnership proposal to Blockbuster (Satell, 2014).

Failure to build and adapt to digital strategy led to the demise of Blockbuster. It was hindered by its old, workable, rigid business models. Netflix proved to be disruptive innovation to Blockbuster's business despite being a small, niche service at the time when they launched their streaming service. Their digital service moved Netflix from a slightly less convenient but cheaper competitor, to the realm of innovative disruption; an innovator offering better and cheaper goods that eventually destroyed Blockbuster.

9.5.4.2 THE CASE OF NOKIA AND APPLE   Nokia's strategic model was excessively focused on enterprise over consumer tastes and preferences. It was a pervasive bureaucracy, leading to an inability to act, destructive internal competition, and the failure to realise the importance of lifestyle products like the iPhone (Cord, 2014). Apple's management model is completely different compared to that of Nokia. Apple has no official strategy; however, Nokia, in contrast, has articulated its strategic plan meticulously (Peltonen, 2018), which is difficult to change. Apple's management vision is about innovation, simplicity, and intuitive use of guided decisions, without any heavy bureaucratic decision-making machinery or the interference of lower-level managers (Isaacson, 2011), which Nokia lacks. Therefore, Nokia Corporation's failure to develop a successful strategic response to the threats of Apple and Google in the smartphone business worsened its situation through several badly timed decisions (Lamberg, et al., 2021) that eventually ruined Nokia.

9.6 SECURING YOUR DIGITAL BUSINESS IN THE CYBERWORLD

9.6.1 The problem of information system security

Information is an asset which, like other important business assets, has value to an organisation and consequently needs to be suitably protected. Information exists in many forms:

- printed or written on paper
- stored electronically
- transmitted by post or electronic means
- visual, e.g. videos, diagrams
- published on the Web
- verbal/oral, e.g. conversations, phone calls
- intangible, e.g. knowledge, experience, expertise, ideas.

Whatever form the information takes, or means by which it is shared or stored, it should always be appropriately protected. Regarding the Information Lifecycle, information can be created, owned (it is an asset), stored, processed, transmitted/communicated, used (for proper or improper purposes), modified or corrupted, shared or disclosed (whether appropriately or not), destroyed or lost, stolen, controlled, secured, and protected throughout its existence. In the information age, we will be going online more and providing more personal information (email, electronic transfer), and business transactions/e-commerce. The Internet allows an attacker to operate anywhere in the world, from their home desk. They just need to find one weakness, so a security analyst needs to close every vulnerability. By any measure, the problem of data loss or theft due to breaches has reached crisis proportions. For every cyber criminal's gain, it is a great loss to a law-abiding citizen. Aside from individual, national and personal losses, it was estimated that the world economy had lost up to two trillion USD by 2019 (Morgan, 2019).

9.6.2 Security concerns and cyber-attacks on small businesses

Understanding cybersecurity starts with the basic assumption that in cyberspace (a generic name for all online or electronic platforms), we all are attractive targets for attacks by cyber criminals. The intended objects could be our money or data, usernames, passwords, documents, emails, and online presence, among others. Most cyberattacks are generic and can happen to anybody, although personalised attacks do occur. One basic and common enabler of cyberattack is human error. These enablers could be as simple as trusting the electronically sent instructions in a phishing email, to as complex as criminals posing as clients, vendors or even employees or professionals with an aim of gaining access to your assets, both financial and others (Shelby, 2018; Sule et al., 2021). Table 9.2 illustrates some common threats to information systems.

TABLE 9.2   Common threats to information systems

Common threats to information systems: Who is knocking at the door?	
• Hacker, Cracker • Denial-of-Service (DoS) Attacks • Distributed Denial-of-Service (DDoS) Attacks • Smurfing • Spoofing attacks • Sniffer • Network scanning tools • Operating System (OS) attacks • Remote Access • Phishing • Pharming • Click fraud • Social engineering attacks • Identity thieves • Human error • Intellectual property theft • Expenses fraud • Hardware issues (computer power supply failure, lack of capacity) • Software issue (bugs or design flaws, data corruption)	• Accidents • Natural disasters (fire, flood, storm, earthquake, lightning, tsunami, volcanic eruption) • Sabotage (industrial and individual) • Vandalism • Theft • Data breach • Unauthorised access to company information • Unauthorised access to customer information • Computer viruses and malware • Trajan horses • Worms • Ransomware • Spyware • Adware • Cyberterrorism and cyberwarfare • Services issues (power cuts, network outages)

The digital space, and digital systems, are core operating contexts for most businesses and their associated activities, whether entering economic relations with customers purchasing goods and services, storing and sharing data, or undertaking commercially sensitive activities that involve confidential information (Office for National Statistics, 2019; Buil-Gil et al., 2021).

9.6.3 Information security standard

Over the years, ISS standards and frameworks have been playing a pivotal role in the dissemination of now much-needed holistic (technical, organisational, and managerial) approaches (Von Solms, 1999). Among them, ISO/IEC 27001 is probably the most renowned one, being the third most widespread ISO certification worldwide, following ISO 9001 and ISO 14001 (ISO, 2019). The standard was designed and published jointly by the International Organization for Standardization (ISO) and the International Electrotechnical Commission (IEC) in 2005, as an evolution of BS 7799 (Culot et al., 2021). It '[…] specifies the requirements for establishing, implementing, maintaining, and continually improving an information security management system (ISMS) within the context of the organization'. The requirements '[…] are generic and are intended to be applicable to all organizations, regardless of type, size or nature' (ISO/IEC 27001:2013). Several leading organisations ask their business partners to be

ISO/IEC 27001 certified (for example, Netflix for post-production partners), and widespread publicity has been given over the years to the attainment of ISO/IEC 27001 certification by prominent technological providers. These include Apple Internet Services, Amazon Web Services, GE Digital, several Microsoft business units, and, more recently, Facebook's Workplace (e.g. Venters and Whitley, 2012).

9.7 CHAPTER SUMMARY

The discussion in this chapter begins with a summary of emergence of e-commerce. E-commerce encompasses business that involves buying and selling goods, transmitting funds or data over the Internet. E-commerce originated as a standard for the exchange of business documents like orders or invoices, between suppliers and business customers. World Wide Web (WWW) technology has unceasingly improved to enhance the security standards and e-commerce needs over the Internet. The main goal of e-commerce is to reach the maximum customers at the right time in order to increase sales and profitability of business, which WWW technology is playing a major role in fulfilling.

Digital business models rely on technology to create digital services and products that customers are willing to buy. It assists in creating and delivering value added products and services, at reduced cost, that could be personalised to enhance customer experiences. However, it could be highly disruptive to established businesses.

The success of digital transformation depends on a well-designed and well-executed digital strategy. As enterprises are continuously integrating technology into their businesses, it is changing the way in which they carry out their work and deliver their products and services. The technological changes involve digital innovation strategy to remain competitive. This requires a plan of action that is designed to achieve business goals through the implementation of digital initiatives. It entails the support of tools and frameworks to enhance digital innovation processes.

CASE STUDY 1 How Amazon became a world brand through innovation and digital strategy

Amazon was founded in 1994, by Jeff Bezos, as a virtual bookstore start-up company in Seattle, USA, after quitting his job as a senior vice-president at an investment bank. He developed the software for the www.amazon.com site and sold his first book in July 1995. As of 2020, the revenue of the company was 386.1 billion USD. Today, amazon is a worldwide e-commerce company that operates in 13 countries and ships to more than 100 countries. Amazon's mission is to continually raise the bar of the customer experience by using the Internet and technology to help consumers find, discover, and buy anything, and empower businesses and content creators to maximise their success. Amazon has succeeded where several giant online companies have failed, because of its customer-centric focus and commitment to a world-class customer service. Their shopping digital models and tactics has led to reduced cost, simplicity, and convenience to online shopping experiences that many high street retailers could not match.

According to Bezos, Amazon's business model is based on three value propositions: low price, fast delivery, and a wide range of products for customers to select from. The success relies on innovative digital models, powered by contemporary digital technology, that supports seamless growth, novel development and deployment of changes across multi-related platforms. Amazon's digital marketing, apart from its online advertisements, maximises listings in search results using search engine optimisation (SEO) and targeted social media channels that direct customers to Amazon's website. Their digital marketing strategy tactics, among others, includes email marketing, video marketing, dedicated websites and designs, conversion rate optimisation (CRO), pay-per-click (PPC) advertising, user data, and user-generated content. Its digital plan includes cashless stores, home robots, cashier-free stores, delivery drones, Amazon scouts, Alexa, games streaming services, and biometric payments.

CASE STUDY 2 How digital strategy made Netflix successful

Netflix is a world-leading entertainment service, with over 222 million paid memberships in over 190 countries. The company's innovative digital model enables its customers to watch as much as they want, anytime, anywhere, without commercials or commitments. Ability to envision a future for home streaming and success to innovate their digital marketing led to the success of Netflix digital business. Netflix was able to achieve higher strategic tactics than its rival, Blockbuster, by targeting different segments of video rentals. Customers were turning digital to rent their DVDs online instead of visiting high street rental shops, as the brick-and-mortar film-rental model was turning obsolete (Forbes, 2014).

Netflix's digital marketing strategy focuses on building strong relationships between the brand and its viewers. Despite Netflix's disruptive technological innovation (PwC., 2022) that displaced several established market-leading firms, products, and alliances, it has been able to use technology to deliver its business objectives effectively to its current and aspiring customers. As part of their digital strategy, Netflix efficiently uses machine learning without human help, to assist their algorithms to learn about their platform. The use of AI knowledge enables the platform to automate millions of decisions based on user activities (Gomez-Uribe & Hunt, 2015); thus, users could spend hours watching several movies and TV shows without recommendations.

Seminar exercises

Discussion topics:

1. We are witnessing the death of the high street in the UK. Why is this happening? Can we do something about this? What is the future of shopping?
2. Have you purchased music online or subscribed to a music service? What was your experience?
3. When you want to purchase a product or a service for yourself, or a company you work for, what is your thinking process and the steps that you follow from the moment you have the idea to the moment you complete the purchase?
4. Which business models and revenue models should we consider to exploit the power the Internet effectively?

Group exercises:

1. Think about the innovation that you have witnessed during the time you have used a mobile device.
   - What would you say are the main digital businesses that work in your country of origin that have changed the way people spend their time or buy online?
   - We talk about these businesses being 'successful', but what is success for a start-up business? When does a start-up stop being a start-up?
   - What do these services have in common that you think has made them successful?
2. Think about an innovative digital business idea using the business model canvas.
   - Explain the nature of your digital business.
   - Conduct an initial assessment of the industry you have selected and the needs of its consumers, then consider the market niche to which your new business is applicable.
   - Carry out simple competitive analysis to predict how the digital business will stand up against competitors in the industry.
   - Create a digital artefact in the form of a business pitch appropriate for board level audience.

References

Alameda, T. (2020) Data, AI and Financial Inclusion: The Future of Global Banking Responsible Finance Forum, Responsible Finance Forum BBVA 2020. Available online: https://responsiblefinanceforum.org/data-ai-financial-inclusion-future-global-banking/ [Accessed on 15 March 2022].

Asquith, A., & Horsman, G. (2019) Let the robots do it! Taking a look at Robotic Process Automation and its potential application in digital forensics. Forensic Science International: Reports, 1, 100007.

Beck, R., Muller-Bloch, C., King, J.L. (2018) Governance in the blockchain economy: a framework and research agenda. *J Assoc Inf Syst* 19(10), 1020–1034

Bharadwaj, A., Sawy, O., Pavlou, P. & Venkatraman, N. (2013) Digital business strategy: toward a next generation of insights. *MIS Quarterly*, 37(2), 471–482.

Bibri, S.E., Krogstie, J. (2017) Smart sustainable cities of the future: An extensive interdisciplinary literature review. *Sustain. Cities Soc.* 31, 183–212.

Bryson, J. R. (1997) Obsolescence and the process of creative reconstruction. *Urban Studies*, 34, 1439–1458.

Buil-Gil, D., Lord, N. & Barrett, E. (2021) *The Dynamics of Business, Cybersecurity and Cyber-Victimization: Foregrounding the Internal Guardian in Prevention, Victims & Offenders*, 16(3), 286–315, DOI: 10.1080/15564886.2020.1814468

Cord, D. (2014) *The Decline and Fall of Nokia*. Stairway Press; Seattle.

Correani, A., De-Massis, A., Frattini, F. & Petruzzelli, A. (2020) Implementing a digital strategy: Learning from the experience of three digital transformation projects. *California Management Review*, 62(4), 27–56.

Culot, G., Nassimbeni, G., Podrecca, M., Sartor, M. (2021) The ISO/IEC 27001 information security management standard: Literature review and theory-based research agenda. *TQM J.*, 33 (7), 76–105.

Downes, L., & Nunes, P. F. (2013) Big-bang disruption. *Harvard Business Review*, 91(3), 44–56.

Downes, L. & Nunes, P. (2013) *Blockbuster Becomes a Casualty of Big Bang Disruption*. [Online] Available at: https://hbr.org/2013/11/blockbuster-becomes-a-casualty-of-big-bang-disruption [Accessed 13 March 2022].

Enríquez, J.G., Jiménez-Ramírez, A., Domínguez-Mayo, F.J., & García-García, J.A. (2020) Robotic process automation: A scientific and industrial systematic mapping study. *IEEE Access*, 8, 39113–39129.

Evans, D. S., Hagiu, A. & Schmalensee, R. (2008) *Invisible Engines: How Software Platforms Drive Innovation and Transform Industries*. Cambridge, MA: MIT Press.

Ferreira, J. (2013) Business strategy – applications and advancing tools. *Management decision*, 51(7). DOI: http://dx.doi.org/10.1108/MD-04-2013-0200

Forbes (2014) *A Look Back At Why Blockbuster Really Failed And Why It Didn't Have To.* [Online] Available at: www.forbes.com/sites/gregsatell/2014/09/05/a-look-back-at-why-blockbuster-really-failed-and-why-it-didnt-have-to/?sh=51758a6c1d64 [Accessed 20 March 2022].

Fridgen, G., Lockl, J., Radszuwill, S., Rieger, A., Schweizer, A., & Urbach, N. (2018) A solution in search of a problem: a method for the development of blockchain use cases. In: 24th Americas Conference on Information Systems, 1–10.

Glueck, W. & Jauch, L. (1989) *Strategic Management and Business Policy*, McGraw-Hill Education, New York.

Gobble, M. (2018) Digital strategy and digital transformation. *Research-Technology Management*, 61(5), 66–71.

Gomez-Uribe, C. & Hunt, N. (2015) The netflix recommender system: Algorithms, business value, and innovation. *ACM Transactions on Management Information Systems, 6*(4), 1–19.

Harvey, D. (1978) The urban process under capitalism. *International Journal of Urban and Regional Research*, 2, 101–131.

Hess, T., Matt, C., Benlian, A., & Wiesböck, F. (2016) Options for formulating a digital transformation strategy. *MIS Quarterly Executive*, 15(2), 123–139.

Hughes, C. & Jackson, C. (2015) Death of the high street: identification, prevention, reinvention, Regional Studies, Regional Science, 2:1, 237–256, DOI: 10.1080/21681376.2015.1016098

Isaacson, W., (2011) *Steve Jobs*. Helsinki: Otava.

Jarry, A. (2021) *How much has consumer behaviour changed in the past year – and how can marketers adapt?* [Online] Available at: https://marketingtechnews.net/news/2021/mar/01/how-much-has-consumer-behaviour-changed-in-the-past-year-and-how-can-marketers-adapt/[Accessed 13 March 2022].

Kumar, H., Singh, M. K., Gupta, M. P., Madaan, J. (2020) Moving towards smart cities: Solutions that lead to the Smart City Transformation Framework. *Technological Forecasting and Social Change.* Elsevier, vol. 153. Issue C.

Labazova, O., Dehling, T., Sunyaev, A. (2019) From hype to reality: A taxonomy of blockchain applications. In: *Proceedings of the 52nd Hawaii I International Conference on System Sciences.*

Lamberg, J.-A., Lubinaitė, S., Ojala, J. & Tikkanen, H. (2021) The curse of agility: The Nokia Corporation and the loss of market dominance in mobile phones, 2003–2013. *Business History,* 63(4), 574–605.

Lansiti, M., & Lakhani, K.R. (2014) Digital ubiquity: How connections, sensors, and data are revolutionizing business. *Harvard Business Review,* 92(11), 90–99.

Lau, Y. (2020) *Modern Businesses Need Modern Strategy.* [Online] Available at: www.forbes.com/sites/forbeshumanresourcescouncil/2020/11/16/modern-businesses-need-modern-strategy/?sh=5d3ef6003752 [Accessed 12 March 2021].

Lee, J.H., Phaal, R., Lee, S.H. (2013) An integrated service-device-technology roadmap for smart city development. *Technol. Forecast. Soc. Chang.,* 80(2), 286–306.

Lockl, J., Schlatt, V., Schweizer, A., Urbach, N., Harth, N. (2020) Toward trust in internet of things (IoT) ecosystems: design principles for blockchain-based IoT applications. *IEEE Transact Eng Manag,* to appear in Lopes, Jorge, and José Luís Pereira. (2019) Blockchain projects ecosystem: A review of current technical and legal challenges. In *Advances in*

Intelligent Systems and Computing. Cham: Springer, 83–92.

Madakam, S., Holmukhe, R. M., & Jaiswal, D. K. (2019) The future digital work force: Robotic process automation (RPA). *J ISTEM-Journal of Information Systems and Technology Management,* 16. Doi: https://doi.org/10.4301/S1807-1775201916001 10.4301/S1807-1775201916001

Mamoshina, P., Ojomoko, L., Yanovich, Y., Ostrovski, A., Botezatu, A., Prikhodko, P., Izumchenko, E., Aliper, A., Romantsov, K., and Zhebrak, A. (2018) Converging blockchain and next-generation artificial intelligence technologies to decentralize and accelerate biomedical research and healthcare. *Oncotarget,* 9, 5665–90.

Massey, D. (1984) *Spatial Divisions of Labour: Social Structures and the Geography of Production.* Basingstoke: Macmillan.

McCrudden, C. (2019) 'We are witnessing the death of the high street –but here's why we don't need to be sad about it. Available at www.proquest.com/other-sources/we-are-witnessing-death-high-street-here-s-why/docview/2241827031/se-2?accountid=12834 [accessed on 09/03/2022].

Moffitt, K.C., Rozario, A.M., & Vasarhelyi, M.A. (2018) Robotic process automation for auditing. *Journal of Emerging Technologies in Accounting,* 15(1), 1–10.

Morgan, S. (2019) Cyber crime costs projected to reach $2 trillion by Available: www.forbes.com/sites/stevemorgan/2016/01/17/cyber-crime-costs-projected-to-reach-2-trillion-by-2019/#554e45a53a91 [Accessed 20 March 2022].

Nakamoto, S. (2008) Bitcoin: a peer-to-peer electronic cash system https://bitcoin.org/bitcoin.pdf. [Accessed 19 March 2022].

Neirotti, P., De Marco, A., Cagliano, A.C., Mangano, G., Scorrano, F. (2014) Current trends in smart city initiatives: some stylised facts. *Cities,* 38, 25–36.

Office for National Statistics. (2019) *E-commerce and ICT Activity*, UK: 2018, (Statistical bulletin).

Osterwalder, A., & Pigneur, Y. (2010) *Business Model Generation: A Handbook for Visionaries, Game Changers, and Challengers*. Wiley; Hoboken, New Jersey.

Paul, S. (2019) *Use of Blockchain and Artificial Intelligence to Promote Financial Inclusion in India Smita Miglani Indian Council for Research on International Economic Relations*. Available online: https://economicti mes [accessed on 15 March 2022].

Peltonen, T. (2018) Case Study 4: The collapse of Nokia's mobile phone business. In *Towards Wise Management: Wisdom and Stupidity in Strategic Decision-making*. Springer, Cham. 163–189.

Peric, K. (2015) Digital financial inclusion. *Journal of Payments Strategy & Systems*, 9, 212–14. Available online: www.ing entaconnect.com/content/hsp/jpss/ 2015/00000009/00000003/art00001 (accessed on 15 March 2022).

Porter, M. (1996) What is strategy? *Harvard Business Review*, 74(6), pp. 61–78.

PwC. (2022) *Disruption, Innovation and Emerging Technologies*. [Online] Available at: www.pwc.co.uk/issues/ intelligent-digital/disruptive-inn ovation-emerging-technology.html [Accessed 20 March 2022].

Reyes, C. (2022) *What is Digital Strategy?* [Online] Available at: www.liferay. com/resources/l/digital-strategy [Accessed 12 March 2022].

Santos, M.F., Carvalhosa, P., Portela, F., Abelha, A., & Machado, J. (2017) Pervasiveness in digital marketing–a global overview. In *World Conference on Information Systems and Technologies*. Springer, Cham. 391–398.

Satell, G. (2014) *A Look Back At Why Blockbuster Really Failed And Why It Didn't Have To*. [Online] Available at: www.forbes.com/sites/gregsat ell/2014/09/05/a-look-back-at-why-blockbuster-really-failed-and-why-it-didnt-have-to/?sh=25bdddc41d64 [Accessed 13 March 2022].

Shelby, J. (2018) *Cyber Security Trends Driven by Digital Identity Protection*, May.

Sule, M.J., Zennaro, M., Thomas, G. (2021) *Cybersecurity through the lens of Digital Identity and Data Protection: Issues and Trends*, https://doi.org/10.1016/ j.techsoc.2021.101734

Van der Aalst, W. M., Bichler, M., & Heinzl, A. (2018). *Robotic Process Automation Bus Inf Syst Eng*, 60, pp. 269–272. https://doi.org/10.1007/s12 599-018-0542-4

Venters, W. & Whitley, E. (2012) A critical review of cloud computing: researching desires and realities. *Journal of Information Technology*. 27, 3, 179–197.

Von Solms, R. (1999) Information security management: Why standards are important. *Information Management & Computer Security*, 7, 1, 50–57.

Williams, D., & Allen, I. (2017) Using artificial intelligence to optimize the value of robotic process automation. Available from: www.ibm.com/ downloads/cas/KDKAAK29

Zukin, S. (1991) *Landscapes of Power: From Detroit to Disney World*. Berkeley University of California Press, Oakland, California.

INDEX

Note: Endnotes are indicated by the page number followed by "n" and the note number